MASTERING THE MARKETPLACE

Mastering the Marketplace

Popular Literature in Nineteenth-Century France

ANNE O'NEIL-HENRY

UNIVERSITY OF NEBRASKA PRESS · LINCOLN AND LONDON

Acknowledgments for the use of copyrighted
material appear on page 161, which constitutes
an extension of the copyright page.

Library of Congress Cataloging-in-Publication Data
Names: O'Neil-Henry, Anne, author.
Title: Mastering the marketplace: popular literature
in nineteenth-century France / Anne O'Neil-Henry.
Description: Lincoln: University of Nebraska Press,
2017. | Includes bibliographical references and index.
Identifiers: LCCN 2017025011 (print)
LCCN 2017034830 (ebook)
ISBN 9781496204653 (epub)
ISBN 9781496204660 (mobi)
ISBN 9781496204677 (pdf)
ISBN 9781496201980 (cloth: alk. paper)
Subjects: LCSH: French fiction—19th
century—History and criticism. | Literature
publishing—France—History—19th century.
Classification: LCC PQ653 (ebook) | LCC PQ653
.O54 2017 (print) | DDC 840.9/007—dc23
LC record available at https://lccn.loc.gov/2017025011

Set in Garamond Premier by Rachel Gould.
Designed by N. Putens.

To Nathan, June, and Irene

Contents

Illustrations

Acknowledgments

I feel fortunate to have received so much support—professional and personal—from many people over the course of this project. I would first like to thank my professors and mentors in the Romance Studies Department at Duke University. In particular, David Bell provided wonderful mentorship in all areas of the profession, and I am so glad to have worked with him. Thanks too to Deborah Jenson, Stephanie Sieburth, and Neil McWilliam, who gave me invaluable advice and guidance. I want to thank Helen Solterer and Linda Orr, who pushed me to think in challenging and creative ways. I am sincerely grateful for the encouragement and friendship of all my Duke graduate school colleagues.

Since my arrival in the Department of French and Francophone Studies at Georgetown University, I have felt welcomed and supported, and I am grateful to all of my colleagues for their help. Special thanks go to Sylvie Durmelat, Susanna Lee, Miléna Santoro, Susan Terrio, and Paul Young for their feedback on my work and their support and friendship. I am especially indebted to Andrew Sobanet and Deborah Lesko Baker; they have helped me immeasurably in matters both personal and professional. Outside of my department I am grateful for my other Georgetown colleagues: Daniel Shore and Brian Hochman for their support and friendship, and Ashley Cohen and Nicole Rizzuto for reading portions of this book. We have a wonderful community of scholars in the DC area with whom I have had the pleasure of trading work. Lisa Leff, Elise Lipkovitz, Katrin Schultheiss, Urvashi Chakravarty, and Lindsay DiCuirci all read and gave important feedback on portions of this book. I want to extend very special thanks to Masha Belenky, Kathryn Kleppinger, Chelsea Stieber, and Erin Twohig for their attentive and patient readings of multiple parts of this project and for their collaboration and friendship.

This book is the product of research trips and archival work that would not have been possible without material support from the Department of French and Francophone Studies at Georgetown, the Graduate School of Georgetown, and the Faculty of Languages and Linguistics at Georgetown, for which I am thankful. I am thankful too for the help of research librarians at the Bibliothèque Nationale de France, the Library of Congress, Harvard University's Houghton Library, and the McGill University Library. Rebecca Saltzman, my student research assistant, was invaluable in helping with translations and bibliographical work; Joan Matus was incredible in her administrative support. I thank Alisa Plant, Courtney Ochsner, and Elizabeth Zaleski at the University of Nebraska Press for shepherding me through the publication process, and Judith Hoover for her attentive reading. I am thankful as well for the two readers of my book, who offered important and much-welcome feedback. Reworked portions of chapters appeared as articles in *French Forum* and *Dix-Neuf*, and I am grateful to both journals for their permission for the work to appear here.

A few more personal thanks are in order. First and foremost to my wonderful parents, Patrick Henry and Mary Anne O'Neil, for their immeasurable support of my education and for all their professional and personal advice, and to my late grandmother Cornelia O'Neil, the best role model imaginable. Thanks to my Hensley and Solomon in-laws for their love and support throughout this project; to Rachel Winkelman for being my expert consultant on all matters related to business, to Elinor Hutton for her brilliant design advice, and to Rebecca Corvino for her copyediting genius and encouragement. Finally, I could not have completed this project without the support of Nathan Hensley, who has been beside me since before this project began and who is the most patient editor, insightful colleague, and thoughtful friend imaginable. June and Irene Hensley make our lives full and lovely, and this book is dedicated to them.

INTRODUCTION

In 1851, while in the midst of composing *Madame Bovary*, Gustave Flaubert noted that he was experiencing difficulties in his writing and worried he might "tomber dans le Paul de Kock."[1] A year later he lamented, "Ce que j'écris présentement risque d'être du Paul de Kock si je n'y mets une forme profondément littéraire."[2] The Paul de Kock so repeatedly maligned by Flaubert was actually a best-selling and prolific novelist, who had a long and lucrative career spanning nearly fifty years until his death in 1870. Despite or perhaps because of this commercial success, de Kock had already in his own day come to embody the very idea of lowbrow literature, exactly the type from which Flaubert hoped to distinguish himself. The author of *Madame Bovary* was hardly the only one to employ "Paul de Kock" as shorthand for "bad" literature in order to expose hierarchies in his contemporary literary field. Honoré de Balzac, who initially enjoyed a friendly relationship with the popular novelist Eugène Sue until sales of Sue's serialized fiction began to dwarf his own, accused the well-known dandy of being "Paul de Kock en satin et à paillettes."[3] Effectively charging Sue, the author of the best-selling serial novel *Les Mystères de Paris* (1842–43), with being a philistine disguised in fancy trappings, Balzac later admitted, as he wrote of the disfigurement of his character Vautrin in *Splendeurs et misères de courtisanes*, "Je fais du Sue tout pur."[4] By using Sue's name to signify excessively violent description, Balzac evinced his familiarity with but also his contempt for Sue's work.

These examples from Balzac's and Flaubert's correspondence reveal the overlapping and often interconnected nature of the burgeoning literary marketplace of early to mid-nineteenth-century France. Now-canonical authors and mass cultural impresarios collaborated with, borrowed from, and positioned themselves against one another in the particularly dynamic literary environment of this period, a battleground of cultural and economic value productively viewed as the birthplace of our own modern mass-media culture. This was a cultural field in the process of undergoing radical changes due to a rise in literacy rates, the proliferation of lending libraries and reading rooms, the explosion of literary journals and political newspapers, the rise of the figure of the publisher, the development of advertising techniques in the press, and the advent of the serial novel, among other factors. At this time authors faced the challenge of developing sophisticated tactics for selling their books, working with the new figure of the publisher, and situating themselves within what the sociologist Pierre Bourdieu has theorized as "the literary field." In this postrevolutionary period, itself one of great social and political upheaval, the author became, more and more, a professional who wrote for a living and had to negotiate the delicate balance between aesthetic concerns and popular tastes. These commercial demands effectively changed how authors wrote about and altered their conceptions of literary practice. For authors and their critics, in other words, this nascent marketplace generated opportunities for aesthetic and generic innovation as well as demands to meet rapidly changing preferences. My study demonstrates how the material, commercial, and cultural pressures of this new media environment manifested not just in the correspondence or explicit statements of authors, critics, and publishers but in the form of the literary texts themselves. In tracking how these material changes shaped the literary artifacts of this early media environment, we gain access to a more nuanced picture of literary practice during this key period, one that challenges the still powerful categories of "high" and "low" literature. What we see, ultimately, is a world in which Flaubert and de Kock, Balzac and Sue, were not opposite figures so much as rival players on the same stage.

A NEW MARKETPLACE FOR BOOKS

Book and cultural historians, including Yves Mollier, Martyn Lyons, James Smith Allen, and more recently Christine Haynes, have scrupulously studied the material changes to France's literary marketplace across the early to mid-nineteenth century. A brief overview of this history helps establish how literature was produced, marketed, and sold and provides a framework for the literary analysis constituting the main contribution of this study. Mechanical presses and ink rollers, paper from wood pulp now produced in continuous rolls rather than sheets, the mechanization of book binding: these and other improvements in press and paper technology enabled books to be printed and disseminated more easily and cheaply than ever before.[5] National literacy rates had risen, thanks in part, but not exclusively, to educational reforms such as the 1833 Guizot Law, requiring an elementary school in each commune, and the Falloux Law of 1850, requiring a girls school in each commune as well.[6] Yet as Martyn Lyons reminds us, especially in urban areas, literacy had already been climbing by the eighteenth century; in fact "expanding opportunities for female employment ... did [even] more to raise the level of female literacy."[7] The growing reading public in any case stretched the demographics for authors' works and helped establish the author as a professional who, due to declining literary patronage, increasingly had to sell his or her works in this expanding market to make a living.[8]

How readers learned about and accessed literary works changed too. In the earlier part of the century, publishers tasked sales assistants with disseminating their products. Some of them eventually worked independently, on commission, for multiple publishers; *colporteurs,* whom John Barberet calls the "traveling salesmen of the literary market," typically sold these books outside of urban centers.[9] The development of and increase in lending libraries and the *cabinet de lecture* granted access to books and newspapers, for a small fee, to those readers not otherwise able to afford their own copies.[10] These developments, among others, illuminate the growing accessibility of literature alongside the rising reading public.[11] Another way literature gained a larger audience during this period was through the press. In 1836 Emile de Girardin and Armand Dutacq launched, respectively, *La Presse* and *Le Siècle*, both of whose subscription prices (40 francs) were half those of the most widely read political daily newspapers (80 francs).[12] What these publications lost from subscriptions they made up for in paid advertisements, ushering in what Marc Martin calls the massive "entrée de la publicité dans la presse" at a time when, around the early 1830s, "le marché des annonces s'organise."[13] This *presse à bon marché* (penny press) sought to be seen as "information-based and politically neutral," no doubt a strategy for these money-making machines to alienate as few readers as possible, though rarely did their neutrality remain constant over the course of publication.[14] Newspaper readership surged: by 1858 "the Parisian dailies could claim sales of 235,000 copies," even if these less expensive *quotidiens* (dailies) did not always sell as consistently as their counterparts that kept subscription prices elevated.[15]

Another factor contributing to these newspapers' readership was the development of the *roman-feuilleton* (serial novel), whose success was related to these newspapers' high readership. The *feuilleton* was a space initially at the bottom of the newspaper—included to expand the size of the publication without paying extra taxes—and was conceived as an area "in which the era's journalistic conventions did not apply."[16] There, in 1836, Girardin published France's first serial novel, "un roman publié par tranches dans le 'feuilleton' des quotidiens," in this case Balzac's *La Vieille fille.*[17] Balzac's text did serve to promote and sell Girardin's *La Presse*, but the most famous writer of the *roman-feuilleton* of this period was Sue; his *Mystères de Paris* was published in the *Journal des débats*, whose subscriptions "increased by many thousands in the early months of [Sue's] publication."[18] Though readership of the *roman-feuilleton* was remarkable, it is important to remember that the subscription rates of these journals were still prohibitively expensive for many working-class readers.[19] Nevertheless, as we will see in detail, in addition to generating new readers and sales for the newspapers in which it appeared, the *roman-feuilleton* sparked intense debate among literary critics and politicians alike, who feared the dangers of its mass dissemination. The advent of the serial novel provoked the transformation of the newspaper from a political publication to one more accessible to a general public; in turn serial publication transformed the shape of the novel itself. The recent work of critics on the press and media culture, notably that of Marie-Eve Thérenty, Alain Vaillant, and Gillaume Pinson, has generated new understandings of the importance of this medium in sponsoring overlap between the press and literature, news and fiction, authors and journalists.[20]

It was not, however, merely these social and technological forces that altered the business of selling books. As Haynes has recently argued, "the literary marketplace was a contingent outcome of political struggle, on both the professional and national levels," and at the heart of this struggle was the *éditeur*, a figure "who specialized in commissioning, financing, and coordinating the creation, production, and marketing of books by others."[21] These new professionals, who ultimately formed the trade association Cercle de la Librairie in 1847, lobbied for fewer state regulations of the book trade, a stance that clashed with the position of what Haynes calls the corporatist camp: "largely printers and booksellers who were descended . . . from members of the old guilds."[22] Decades-long debates about the state's regulation of publishing ultimately led to the liberalization of the marketplace. Debates were also waged throughout the century over laws dealing with literary property rights, or *droits d'auteur*, laws that had financial implications for both the author and the publisher. As a consequence, the term of authors' rights was prolonged a number of times throughout the century: in 1793 rights were given to an author over the course of his or her lifetime, and then for the ten years following the author's death to his or her family; under Napoleon, in 1810 rights were given for twenty years after the death of the author; under Napoleon III they were further extended in 1854 to thirty years after the author's death and in 1866 to fifty years.[23] The importance of the political debates associated with publishing, which crystallized in no small part around the new figure of the *éditeur*, cannot be overstated in developments of the industry in the nineteenth century.

If the figure of the publisher emerged at the beginning of the nineteenth century, by the end of the century these successful entrepreneurs of *l'édition* (publishing) had established the *maison d'édition* (publishing houses): "Ces fabriques de best-sellers deviennent peu à peu de véritables entreprises, gérées intelligemment ou négligemment selon les cas . . . l'artisanat et l'amateurisme cèdent souvent la place à la direction attentive et fine d'une grande affaire."[24] In other words, the impact of a growing capitalist economy on the profession of publishing was palpable, as it was in the case of other industries. Throughout the century, not just in the second half, publishers were responsible for major innovations in the way books were formatted and sold. For example, in 1838 the *éditeur* Gervais Charpentier debuted volumes sold in what became known as the "format-Charpentier": a book in octodecimo format (in-18), which contained the length of a book in octavo format (in-8°; this was a more standard format) and was priced at 3.5 francs, much less than the more typical 7.5 to 9 francs. At a price that represented "le salaire quotidien d'un bon ouvrier," this size offered a cheaper option to engage a wider readership, and the *cabinets de lecture* often purchased volumes of these economical works.[25] Charpentier would then launch his series *La Bibliothèque Charpentier*, which boasted contemporary authors (Balzac, Hugo, Musset) but also classic French and foreign writers—Shakespeare, for example.[26] This series was one of a number of collections from this period popularized by these entrepreneurial publishers who repackaged works for profit and significantly shaped the new marketplace.[27] If the mass marketplace was more fully formed by the end of the century, we can nonetheless see traces of it in the century's beginning decades.

This material history of the early to mid-nineteenth-century marketplace for culture enables us to see the many and competing factors generating literary innovation in this period. Nowhere are these changes more obvious than in the *Feuilleton du journal de la librairie*, a short publication dedicated to professionals in the book trade. The publication's subtitle elucidated the wide array of topics this short publication encompassed: *Tout ce qui se rattache aux intérêts de l'imprimerie et de la librairie, fonderie, papeterie, gravure, musique, etc.*[28] Created in 1825 as a supplement to the *Bibliographie de la France*—France's official record of all printed works—the *Feuilleton* appeared weekly from 1834 until the acquisition of the journal by the Cercle de la Librairie in 1857, when its format changed.[29] Issues of this supplement dedicated to professionals in the book trade included, among other matters, advertisements for new works spanning several different genres, announcements of book acquisitions, job offers, and rulings on legal matters relating to the industry in the column "Décisions judiciaires en matière de librairie" (Legal Decisions related to Bookselling). This small emporium for the sharing of professional knowledge among a newly linked set of cultural producers is a kind of microcosm of the literary field at this period. The *Feuilleton* served as an important professional resource, and its existence and hybrid form restores visibility to the dense network of actors at the center of nineteenth-century literary production. Here the names of popular writers mingled with those of now canonical ones, debates over publishers' rights played out, and professional readers tracked developments in and general practices of their evolving industry.[30] Seemingly a minor detail in the history of print culture, the *Feuilleton* nonetheless gives evidence of the dynamic and increasingly interconnected marketplace that took shape in the first half of the nineteenth century.

The *Feuilleton's* "Décisions judiciaires" column is particularly revealing of how this publication mediated a changing literary field. This subsection featured coverage of the many legal debates occasioned by the new marketplace, disputes over authors' rights, increasing problems with foreign and domestic counterfeiting, developments in print technology, and the changing role of the publisher. On the topic of counterfeiting, consider a March 21, 1835, case in which the publisher Eugène Renduel, then proprietor of Victor Hugo's work, brought charges of partial counterfeiting against the publisher M. Guérin, who had included four excerpts of poems from Hugo's *Les Feuilles d'automne* in his lengthy *Livres des Jeunes personnes* without Hugo's or Renduel's consent. Since the reproduction of Hugo's poems represented "une partie si minime" of this work, the case was ultimately dismissed.[31] Among recurrent debates concerning the extension of literary property laws is a case from January 31, 1835, involving de Kock and the publisher Gustave Barba (just one instance in an ongoing struggle between the two). Barba had announced the forthcoming publication of the *Oeuvres complètes de Paul de Kock*; de Kock objected to the use of the word "complètes" (complete), arguing that Barba lacked the rights to a number of his works. The column details how the Court Royal determined that Barba contractually possessed these rights until 1835 and was therefore *not* guilty of counterfeiting, for he had not yet printed the collection with the offending title. These two legal cases demonstrate that, while we would not consider them professional peers today, de Kock and Hugo in fact worked within and negotiated the same shifting rules of the market at a moment when the profession of the publisher and even that of the author became more clearly defined. While the *Bibliographie* itself catalogued the rise of this commercial literature, the *Feuilleton* and within it the "Décisions judiciaires" served as sites where professional knowledge of the modern commercial book trade was made and consolidated.

The formal composition of these short legal accounts also had larger implications for the developing marketplace. Like their counterparts in the *Gazette des tribunaux* and other journals, the "Décisions judiciaires" column often began by stating the general legal question being debated or by noting a ruling before delving into the details of the related case.[32] "Un libraire peut-il publier, sous forme de receuil, les articles insérés dans un journal périodique?" asks a report from a December 21, 1833, issue, ending not with the answer but with the promise "Nous rendrons compte de la décision qui interviendra."[33] A March 8, 1834, report is preceded by the question "Les dépôts ordonnés à l'imprimeur ou à l'éditeur par le décret du 5 février 1810 suffisent-ils pour conserver à l'auteur le droit de propriété? (Oui)."[34] In this case the outcome is stated. Read in the larger context of the *Feuilleton*, this dialogic format—an alternation between question and answer depending on each case—can be seen to mirror the changing nature of the book trade of this period. Still other columns were prefaced by a legal judgment that set up new terms for the supplement's readers, such as "Il est interdit à un sténographe de publier les leçons d'un professeur; un pareil acte est considéré judiciairement comme une contrefaçon" from March 20, 1841, or, from May 6, 1837, "L'auteur qui a traité avec un libraire pour la composition d'un ouvrage est obligé de livrer une copie lisible et de corriger lui-même les épreuves, à peine de résiliation des conventions."[35] These legal proclamations are more definitive than the question-and-answer format. Yet whether through definitive statements or interrogatives, these cases show even at the level of their composition the process of redefining the trade. As Haynes suggests, the *Feuilleton* facilitated publishers' ability to "undertake collective activities"; it also explored, defined, and, in a sense, demonstrated in real time the contemporary developing literary marketplace. Close readings of such cultural artifacts, seen alongside the material historical contexts that produced them, form the basis of *Mastering the Marketplace*'s method.

POPULAR LITERATURE AND ITS CRITICS

Arguments about the prominence of literary figures such as Balzac, Stendhal, Sand, and Hugo and movements like romanticism, realism, and idealism during the first half of the nineteenth century have been well rehearsed. Moving beyond such discussions, newer scholarship has been devoted to what were once considered more marginal genres of this period—that is, works that were widely read but that would not go on to form part of the literary canon at the end of the century. Whether writing on the concept of *para-littérature*, the "roman populaire," "littérature frénétique," crime fiction of the *bas-fonds* (slums), or sentimental fiction, scholars such as Marc Angenot, Anne-Marie Thiesse, Anthony Glinoer, Dominique Kalifa, and Margaret Cohen have offered alternative interpretations of the most dominant genres and tastes of the period. While, for example, the historical novel as practiced by Walter Scott was in fashion in the early part of the century, Judith Lyon-Caen has also shown that readers craved a contemporary "représentation du social" in their works.[36] The *roman gai* (comic novel) enjoyed popular readership alongside the *roman noir* (Gothic novel).[37] This study focuses predominantly on the novelistic form, but the same decades also saw a rise in the prevalence of popular theater, notably vaudeville and melodrama, and a number of authors I focus on (in particular de Kock) were heavily involved in this scene. These popular theatrical forms, which, as Jennifer Terni explains, were associated with commercial bourgeois culture and "infused with . . . stereotypes, situation-based plots, reversals of fortune, mistaken identities, and of course happy endings," resemble in many ways the varied novelistic productions that emerged during the period and represented shifting contemporary tastes.[38] My aim is not to recover another popular genre or reimagine the major literary movements of the period in the context of popular literature but rather to build on the work of these literary critics to show, first, how the varied responses to market pressures helped shape the literature of these authors itself and, second, how such pressures occasioned a dramatic blurring of the hierarchical and generic boundaries that later criticism has often unconsciously worked to enforce.

Along with the proliferation of popular literature during the first half of the nineteenth century, there was a parallel explosion in literary criticism, in literary journals as well as in the newly formed literary press. Some of the most famous critics—Jules Janin, Sainte-Beuve—were themselves writers of literature and saw criticism as a more stable and lucrative profession. Many of the major critics of the July Monarchy became experts of the literature of previous centuries and national traditions; as Lyon-Caen explains, this assured them a certain professional authority, which often coincided with a tendency toward "le dénigrement du roman moderne et le recours à l'histoire . . . comme l'un des moyens les plus efficaces de disqualification du roman."[39] These critics were often professionally or personally connected to the authors they reviewed, and these biases (both positive and negative) became legible in their critiques.[40] In the end, however, much like the commercial authors they disdained, moralizing critics toed the line between providing an intellectual service and staking a claim for themselves within the same market; as Glinoer puts it, the critic was a professional "homme de lettres," required to sell "le produit de son travail aux éditeurs et aux journaux."[41] These caveats about July Monarchy critics—their biases, personal and professional connections, and concerns—are all important to keep in mind as this study mines nineteenth-century reviews to understand the tastes of the period.

Toward the end of the 1830s and the beginning of the 1840s, the concerns and even fears critics had about the rise of popular literature, especially the serial novel, became manifest. These took the form of vigorous debates about and negative campaigns against this literature, waged principally by critics who yearned for a past "grandeur littéraire" in their critique of contemporary literary production, mostly taking up "les positions esthétiques et morales les plus conservatrices."[42] In one of the best-known contributions to this period's considerations of literary value, "De la littérature industrielle" of 1839, Sainte-Beuve addresses the issue of commercial, or "industrial," literature, which, though it may have existed before, had become for him a corrupting force needing to be reined in.[43] He uses mixed metaphors of contamination and militarism to describe what he views as the unprecedented takeover of the literary field by unqualified authors: the literary world had never been "envahi, exploité, réclamé à titre de juste possession, par une bande si nombreuse, si disparate et presque organisée comme nous le voyons, aujourd'hui, et avec cette seule devise inscrite au drapeau *Vivre en écrivain*."[44] He laments the dearth of conscientious and educated writers, claiming that everyone now believes himself capable of becoming a celebrated writer: "Pourquoi pas moi aussi? Se dit chacun."[45] These authors were part of an alarming trend, according to Sainte-Beuve, who also disparages the commercialization of the press and links advertising with the corruption of literature; the execution of sound criticism was impossible, he believed, when, in the same publication, one could find an advertisement for the work in question. Sainte-Beuve insists that this evil ("mal") was neither new nor likely to be totally eliminated, yet he issues a rallying cry to his readers: "Tâchons d'avancer et de mûrir ce jugement en dégageant la bonne [littérature] et en limitant l'autre avec fermeté."[46] By establishing this category of industrial literature, Sainte-Beuve also specifies its opposite: "une autre littérature, vouée à la rareté, à l'inspiration, au travail assidu et à l'excellence esthétique."[47] The critic thus situates the hierarchies of the literary field in absolute terms: intellectual and commercial, high and low, good and bad.

Less than a decade later the conservative critic Alfred Nettement published "Études critiques sur le roman feuilleton" (1845), a treatise that reiterates some of Sainte-Beuve's points but specifically targets the serial novel. For Nettement the commercialization of the press, that is, the lowering of subscription fees and the addition of publicity, was just one of many factors contributing to what he saw as the contemporary "désordre littéraire."[48] This critic attributes the *roman feuilleton* (or "roman immoral, deux mots pour la même idée") to contemporary "atheistic" politics and maintains that as society descended "au-dessous du niveau de la civilisation," it would logically become "inondée par ses égouts."[49] Nettement criticizes the serial novel's depravity, addictive nature, and lack of the good and beautiful qualities he so highly valued, in addition to its style.[50] Though his critique of the genre focuses more on the morality of the content and the dangers to society that such works might engender, and less exclusively on commercialization, Nettement echoes Sainte-Beuve's sentiment that the literary world has been contaminated, and he reiterates its high/low divide. Nettement and Sainte-Beuve, among other vocal critics during this period, railed against developments in popular culture while firmly asserting themselves in hierarchical opposition to the producers of industrial literature.

Bourdieu picks up on the alleged antinomy between industrial literature and a "purer" sort of artistic production in his theorization of the literary field, a space of relations "organized around the opposition between pure art . . . and bourgeois art." For Bourdieu the literary field ultimately "organize[s] itself according to two independent and hierarchized principles of differentiation: the principal opposition, between pure production, destined for a market restricted to producers, and large-scale production, oriented towards the satisfaction of the demands of a wide audience." Relying on the work of Flaubert, Bourdieu describes a space where commerciality and purity are at odds; we might think of this in terms of what he calls "commercial success" and "cultural capital" (the social and symbolic but not financial elements that connote class and distinction), a field that was "constituted as such in and by opposition to a 'bourgeois' world which had never before asserted so bluntly its values and its pretension to control the instruments of legitimation."[51] Bourdieu's binaristic approach has proven to be a powerful critical tool. In the chapters that follow, however, I draw on his key terms but insist on a more complex view of the works that, for Bourdieu and Flaubert alike, appear in stark opposition to a "purer" cultural production. As we will see, close analysis of the aesthetic properties of literature from the early moments in the mass marketplace—and the reception of those works—discloses more ambivalence on the part of authors and their readers and critics than is suggested by the clear distinctions of value that Bourdieu shares with his nineteenth-century critical precursors.[52]

As becomes clear from the work of Sainte-Beuve and Nettement and, later, Bourdieu, what emerges from this period is a distinction between high and low literature, concepts that are still active in today's literary field, if modified from their original meaning. Highbrow literature, as Sainte-Beuve defines it, places emphasis on "aesthetic" as opposed to "commercial" value; it incorporates figurative language, literary tropes (allegory and metaphor, among others), elaborate character studies, and extensive historical or metaphysical themes. Lowbrow, or industrial, literature is more plot-driven, tends to include stock characters, places less emphasis on figurative language, and reliably offers a simple moral lesson. The majority of authors that would become part of the literary canon at the end of the century fall into what the nineteenth-century critics who judged them would deem highbrow. This canonization process therefore reified the categories of high and low that in the earlier period were being actively redefined and contested. This book's aim is to show that at the very time these notions were emerging, authors who now connote highbrow and lowbrow literature actually blurred the boundaries of these now seemingly static categories.

METHOD AND PRACTICE

In *Mastering the Marketplace* I show how both high- and lowbrow authors together responded to the changing needs of the dynamic literary market-place of early to mid-nineteenth-century France. To do so I examine those authors' reception, reputation, and most especially the formal elements of their literary works (style, plot, characters, tropes: all of which I refer to here as "form"). I analyze the spectrum of literary production: the work of Balzac, de Kock, and Sue, as well as a literary phenomenon known as "panoramic literature," a proliferation of short, typological texts that aimed at documenting and categorizing all types of Parisian phenomena throughout the 1820s, 1830s, and 1840s, written by well-known and unknown authors alike. By closely studying these texts as well as the advertisements, book reviews, publication history, sales tactics, and promotional tools associated with them, I expose a more nuanced picture of the relationship among these authors: a jumbled, interconnected sphere in which critics and authors grappled, in different ways, with the common task of coordinating commercial and cultural success. More specifically I demonstrate how popular authors in the late Restoration and July Monarchy understood and profited from the nascent literary market; how, for example, Balzac, now a canonical author, actually engaged in trends that placed him closer to commercial writers than his later critics, following the author himself, would have recognized. I show how the broader social and material conditions under which this literature was produced—the innovations in print technology, reading demographics, advertising campaigns, market competition—becomes manifest in the literature itself.

The digitization of large swaths of the nineteenth-century press and of popular texts previously difficult to access, as well as the creation of *Médias 19*, an online platform and database for scholars working on nineteenth-century media, have rightly aroused scholarly interest in these previously understudied domains. Yet while the *roman-feuilleton* and the press more generally have been the topics of important recent scholarly work, I offer sustained readings of once important but now neglected popular authors—de Kock, Sue (especially his work predating *Les Mystères de Paris*), and the authors of panoramic literary texts—read by so many in the early to mid-nineteenth century. *Mastering the Marketplace* restores visibility to these figures and therefore further revises well-established conventions of this period's literary history. Such literary readings, alongside original archival research and coupled with attention to historical and cultural context, help us revise existing understandings of this crucial moment in the development of industrialized culture. Ultimately such readings enable us to link this formative period with our own, in which mobile electronic devices, Internet-based bookstores, and massive publishing conglomerates alter, once again, the way literature is written, sold, and read.

Mastering the Marketplace draws on a variety of fields often considered distinct from one another, including literary studies, cultural and material history, and cultural studies. This varied methodology is informed by a number of key works. I draw, for example, on Margaret Cohen's *The Sentimental Education of the Novel* for a model of reading "literature *hors d'usage*" and for an understanding of this period in literary history as one in which canonical authors like Balzac "emerge as literary producers among other producers, seeking a niche in a generic market promising both economic and cultural return."[53] I use the cultural historian Judith Lyon-Caen's *La lecture et la vie: Les usages du roman au temps de Balzac*, in which she studies the letters written to Balzac and Sue, to solidify my comprehension of the reading culture and practices of this period. I rely on Christine Haynes's historical study, *Lost Illusions: The Politics of Publishing in Nineteenth-Century France*, to establish my conception of the literary marketplace of this period as one shaped significantly by the political struggles among publishers. In its focus on individual authors and their texts, this study does not aim to intervene in the field of book history; it remains rather a work of literary and cultural criticism informed by the work of book historians.

Studies of book history that tackle the literary marketplace tend to focus on the material, empirical elements of the relationship of author and publisher. In their reconstruction of the historical phenomenon, these studies have helped offer specific details about the physical format of the works produced, the quality of the paper, and the print runs of the best sellers, among other important material matters. Such empirical studies do not therefore focus on the content of the literary works: the tropes that recur throughout an author's oeuvre, the formal distinctions of different genres in which authors work, or the way the content of that work reflects the developing taste of the period. Literary scholars practicing methods of distant reading, influenced most notably by Franco Moretti and enabled by the mass digitization of literary works, advocate for an understanding of the totality of the literary field as opposed to the proportionally small fraction of canonical works we currently consume. Like the more synoptic studies of book historians, distant readers' statistical analysis of literature examines the conditions of the literary field without using close literary readings to make their claims.[54] On the other hand, literary studies that do focus on the content of literary works can at times overlook the important historical contexts of their production. *Mastering the Marketplace* draws from these dialectically opposed methods and thus is able to offer a new perspective on the wider-scaled analyses while opening up broader vistas for these closer readings more typically concerned with individual textual objects.

By analyzing writers who borrowed from and recycled elements of their own literary corpus across genres and who repurposed clichés and types from the works of others, I also draw on concepts that contemporary new media scholars have explored, namely recirculation and remediation. Jay Bolter and Richard Grusin's work on remediation, a term they study in the context of newer digital technologies, describes it as an act by which "media are continually commenting on, reproducing, and replacing each other."[55] Any new medium thus appropriates or repurposes older ones. Ellen Gruber

Garvey, writing on the medium of scrapbooking in nineteenth- and early twentieth-century America, notes that, in this context, "writing is understood as a process of recirculation, in which information is sorted and stockpiled until it can acquire value by being inserted into a new context. As often appears to be true on web pages, the origin of the material is less important than the new form it takes, resorted and made available in new ways."[56] Both nineteenth-century and contemporary critics often accused de Kock and other popular writers of the period of writing the same novel again and again and merely changing the title or of simply regurgitating clichés. These insights from new media studies, a field interested in the creation and consumption of cultural production, might enable us to see these processes of literary recycling across genres, so common in the works of these popular authors (and more elite ones for that matter), as fundamental to the creation of a new media environment. The novels and "panoramic literature" cited earlier—all of which were reworked, reissued, and remediated with great success in the literary market—might thus help uncover new understandings of the dynamic origins of the nineteenth-century literary market and establish links between nineteenth-century "new media" and that of the twenty-first century.

Given my desire to enter in depth into the intricacies of the style, genre, and reception of writers grappling differently with changing market pressures, I have limited myself to the works of three major figures (de Kock, Sue, and Balzac), in whose work and correspondence the relationship to the marketplace is made explicit, and the phenomenon of panoramic literature, to which many types of authors—popular, elite, male, female—contributed. In the case of panoramic literature, we see an urban genre with a common set of aesthetic and thematic goals that targeted a range of audiences and came to connote a literary formula that was sure to sell. De Kock too established a formulaic style of writing that drew in scores of readers and made him a domestic and international success, while Sue dabbled, with commercial and some critical success, across genres before achieving global stardom with the publication of *Les Mystères de Paris*. So central to the developing market were de Kock and Sue that even their names connoted meaning in the nineteenth-century literary field. Balzac offers a counterpoint to these more overtly lowbrow authors; while he promoted himself and came to be seen as a serious author, he also contributed to more commercial publications and incorporated these forms of writing into his more highbrow works.

This deliberately narrowed focus means a comparative neglect of other key best-selling authors like Frédéric Soulié and Alexandre Dumas, as well as writers, like George Sand, whom we would now consider canonical but who were intimately involved in the same literary networks as the authors studied here. Hugo also of course produced best-selling novels both at the beginning of the period I study here (*Notre-Dame de Paris*) and later in the century (*Les Misérables*). While the case of Dumas is a particularly pertinent one—he was associated with commercial literature to such a degree he was accused of running a "fabrique de romans," or "novel factory," with his collaborators—I have chosen authors for this study who, aside from Balzac, have received less scholarly attention.[57] It is my hope that this book's close engagements with the work of the popular authors I examine will serve as a jumping-off point for further study. I have chosen not to concentrate specifically on the question of popular women writers during this period, a topic studied in depth by Cohen, Catherine Nesci, Margaret Waller, and Thérenty, among others. Major authors like Sand, who wrote prolifically but did not consistently produce best-selling works, figured prominently in the literary field of the mid-nineteenth century; even after both of their deaths, Sophie Cottin and Madame de Staël's works were best sellers; and as much as or more than her husband Emile, Delphine de Girardin was a major media figure who facilitated literary networks through her salons.[58] While my study does not pay sustained attention to these or other significant female authors *as* female authors, their role and importance in the literary field of the early to mid-nineteenth century merits note and has already occasioned important studies.

The chapters of this book are organized according to individual authors and, in the case of so-called panoramic literature, a group of authors and publishers; they share a common focus on exploring the literary recycling, collaboration, and conscious self-positioning that grew out of this emerging literary market. In the first chapter I argue that while the phenomenon of panoramic literature is illustrative of early nineteenth-century readers' taste for urban observation, it also exemplifies the fluidity of generic boundaries and the more openly commercial nature of the literary marketplace. Panoramic literature, a term coined retrospectively by the cultural theorist Walter Benjamin, took the form of what was called the *Physiologie* series or of larger collections, such as *Paris ou le livre des cent-et-un* (1831), and was in part a phenomenon cooked up for profit by innovative publishers. These observations of Parisian life, often written in a comical tone and illustrated by famous caricaturists of the period, claimed mastery over their urban subjects (the *flâneur*, the working-class woman, or the student, for example) and promised to depict and decipher the city for their public. Especially during the later years of the July Monarchy, these inexpensive works were extremely popular, generating money for their authors and canny publishers and prompting cases of literary recycling. Analyses of these panoramic texts—in particular *Physiologie du flâneur, Physiologie des physiologies*, and de Kock's 1842 *La Grande Ville: Nouveau tableau de Paris*—as well as an examination of the advertisements for these works as the phenomenon developed in real time, demonstrate their self-conscious commerciality, an awareness of their place in the marketplace. The typological descriptions so frequent in these panoramic literary texts also circulated throughout the novels of contributors to the movement and those of their contemporaries. Attention to the reuse of this trope across genres exposes a more connected literary field despite perceived differences of value.

Moving from panoramic literature to popular novels, the second chapter focuses on de Kock. Thanks to his inexhaustible production of vaudevilles, novels, and occasional writings on Paris, de Kock's lucrative career spanned the better part of the nineteenth century. By the July Monarchy he had established himself as the bourgeois writer par excellence, to such a degree that by the 1830s his name itself carried a specific negative connotation. I chart the use of "Paul de Kock" as a brand name for "bad" literature through detailed reception history, exposing complexities that nineteenth-century and contemporary received ideas about de Kock overlook. Additionally I focus on his own literary recycling and on close readings of his work. De Kock republished passages of urban descriptions from one text to another and across genres. This recycling, as well as his frequent use of certain stock characters, repetitive plotlines, and recurring digressive passages, must be considered alongside his extraordinary commercial success. In other words, he and his publishers were able to convince his public of the variety in his texts and create a type of writing for which there was lucrative commercial demand. Through the keen manipulation of the forms and formats in which his work appeared, de Kock's narrative and publishing practices challenge our understanding of literary form and teach us about nineteenth-century mass-media culture.

The third chapter turns to the figure who, for Balzac, embodied commercialized literature: Eugène Sue, author of, among other works, *Les Mystères de Paris*, a media phenomenon of unparalleled proportions. This serial novel, published in the *Journal des débats*, not only generated huge numbers of subscribers for the *Journal* and sold unprecedented numbers of copies once it was published in volumes but also occasioned the publication of many international adaptations of the urban mystery genre. Multiple translations, editions, and interpretations of Sue's work were produced in the years following its initial appearance. While I address *Les Mystères* as a literary phenomenon by examining the publicity surrounding its publication, this chapter departs from recent criticism on Sue as part of the network of "mystères urbains" in its focus on Sue's oeuvre as a whole. With few exceptions virtually all scholarship on Sue focuses exclusively on *Les Mystères*. I maintain instead that Sue was a market-savvy author who made multiple attempts to achieve commercial success by exploiting his literary network and by writing in disparate, already established novelistic genres—maritime novels and *romans de moeurs* (novel of manners)—before he attained his exceptional success with *Les Mystères*. His serialized fiction became a blockbusting phenomenon in part because of his previous literary and professional strategies. For example, tropes, subplots, and types reappear in his novels throughout his career, demonstrating that he recycled elements of his work and modified them according to the relevant subgenre. Through analyses of his lesser-known (and critically unexamined) works leading up to *Les Mystères* (*Kernok le pirate* [1830], *Mathilde* [1841], and *Paula Monti* [1842]), as well as an examination of their marketing, publishing, and promotion, I argue that Sue made tactical, profitable moves in his choice of literary genres.

This chapter ultimately illustrates that Sue's mega–best sellers, as well as his more minor commercial hits (and failures), inform us about the changing marketplace and contemporary literary tastes.

In the fourth chapter I analyze Balzac's complicated relationship to the literary marketplace, a milieu he famously depicted in his novel *Illusions perdues* (1837–44). He envied the commercial success of authors like Sue while at the same time consciously positioning his works against those of popular authors. Balzac was both a contributor to and a critic of the early commercialized mass market, in particular the movement of panoramic literature. I explore how Balzac adopts and overtly repurposes text from his contributions to panoramic literature, exploiting a marketable trope that he elsewhere disdained. Accordingly, after the 1841 publication of *Physiologie de l'employé*, he transformed his serial novella *La Femme supérieure* (1837) into the 1844 version titled *Les Employés*, a more lengthy sociological study of the world of bureaucracy during the early nineteenth century. Through close readings I demonstrate how this ambiguous stance toward popular contemporary literary tropes is also evident in his trilogy *Histoire des Treize* (*Ferragus, La Duchesse de Langeais, La Fille aux yeux d'or* [1833–34]). In these three short novels the author openly reuses passages from other, nonfiction panoramic publications. At the same time he renders other examples of his typological urban writing extremely figurative and thus more overtly focused on aesthetics than the panoramic texts. Critics have deemed Balzac a more serious writer than his popular contemporaries, whose works purportedly connoted less cultural capital. Balzac's works and correspondence evince too his own preoccupations with literary value in the emerging midcentury literary marketplace. My examination of Balzac's engagement with the tropes of panoramic literature focuses less on his publishing practices or sales figures. Instead, through these close readings of works spanning a decade of his career, a more complex picture of the author emerges, blurring lines between high and low literature that are often replicated in past and current scholarship on Balzac.

I conclude my study with a brief overview of developments in the twenty-first-century French literary market and a short analysis of a contemporary best-selling novel, *L'Elégance du hérisson* by Muriel Barbery (2006), which, like its nineteenth-century predecessors, addresses and challenges extant definitions of high and low literature. This contemporary surprise best seller, though published by the elite publishing house Gallimard, both straddles the line between what we would now call a literary best seller and commercial fiction, and exposes tensions between high and low culture throughout the novel itself. By comparing Barbery's novel to novels more clearly identifiable as highbrow or lowbrow published that same year, I offer a recent example of a work that like my nineteenth-century examples self-consciously negotiates the balance between the commercial and the critical. I draw parallels between the early nineteenth-century literary market in France, which saw the changing status of the writer, the boom in the literate population, the mass democratization of literature, the rise of the novel, and the birth of the modern publishing industry, and the market of the global twenty-first century, in which e-readers and the Internet have once again altered the shape of the literary field. If the scope and scale of the market have changed drastically since the period studied in this book, we can nonetheless read in the very form of contemporary cultural productions how writers—and their works—continue to respond to and adapt within the always changing literary field.

Chapter One

POPULAR PANORAMAS

The May 28, 1842, issue of the daily newspaper *La Presse* contained two ads on its back page, one directly above the other, that publicized the sale of similar yet importantly different works—one a larger volume, the other a smaller and less expensive one (fig. 1). The first advertised *La Grande Ville: Nouveau tableau de Paris*, a compilation of short chapters depicting diverse urban types and occurrences by one of the period's best-known writers: Paul de Kock. The name of this exceptionally popular, prolific novelist and playwright, the subject of chapter 4 of this book, was in boldface and centered across the top of the ad, a sure draw for his abundant readers. The names of a number of similarly famous illustrators who contributed to the work were also included: Gavarni and Daumier, to name only two. The advertisement gives little indication of the content of the work; instead it focuses principally on the material features of the different formats in which it will be sold. With one installment for each week of the year, *La Grande Ville*, the ad explains, could be purchased individually as illustrated installments for the price of 40 centimes apiece ("52 Livraisons de 16 pages, papier jésus vélin, ornées de quatre à six dessins gravés sur bois par Andrew, Best et Leloir,

FIG. 1. Ads for Paul de Kock's *La Grande Ville* and La Maison
Aubert's *Physiologie* series. *La Presse*, May 28, 1842. Bibliothèque
Nationale de France.

et intercalés dans le texte)."[1] Once all the installments had been produced,
clients could alternatively buy "2 beaux volumes grand in-8° jésus vélin, ornés
d'une riche couverture imprimée en couleur, et dessinée par Victor Adam."[2]
This announcement calls attention to the high quality of the large-format
paper, cover, and craftsmanship of the product, underscored by the use of the
adjectives *beaux*, *grand*, and *riche* as well as the names of known illustrators.
Either as a luxury item or a series of installments, the physical qualities of
these two versions of *La Grande Ville* were theoretically different enough
that clients could in fact purchase both products. As the promotion for this
text makes clear then, *La Grande Ville* was packaged as a work that was sure
to sell and, as such, a profitable gamble for its publishers.

Directly below the advertisement for *La Grande Ville* there is one announcing the availability of the complete collection of *Physiologie-Aubert*, a series
of texts sold cheaply at 1 franc per volume, whose twenty-five titles are listed
in three columns below. The works include *Physiologie de l'employé* by Balzac,
Physiologie du bourgeois by the caricaturist Henri Monnier, *Physiologie du
bas-bleu* by the popular novelist Frédéric Soulié, and *Physiologie de l'homme
marié* by de Kock, all names either evoked in the previous ad or that would
eventually become associated with the second volume of *La Grande Ville*,
published the following year. Each volume in this series, we read, contains
sketches by many of the same illustrators as *La Grande Ville* (Gavarni and

Daumier). As if to showcase their talent, the ad boasts two of these illustrations, one a comical rendering of Eve being tempted by a snake with a human head, from the recently issued *Physiologie du floueur*. As opposed to the publicity for *La Grande Ville*, this second ad makes no mention of the quality of paper or of the physical properties of the works being promoted. Rather it underscores the inexpensive price of the publications and devotes space to the long lists of titles in the collection, so many that, after the first title in each column, the shorter *idem* is used in place of *Physiologie*. Stacked one on top of the other in this issue of *La Presse*, these two ads publicized works that shared common illustrators, authors, and urban subjects yet were packaged differently, with disparate price points, and seemed to target different audiences. The content, form, and marketing of these related works not only reveal the fluid nature of a particular subgenre but also expose contemporary tensions about literary value and reflect the developments of an increasingly profit-driven marketplace.

La *Grande Ville* and the *Physiologie-Aubert* collection are examples of a highly commercialized and self-consciously trendy literary phenomenon that became known in the twentieth century as "panoramic literature," a concept first evoked by Walter Benjamin. In his essay *Charles Baudelaire, a Lyric Poet in the Era of High Capitalism*, Benjamin likens these works to the visual spectacle of the painted panoramas—displayed in a rotunda for a complete immersive experience—that were fashionable throughout Europe toward the end of the eighteenth and the beginning of the nineteenth century: "These books consist of individual sketches which, as it were, reproduce the plastic foreground of those panoramas with their anecdotal form and the extensive background of the panoramas with their store of information."[3] This so-called panoramic literature dated roughly from the early July Monarchy (1830) until about 1845, peaked around 1840–42 as the above advertising suggests, and comprised a number of texts featuring nonfiction observations on urban life written by well-known and obscure authors alike. These authors, and especially their publishers, adopted strategies—both formal and promotional—to capitalize on current trends and appeal to as wide an audience as possible. The panoramic literary texts serve, then, as one of many examples of the successful ways products were packaged and sold to

France's growing readership during this early moment of mass culture. Their manifest hybridity and self-conscious commerciality also help to underscore explicitly the formal and promotional tactics with which the other authors (and publishers) I explore in this book experimented in order to comprehend, master, and profit from contemporary popular and critical tastes.

PANORAMIC LITERATURE IN CONTEXT

Panoramic literary texts were varied and came in different formats. Nineteenth-century literary dictionaries and catalogues seemed unable to classify them uniformly, as we will see, an inability that suggests a hybridity or blurring inherent in the genre. The *physiologies*, for example, were short studies of urban social types that were inexpensive to purchase, made for quick and easy consumption, and resembled a sort of humorous biological or ethnographic study. They were published by the hundreds, especially between 1840 and 1842, principally (but not exclusively) by La Maison Aubert, a publishing house run by Gabriel Aubert and Charles Philipon that also produced lithographic prints, caricatures, and the well-known satirical journals *La Caricature* and *Le Charivari*. The series' titles, including *Physiologie du flâneur*, *Physiologie de la grisette*, and *Physiologie du tailleur*, evoked the emerging scientific discipline of physiology, and the works themselves mimicked the language of the natural sciences in their classifying of social types.[4] Their style was witty, however, rather than scientific, and they focused on specifically contemporary types and mores through vignettes, dialogues, and descriptions.[5] Richard Sieburth has pointed out that some of the origins of this genre can be traced to earlier *études de moeurs* (studies of manners) and satirical journals like *La Silhouette* and *La Caricature* (both run, at least in part, by Philipon) that contained comical illustrated vignettes.[6] The illustrated *Physiologie de la poire*, a work published on the heels of Philipon and Daumier's famous caricatures of King Louis-Philippe as a pear, was not the first work to bear this title: Brillat-Savarin's 1825 *Physiologie du goût* and Balzac's 1829 *Physiologie du mariage* are often seen as precursors of this subgenre.[7] The formulaic nature of these *physiologies* is reminiscent too of other modes of popular culture being produced at the same time, like vaudevilles, which, Jennifer Terni has noted, "were formulaic and mass produced, and . . .

their popularity depended, at least in part, on their formulaic predictability."[8] Although clearly distinct in their formal composition from the vaudevilles, the *physiologies* nonetheless relied on the use of types and a predictable structure that made them appealing to readers.

There existed pricier counterparts to the *physiologies*, like *La Grande Ville*, referred to at times as *tableaux de Paris* or, as Priscilla Ferguson has classified them more generally, "literary guidebooks."[9] They included the 1831 *Paris, ou le livre des cent-et-un* ("Paris, or the Book of the One Hundred and One"), authored, as its title suggests, by 101 different writers in an attempt to keep publisher Pierre-François Ladvocat's business afloat; the 1839–42 *Français peints par eux-mêmes* ("The French Depicted by Themselves") by the publisher Leon Curmer; and numerous works called new or *"nouveaux" tableaux de Paris*, referencing Louis-Sebastien Mercier's *Le Tableau de Paris*.[10] These works could be purchased in installments or as elegantly bound editions and were usually geared toward a middle-class public.[11] The larger volumes were similar to the *physiologies* in their episodic depiction of everyday urban phenomena (types, events, places, professions), yet they were less prescribed in their format. The chapters in these works varied—at times as a result of their different authors—and could take the form of a short story, a dialogue, an essay, or straight typological description, as in the *physiologies*. Affirming that the "panoramic text uses clearly differentiated genres to represent differing social species," Margaret Cohen has termed this characteristic of panoramic literature "heterogenericity."[12] The more expensive examples of panoramic literature, then, as opposed to the more fixed *physiologies*, were models of hybridity in their generic composition, and nineteenth-century cataloguers and bibliographers alike recognized this blurring of generic boundaries.

Much of the commercial success of these works can be attributed to their humorous style and appealing illustrations and, to be sure, the careful publicity campaigns by their publishers. Scholars have argued that these panoramic literary texts enabled readers to navigate and comprehend changing urban spaces and social categories.[13] Such *mises en types* ("rendering as types," Judith Lyon-Caen's term) sought to classify and understand cultural codes and types during a moment of great social and political upheaval. Lyon-Caen in particular sees connections between panoramic literature and contemporary social investigations, or *enquêtes sociales*, works on public hygiene and prostitution.[14] For her, "littérature panoramique et romans et enquêtes sociales de la monarchie de Juillet forment ainsi un voisinage textuel qui brouille les frontières de genres et de registres."[15] Meanwhile critics like Karlheinz Stierle locate in the subgenre of the *tableaux de Paris* the origins of Baudelaire's theories of modernity.[16] In addition to exposing the inner workings of the dynamic literary marketplace, this short-lived phenomenon demonstrates both proto-sociological and literary significance, despite its superficially lowbrow pretentions.

Benjamin's notion of panoramic literature as a "petit bourgeois genre virtually devoid of genuine social insight," the textual equivalent of the painted panoramas, has long been accepted as the critical model for analyzing this body of work.[17] Recently, however, Martina Lauster, Nathalie Preiss, Valérie Stiénon, and other scholars have encouraged specialists to push past the almost universally accepted Benjaminian understanding of the *physiologies* and the larger collections of *tableaux*. Lauster argues that Benjamin's approach, which views the *physiologies* and other sketches as part of a "middle-class attempt to gain control over a threatening social body," ultimately obscures "the dynamism of the text-image relationships which makes the [p]hysiologies the most advanced journalistic meta-medium of the time."[18] Likewise Preiss and Stiénon resist the totalizing vision of Benjamin's panorama because, they write, the *physiologies* "privilégient l'écriture non du fragment mais de la fraction et du fait détaché, nulle totalité."[19] Stiénon suggests even looking to the model of the kaleidoscope rather than the panorama for a visual analogy for these texts.[20] While I employ the term "panoramic literature" for ease of reference, I align my thinking with that of recent critics for whom these texts are more ambiguous and dynamic than initially characterized by Benjamin.

These panoramic literary texts may have achieved commercial success for many reasons, such as their "proto-sociological" attempts to render contemporary Parisian society legible to their readers, their embodiment of mid-nineteenth-century French readers' taste for urban observations, their high-quality illustrations, and their humorous tone, among other reasons.[21] They also clearly exposed the complex changes taking place in the new literary marketplace. The advertisements for and content of these panoramic works show the developing influence of publishers on their authors.[22] Publishers produced and publicized these trendy works; authors too took advantage of popular tastes to capitalize on the trend. If the packaging and advertising of these works call attention to themselves as, in Richard Sieburth's words, "commodities destined for mass consumption," the phenomenon of panoramic literature is at once indicative of early mass culture and conscious of the tensions that arose from nineteenth-century popular tastes.[23] The frequent evocation of the notion of literary value found in many of these texts shows the panoramic literary works staging contemporary debates about the tensions between high and low literature. Moreover the consistently mixed categorization of these works in book industry publications and dictionaries demonstrates panoramic literature resisting generic conventions and suggesting more generally the fluid boundaries of the literary field in which they were produced. What follows is a close analysis of the panoramic texts themselves, in particular *Physiologie des physiologies* and de Kock's *La Grande Ville: Nouveau tableau de Paris*, and the promotional materials associated with them, as well as an examination of their classification in the *Bibliographie de la France*. Where previous critics have deemed them "innocuous" and a "nearly perfect example of that transformation of book into commodity," I will show, through an examination of the content and promotion of these works, that their rapid popularity and commercial success embody, perhaps more overtly than other best sellers of the period, not just the merchandising of literature but also the intricate developments in marketing, publishing, and even literary form taking place in this dynamic new marketplace.[24]

PHYSIOLOGIE DES PHYSIOLOGIES

The *Physiologies* were a self-consciously commercial series; they were essentially marketed both from the inside and the outside of the text. In order to understand the way the *physiologie* series exposed the inner workings of the marketplace for popular literature, it is helpful to comprehend fully the form and content of this peculiar subgenre. The 1820s saw the publication of occasional texts, unrelated to the scientific study of physiology, which bore the title *Physiologie* (notably by Brillat-Savarin and Balzac). But during the real boom of their production (1840–42) an estimated 130 were produced, and they sold by the thousands.[25] What is notable about these texts is their uniform structure: "C'est la constance du même format in-32, du même nombre de pages (une centaine environ), le même prix, 1 franc, prix relativement bon marché à cette époque."[26] Though comical in nature, these typological studies, as we have seen, functioned in multiple ways: to render the city readable, allowing readers a chance to master their chaotic urban space; to ironize the notion of the great writer; to ape the language of scientific discourse; to categorize urban phenomena; and to respond to the market's desire for hypercontemporary literary works that depicted their readers' everyday lives.[27]

Take, for example, arguably the most famous instance of the genre, *Physiologie du flâneur* by Louis Huart, a frequent contributor to the genre. The text begins, with mock philosophical pretentions, by disproving previous definitions of man so as to redefine him in the following way: "Un animal à deux pieds, sans plumes, à paletot, fumant et flânant."[28] What characterizes man, according to this text, is his ability to "perdre son temps."[29] The next several chapters explain how to discriminate the legitimate *flâneur* from others, prove how the *flâneur* is fundamentally a moral creature (so empty is his mind that he is incapable of thinking immoral thoughts), and demonstrate how to distinguish among the subgenera of *flâneurs* (from the "flâneur parfait" [perfect *flâneur*] to the "flâneur militaire" [military *flâneur*]). The narrator explains the pleasures and inconveniences of *flânerie* (enjoying colorful signs posted throughout the city; getting thwacked by shutters put out inattentively by shop workers anxious to close up), notes the typical urban spaces in which the *flâneur* circulates, and finally offers helpful hints to new *flâneurs*, including useful vocabulary. Huart breaks down the characteristics of this specific urban type while humorously mimicking philosophical and scientific discourse. This example illustrates the *physiologie*'s fixed format and style despite variations in subjects across the series, a purposeful standardization "par les impératifs éditoriaux de collections destinées à fidéliser un lectorat et à susciter des effets de modes."[30] By 1841 the genre was so popular that an anonymous author published *Physiologie*

SOUS PRESSE. . . . .

L'abondance de matière nous force à reculer
devant l'*annonce!*

FIG. 2. Back cover of *Physiologie des physiologies* (1841).
Bibliothèque Nationale de France.

des physiologies, a parody of an already parodic text.[31] Reading this work gives
insight into the style and format of the genre and also into the way these
works were understood at the time of their publication as a commercial
genre that highlighted tensions about literary value.

On the back cover of *Physiologie des physiologies* there is a sketch of a
tired or even jaded writer, his head resting on one hand as he dips his quill
into the ink with the other and stares dazedly at the text before him, where
several squiggles are drawn but no letters are distinguishable (fig. 2). Below
this sketch, which is not attributed to an artist but resembles the work of
Gavarni and other well-known illustrators of the *Physiologie* series, in bold
type is written the following: "SOUS PRESSE. . . . L'abondance de matière
nous force à reculer devant l'*annonce!*"[32] This cheeky statement occupying

the place that ordinarily offered a list of forthcoming or available texts—and most often *physiologies*—along with the image of the blasé writer work in concert to capture the content of the text that has preceded this back cover. The sheer number of *physiologies* published then and in the previous year, and the almost obligatory need for all authors to produce one of these short texts, are treated in depth in this satirical *physiologie*, a tongue-and-cheek analysis of the ongoing trend.

Physiologie des physiologies begins with a seven-stanza poem that also functions as a summary of what is found in the subsequent text. From the start the author evokes two commonplaces of the *physiologie* genre: that all authors think themselves capable of writing a *physiologie* and that the texts are hastily cobbled together:

> La mine est féconde
> Se dit à part soi tout bas,
> Chacun à la ronde
> Avant de sortir d'ici
> Je m'en vais bâcler aussi
> Ma Physiologie O gué! Ma physiologie.[33]

In addition to the use of the term *bâcler* (to botch or dash off), the ease with which the *physiologies* are produced is repeated when the poet describes the writing process as "une oeuvre en quelques instants est toute finie" and, in a longer passage, explains, "Qu'on me donne seulement . . . de l'encre et du papier blanc, et je vous parie / que sans gêne avant demain / je mets tout le genre humain / en physiologie."[34] Ruth Amossy suggests that this song attests to the fact that "le mérite essentiel de ces petits livres est de s'écouler facilement sur le marché."[35] Not only do all writers feel the need to create their own *physiologie*, but all readers are desperate to read them and to see themselves recognized in them; this need for familiarity motivated not only the writers of panoramic literature but also novelists like Eugène Sue to focus on the urban subject. Likening the short texts to "champignons après une pluie" the poet writes that "chaque homme voulut avoir sa physiologie."[36] The poet also addresses the extreme popularity of these most modern of texts, comparing them to the satirical review *Les Guêpes* and a larger panoramic literary text currently being published, *Les Français peints par eux-mêmes*, but suggests that these two publications "ne font plus furie" and that "les lecteurs en ont assez, leur veine est tarie."[37] Instead it is the age of the *physiologie*: "Vive en ce jour heureux la physiologie."[38] In a dynamic market where need for the newest and greatest product grows daily, the *physiologie* subgenre is the latest trend to surpass these others. Both the introductory poem and the paratextual material at the back emphasize the popularity and prevalence of these works as a way, it seems, to sell more; they build on the commercial phenomenon of the *physiologies* to advance it.

Throughout the remainder of the work, all of these themes (the facility of writing *physiologies*, their omnipresence in the marketplace, their questionable value) are developed at length, indicating engagement with the pressing tensions in the evolving literary field. The author comically cites both the scientific and literary pretentions of these trendy works, noting, "Grâce à ces petits livres, pétris de science et d'esprit, l'homme sera mieux classé, mieux divisé, mieux subdivisé que les animaux ses confrères," and also states that to create a *physiologie* one must simply mix together some simple ingredients, like following a recipe: "Prenez une pincée de Labruyère—une cuillerée des *Lettres Persanes*. Faites infuser les *Guêpes*; *Les Papillons noirs*; *Les Lettres Cochinchinoises*; *La Revue Parisienne*; les *Nouvelles à la main*; Mettez à contribution les feuilletons du *Corsaire* et du *Charivari*"; wrap it all up in "des *Français*, inventés par M. Curmer" and the product is complete.[39] According to Stiénon, this recipe, composed of "ingredients de base, plutôt faciles à trouver," is one of many examples of the genre's "moquerie du créateur incréé," the puncturing of the image of the "genie créateur"; in other words, it gestures toward critical debates surrounding the production of literature, in particular of industrial literature detailed most notably just two years earlier by Sainte-Beuve in his essay "De la littérature industrielle."[40] This parodic text reiterates commonplaces about the dual nature of such works: on the one hand they are pseudo-scientific and even early sociological tracts; on the other, they are deeply involved in a literary conversation—even from the margins.[41]

The text speculates as to why these short works have become so popular, once again underscoring their overt engagement in contemporary questions about literary value and commercial literature. In fact it keenly offers one explanation that Lyon-Caen has recently developed: that contemporary readers enjoyed works that depict recognizable types. The text twists this logic a bit in arguing that "chacun croit y reconnaître le portrait de son voisin, et en rit. S'il se reconnaissait lui-même, il crierait au scandale. Voilà pourquoi chacun attend avec impatience sa Physiologie. . . . Afin de reconnaître son voisin et de s'en amuser, sans jamais se reconnaître soi-même."[42] Readers are familiar enough with the types comically described within that they enjoy recognizing their neighbors (but not themselves), and they eagerly anticipate subsequent publications. This is not the only passage of the work to poke fun at its readers—or its writers. The text offers the following "definition" of *physiologie* (these "definitions" are common features of the genre): "Ce mot se compose de deux mots grecs, dont la signification est désormais celle ci: Volume in-18; composé de 124 pages, et d'un nombre illimité de vignettes, de culs de lampes, de sottises et de bavardage à l'usage des gens niais de leur nature."[43] Replete with silly tales and typographical ornamentations, these small texts target "simple" readers, or so the *Physiologie* posits.

The anonymous author further (humorously) maligns the genre by comparing it to the work of the supposed founder of the *physiologie* trend (Brillat-Savarin, with his 1825 *Physiologie du goût*) and chiding him for the fact that he showed "tant d'esprit et de délicatesse de son temps" and therefore calling attention to the supposed poor literary quality of the *physiologies*.[44] The problem is, he explains, that today's writer prefers not to imitate the "high quality" writing of Brillat-Savarin and has thus never "si bien réussi à s'éloigner du maître."[45] Although the works share the same title of *Physiologie*, simply turning the page reveals serious differences between the two: "Dans l'un, l'esprit le plus gai, le plus fin, le plus charmant, le plus exquis; Dans ceux-ci, l'esprit le plus lourd, le plus épais, le plus fastidieux, le plus grossier."[46] The author highlights the reductive nature of the genre—"Le volume entier est sur la première page"—and even offers a mock *physiologie de l'homme mort* to parody the genre.[47] These works, we are meant to understand, are both simple to write and to read, can be quickly thrown together, and are enjoyed by a large audience. In characterizing the genre in this fashion, the author repeats many contemporary and modern commonplaces about its style and quality. These witty barbs about the quality of the questionable literary value of the *physiologie* can be found throughout the series, not only in this parodic text. In focusing on what she calls the "dimension autoréflexive" (self-reflective dimension) of the *physiologie*, Stiénon notes in particular its tendency to call attention to the inferior literary quality of the works: "Ces monographies s'autodéfinissent comme illégitimes à travers une écriture qui exhibe volontiers leur statu de textes mineurs, faciles, voire de piètre qualité."[48] They enter, in an explicit way, into the contemporary debate about the literary value of commercialized literature.

However, while *Physiologies des physiologies* does focus on the conventions about the facility of writing in this genre and the stereotypes about its readers, it is also at pains to describe the prevalence and commercial success of the genre, despite what the author critiques as its inferior literary qualities; as such, *Physiologie des physiologies* can be said to be marketing itself, and the series as a whole, from within the work itself. Over and over again the author repeats that the *physiologies* are in demand and taking the literary marketplace by storm. There is, for example, the short chapter entitled "Physiologies—Physiologies, et tout est physiologie" in which the author claims that "un livre sérieux aujourd'hui, c'est un non sens," before staging a scene in which the reader enters a bookstore and is confronted with the choice of which book to purchase.[49]

Voyez pluôt—Vous entrez chez un libraire, et vous lui demandez un bon livre.

Que fait le libraire?

Il vous offre une Physiologie.

Vous repoussez cela du doigt avec mépris et vous avez raison—Mais regardez autour de vous;

Parcourez d'un regard tout le magasin de votre libraire. Où sont donc Molière, Racine, Corneille, Montesquieu, Fénelon, Chateaubriand, Lamartine, Hugo? Là-bas, tout au fond dans l'ombre. Ils dorment, en attendant la résurrection. Mais qu'est-ce que donc que tous ces petits livres, jaunes …—bleus,—rouges,—qui se présentent pêle-mêle dans les rayons,—qui encombrent les tables jusqu'au plafond, et dont les longues files se roulent.—s'enroulent et se déroulent comme d'énormes serpents aux écailles changeantes? *Physiologies, Physiologies,—et tout est Physiologie!*[50]

While disparaging the quality of the *physiologie* as opposed to the work of other contemporary and classical writers, the author nevertheless depicts these other writers (both literary greats of seventeenth- and eighteenth-century France as well as contemporary romantic heroes) as being in retreat, waiting out the phenomenon of the *physiologie*. The shadow cast over these more critically accepted works is contrasted with the flashy colors of the *physiologie*, which seem to take over the tables of the bookstore. Even if the reader prefers to buy a work by Molière or even Hugo, the bookseller will push him to buy a *physiologie*. This depiction implies both that the popular texts overshadowed all other available works on the market and also that the never-ending supply of these texts offered all the more incentive for booksellers to push them on their clients. Further still, the author (comically to be sure) claims that his appetite has only been whet by the available *physiologies*—"Vous n'avez fait qu'aiguiser notre soif"—and ends the book with a list of subjects for possible future *physiologies*, entreating his fellow authors to write and promising financial gain: "Vous serez béni par les cordonniers, les chapeliers et les gantiers—ce qui est beau; et vos réclames seront grassement payées,—ce qui est mieux."[51]

In the end both the content and the material surrounding *Physiologie des physiologies* offer insight into the understanding of the genre in the moment that the phenomenon was playing out. On the whole the *physiologies* were very self-conscious about their style and commercial nature, and this particular work—distilling all of the genre's qualities into yet another cheaply formatted (in-32) 124 pages—calls attention to all the genre's characteristics. Denis Saint-Armand and Stiénon view *Physiologie des physiologies* as the culmination of the genre, calling it a "texte contre-programmatique," and highlighting the tendency of the genre to contain a metacommentary regarding "sa médiocrité, sa facilité, ses visées commerciales."[52] This parodic work, in other words, takes to the extreme the *physiologies'* already explicit awareness of their relationship to the literary field. Saint-Armand and Stiénon remind us too that this 1841 text was not without precedent.[53] On October 11, 1840, slightly earlier in the success of the short phenomenon,

La Caricature, a journal that was run out of La Maison Aubert, published an anonymous article also entitled "Physiologie des Physiologies" that took up many of the same themes and repeated some of the same language as the 1841 *physiologie*. The article called attention to the scientific origins of the term, before citing Brillat-Savarin as the founder of the nonscientific version of the genre and finally giving the most "modern" definition of it: "La physiologie est l'art de parler et d'écrire incorrectement, sous la forme d'un petit livre vert, bleu, rouge, jaune, qui fait de son mieux pour soutirer une pièce de vingt sous au passant, et qui l'ennuie tout son saoul en retour."[54] In chapter 4 I will produce a similar version—almost verbatim—of this quotation attributed to Balzac in his *Monographie de la Presse parisienne*, indicating a certain amount of recycling in the critical discourse about these texts as well as in them, a trait so characteristic of the repackaging of language and genres during this period. Notable in *La Caricature*'s article, however, is the consistent reference to the poor quality of these prolific and cheaply sold texts. Further recycling from this piece to the *Physiologie* can be found in the "recipe" this article offers for creating a *physiologie*: "Vous remplissez cela de fadaises, bons mots, balivernes, gaudrioles, anas, coqs à l'âne, sornettes, chansons . . . vous semez le tout de solecismes, jurons. . . . Vous copiez sur la couverture les *Guêpes* ou la *Revue parisienne* . . . et vous servez chaud."[55] Though the steps for concocting *physiologies* are slightly modified here, the references to contemporary publications and the format of this list are quite similar and reinforce the elements of this subgenre that would be crystalized shortly after in *Physiologie des physiologies*. This was a fixed and digestible literary format whose possible topics were virtually infinite; in sum, the recipe laid out by the *Physiologie*'s anonymous author was one that promised commercial success.

AUBERT'S MARKET FOR THE *PHYSIOLOGIES*

Between 1840 and 1842 it was primarily Philipon and his brother-in-law Gabriel Aubert who cornered the market on the short, abundant *physiologies*. Aubert and Philipon's joint publishing venture, La Maison Aubert, maintained "absolute dominance of the city's trade in *les physiologies*."[56] While other publishers tried their hand at the genre (Desloges and Bocquet, to name two), according to Lhéritier, "Aubert, surtout par la qualité de ses illustrations, s'imposa comme le véritable éditeur des physiologies."[57] Between February 1840 and August 1842 La Maison Aubert produced thirty-two *physiologies* "in a combined edition of 161,000 volumes or just over three quarters of the total number of such volumes published in Paris during this period."[58] La Maison Aubert, in other words, profited most from this ephemeral yet lucrative phenomenon. Lhéritier goes as far as calling Philipon the true creator of the particular "genre physiologique": "Il semble bien que les physiologies, telles qu'elles ont été présentées au public, sous petit format et illustrées de nombreuses vignettes soient nées d'une idée de journaliste. L'invention en revient à Philipon . . . et de toutes les productions de la maison Aubert."[59] Whether or not the genre was the brain child of Philipon, it is clear that La Maison Aubert's publications made up the majority of those sold during this short window and that this enterprise took advantage of its experience with and knowledge of the marketplace to dominate and capitalize on the trend. Attention to their publicity campaign, one that keenly seized on market trends for the panoramic literary genre and that would eventually define the brand of the Aubert *physiologie*, evinces the publishing house's use of more modern marketing tactics.

Reasons for the success and volume of La Maison Aubert's series certainly included the existing trend for its satirical, illustrated publications, but its connections with the network of popular publishers, authors, and illustrators, and Philipon's evident understanding of the market, cannot be discounted. Even in the early years of his career, Philipon was actively producing works in line with current trends. Prints attributed to Philipon from the late 1820s "were the gently erotic kind so popular among bourgeois Parisians in the final years of the Restoration." Having opened his own printing shop in 1830, Philipon continued to publish such prints as well as political carica-tures, cannily tapping into the market of the "many print genres that had in common a bourgeois market defined by the commercial culture of the city's Right Bank quarters centered on the Palais Royal." As the popular press began to take hold in Paris, Philipon became involved as one of the shareholders of the new journal *La Silhouette* in 1829 alongside other key figures of the time like Emile de Girardin (who founded *La Presse*) and the journalist and publisher Charles Latour-Mezeray. When he started his own satirical journal, *La Caricature*, in the following years, Philipon "brought to the task not only the valuable administrative and financial experience in the publication of such a journal but also the knowledge of its potential market that must have been relayed to him by his fellow shareholders, all of whom were journalists central to the development of the Parisian popular press." Around the same time Philipon was establishing himself as a preeminent figure of the satirical press, he also joined forces with his brother-in-law and opened La Maison Aubert, a "magasin de caricatures" located, tactically, in the "center of the city's trade in prints and caricatures," the Passage Véro-Dodat. Geographically and professionally Philipon had secured a commercial space that would assure him success.[60]

In 1832 Philipon founded *Le Charivari*, another daily satirical journal. Available by subscription like *La Caricature*, *Le Charivari* differed in price, content, and target audience from the previous paper. *La Caricature* appeared less frequently and was printed on a higher quality paper for more wealthy readers.[61] Both papers, which Philipon controlled, were produced out of Aubert's shop, and Aubert was compensated for the use of this space. In 1835 *La Caricature* folded due to new legislation, so Philipon could pour more resources into *Le Charivari*. Though other newspapers began to include caricatures in their pages, Philipon—with the advent of these two newspapers—was able to "to foresee the potential success of the illustrated satirical journal and to marshal the necessary financial backing to make a go of it in the early years of the July Monarchy."[62] The portrait of Philipon that emerges is of a savvy and well-connected businessman who, as a practitioner and publisher, had an excellent sense of the tastes of readers for light, satirical illustrated texts.[63] With his knowledge of the trade and comprehension of the medium, he was poised to contribute to and profit from the popular literary trend of panoramic literature.

By the time of the phenomenon of the *physiologies*, La Maison Aubert had moved to the Bourse, marking (symbolically, according to Cuno) "the transformation of Philipon's publishing enterprise from one that was struggling, politically contentious, and laden by fines and seizures in the early 1830s to one that was highly successful, commercially diversified, and politically acceptable in the 1840s."[64] At this point Philipon had honed many of his marketing and sales tactics. According to Lhéritier, in the *Charivari*, "on y rencontre souvent, à la dernière page, des annonces pour la collection Aubert et parfois des pages entières reproduisant des vignettes extraites de physiologies."[65] Taking advantage of the free advertising space, Aubert's publishers often placed ads or *réclames* (paid advertisements masquerading as articles) for the *physiologies* within the pages of the *Charivari* as well, a strategy we would call owned media today.[66] These ads also appeared readily from 1840 to 1842 in the daily political papers, notably *La Presse*, whose founder was the former co-shareholder of *La Silhouette* with Philipon. Many of these ads, on which I will linger here briefly, highlighted the exclusivity of the Aubert brand, the famous nature of the authors and illustrators of the series, and the sheer quantity of *physiologies* being produced; at the same time they illustrate the keen marketing tactics of La Maison Aubert.

If we track the ads for the Physiologie-Aubert over the short period of 1841–42, we can see the literary phenomenon of the *physiologies* developing in real time and Aubert's response to this phenomenon in his publicity. In particular, ads from early in 1841 compared with ones in late 1842 show just how prolific these texts became over such a short period and how La Maison Aubert sought to corner the market on them. An ad on April 14, 1841, for the *Physiologie de l'étudiant* by Huart, for example, boasts an illustration of a young man holding an umbrella for his female companion and the word *l'étudiant* in a large, bold type, much larger than the word *physiologie* (fig. 3). The low price of the volume ("1 franc") is centered below the title and author's name, and under the price is a list of six other titles, each in different fonts, the variety of which suggests a lack of cohesion among the volumes despite their common title. On one line of the advertisement, however, the titles of a few works are grouped together—"Physiologies de la Grisette, du Flâneur, du Boutiquier"—and the ad also includes the string "etc, etc, etc, etc," which gesture toward the eventual collection Aubert would advertise and the forthcoming surfeit of *physiologies*.[67] In other words, although La Maison Aubert was actively selling and publishing *physiologies* at this moment, the volumes had not yet become enough of a phenomenon to advertise them as such.

No more than one month later La Maison Aubert had ramped up the

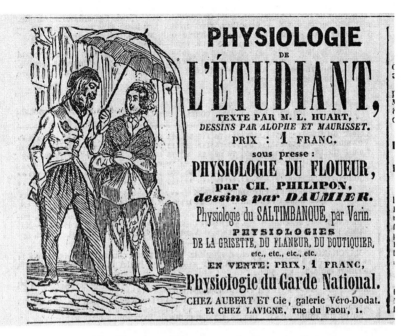

FIG. 3. Ad for *Physiologie de l'étudiant* in *La Presse*, April 14, 1841.
Bibliothèque Nationale de France.

rhetoric surrounding the profusion of *physiologies* in its advertisements. In a *réclame* placed in the May 18, 1841, issue of *La Presse*, the now well-known *Physiologie du flâneur* by Huart was advertized by his publishers as continuing "la piquante collection de volumes in-18, entreprise par MM Aubert et comp., qui mettent sous presse la *Physiologie de la Lorette*, celle du *Flâneur*, du *Boutiquier*, du *Saltimbanque*, et un grand nombre d'autres petits ouvrages du même genre"(fig. 4).[68] Aubert had begun to sell the *physiologies* as individual works and as a collection; as part of his advertising strategy, it seems, his ads now indicated the forthcoming works, as well as already published ones. As if to confirm this approach, below the *réclame* is an ad for the *Physiologie du flâneur* that is visibly more streamlined than the May 14 ad. A sketch of the *flâneur* occupies the left quarter, and the title, centered under the words "Prix: 1 franc," contains the word "FLANEUR" in large boldface. The title hovers above a two-column list of titles "sous presse," which in turn is positioned above a list (in smaller type) of those works currently for sale. All of

FIG. 4. Ad for *Physiologie du flâneur* in *La Presse*, May 18, 1841.
Bibliothèque Nationale de France.

these titles are printed in a relatively similar font—as opposed to the varied fonts in the May 14 ad—giving a sense of uniformity among the works and indicating, by extension, that the genre had begun to coalesce.

Later that year La Maison Aubert's ads show the publishing house defining its brand against those produced by other publishers by highlighting their quality as well as the popular illustrators and authors who contributed to the collection. Though one might assume that the influx of *physiologies* by other authors could only contribute to the popularity of the genre and thus to sales of Aubert's works, by the end of 1841 the publishing house evidently felt the need to distinguish itself from the others and to establish itself as the founder of the genre. The back page of the August 14, 1841, issue of *La Presse* contains promotional material for Balzac's *Physiologie de l'employé* in the form of a *réclame* and an advertisement. Highlighting the quality of Balzac's work, the *réclame* states, "C'est le plus fécond de nos romanciers, M. H. de Balzac, qui a bien voulu se charger de décrire l'employé, et nul ne

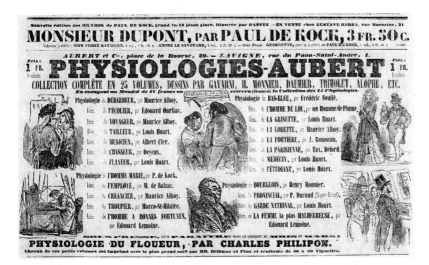

FIG. 5. Ad for La Maison Aubert's *Physiologie* series in *La Presse*,
March 12, 1842. Bibliothèque Nationale de France.

pouvait mieux le faire" before claiming, "Cette collection de petites physiologies est supérieure à toutes celles qui paraissent aujourd'hui."[69] By banking
on the established reputation of Balzac and his incomparable work on this
physiologie, the ad differentiates itself from the other *physiologies* by calling
Aubert's collection, and its contributors, superior. A November 24, 1841, ad
that promoted a variety of works produced at La Maison Aubert included
publicity for the *Physiologies-Aubert* brand, noting, "Il ne faut pas confondre
cette jolie publication avec la foule de mauvais petits livres que son succès
a fait naître."[70] Similarly a *réclame* in the May 28, 1842, issue of *La Presse*
announced the sale of Philipon's own *Physiologie du floueur*, completing "la
collection de 25 jolis petits volumes qu'on désigne sous le titre de *Physiologie-
Aubert*, pour la distinguer de cette foule de petits mauvais ouvrages que son
succèss a fait naître."[71] The *physiologie* was the creation of Aubert, we are
to understand, and all others were not only imitations but inferior ones at
that. Additionally we see Aubert's repackaging of the individual *physiologies*
into a complete collection; he has shrewdly created a new product out of
an existing one—the collection in place of the individual, less expensive
physiologies—thereby further extending the Aubert brand.[72]

Perhaps the zenith of Aubert's *physiologie* publicity came in the form of an ad in *La Presse* on March 12, 1842, that covered over a third of the back page (fig. 5). "PHYSIOLOGIES-AUBERT" runs across the top in block letters, flanked on either side, as had become customary, by the price: "Prix: 1 FR le volume." Underneath we read that the complete collection is available in twenty-five volumes, with illustrations from Gavarni, H. Monnier, and Daumier, among others. To underscore the quality of the volumes' illustrations, the publisher has included six sketches—one, for example, of a man working at his desk to correspond with Balzac's *Physiologie de l'employé*. The large number of sketches is a nod to the trend for caricature and also a reminder of the famous illustrators associated with the *physiologies* and Aubert more generally. Among the illustrations, the ad includes blocks of text containing titles and authors ("*Physiologie de l'employé* par de Balzac"; "*Physiologie du bas-bleu* par Frédéric Soulié"; "*Physiologie du bourgeois*, par Henri Monnier"). Twenty-four works are listed, and "Idem" replaces the word "Physiologie" for all but the first title in each column, reinforcing the sheer number of installments. Although no particular author is highlighted (as was the case in the previous ad for *Physiologie de l'employé*), the names of many of these authors—de Kock, Soulié, Huart, Balzac—should be enough to compel readers into purchasing the complete collection, even if they are less familiar with the other authors.[73] The twenty-fifth volume in the collection is listed along the bottom of the ad as being "sous presse." It is *Physiologie du floueur* by none other than Charles Philipon himself. The boldface text runs along the bottom of the ad, bringing to a close both the Aubert collection and the ad itself. This large advertisement encapsulates the phenomenon of the *physiologie* at the peak of its popularity: it highlights the trendy, well-known artists and their contributions to the series; it repeats and foregrounds the low price; it reinforces the abundance of these short texts by including a list of all the available titles; and without saying so explicitly, as some of the *réclames* do, it emphasizes the exclusivity of the Aubert brand by the size of the title's print, the cachet of the names associated with the collection, and, ultimately, with the inclusion of one of Philipon's own *physiologies*.

A more scaled-down version of this large ad appeared in subsequent issues throughout mid-1842, but at this point ads for and even references to the *physiologie* collection became scarce in *La Presse* and other newspapers. Aubert's name still remained a frequent fixture for his other albums and collections, but the fad for the short typological texts declined. Their popularity seems to have run its course. In fact the lack of advertisements for the *Physiologies-Aubert* speaks once again to La Maison Aubert's keen manipulation of the marketplace; no longer was it deemed profitable to promote a product that was unlikely to sell as well. Philipon and Aubert worked at the beginning of the market for advertising.[74] Analysis of their ads shows a shrewd understanding of the new tools for producing and selling texts and offers insight into the brief but successful run of these short volumes, in particular those of the Aubert brand.

Their promotional strategy was just one of many factors contributing to the predominance of La Maison Aubert's *physiologie* series. In fact the *physiologies* themselves actually served as a vehicle for their own advertising. Huart's *Physiologie du flâneur* contains an illustration of multiple clients crowded in front of the Aubert shop front and a close-up of a *flâneur* intently gazing at the caricatures in the window, so engrossed that he does not realize he is being pickpocketed. It also includes a written description of the riveting storefronts of "Susse, Martinet et Aubert," which, he claims, unwittingly engender the success of Parisian pickpockets: "Il est très difficile d'avoir les yeux à la fois sur une caricature et sur sa poche."[75] The narrator incorporates a reference to La Maison Aubert for the accuracy of his depiction of modern Paris but also to promote the business that will subsequently sell and distribute this very text.[76] For Stiénon and Saint-Amand, this image is typical of the series' references to the texts' own commerciality: "Surcodant leur lisibilité selon les modes de consommation d'une certaine littérature, ces textes insistent sur les mentions que livraient les cabinets de lecture et les boutiques les diffusant."[77] While La Maison Aubert's series were not the only contributors to the genre, their commercial success and visibility testify to Philipon and Aubert's capacity to tap into the market for this in-demand product, as well as to their skill in promoting the *physiologies* by using their already established network of artists and clients.

NOUVEAUX TABLEAUX DE PARIS

The larger, multi-authored texts known to some as the "tableaux de Paris" differed from the *physiologies* in their price and format and through their form, content, marketing, and reception exposed explicit comprehension of their status within the literary field. Indeed Philipon and Aubert were not the only publishers to capitalize on the trend of descriptions of modern Parisian phenomena. Well before the craze of the *physiologies*, a similar but larger text was orchestrated as a commercial venture. In 1831 *Paris, ou le livre des cent-et-un* was produced as a "collective serial" and was "meant to be a lifeline for the publisher Ladvocat whose publishing house . . . was facing ruin. . . . Over one hundred contributors came together . . . to launch a lucrative publishing project that plugged the gap in the market between books and journals."[78] The book included an introduction by the well-known journalist and critic Jules Janin, followed by individual chapters on wide-ranging urban topics. These highly contemporary depictions, or "sketches," as Lauster calls them, "together with 'hundreds' of other sketches, provide[d] a total picture, a 'tableau' or 'physiognomy' of the city."[79] For Cohen, it is *Paris, ou le livre des cent-et-un* that "inaugurated" the trend of "collections of descriptive sketches of contemporary Parisian life and habits."[80]

Though numerous collective volumes appeared in the years following the *Cent-et-un*, the subsequent best-known collection was *Les Français peints par eux-mêmes*, published by Léon Curmer (known for his ornate illustrated editions) between 1839 and 1842, which announced itself as the "encyclopédie morale du XIXe siècle." Almost a decade after Ladvocat's collective work, according to Jillian Taylor-Lerner, "Curmer secured the collaboration of over one hundred writers and artists, soliciting as many celebrity contributors as possible, but also, remarkably, inviting submissions from aspiring amateurs and local informers."[81] Like *La Grande Ville*, *Les Français* could be purchased in different formats of varying prices: "in serial installments for thirty centimes, in softcover volumes for fifteen francs, or in more expensive hardcovers of colored cardboard or gilded leather."[82] Before and during the boom of *physiologies*, publishers took advantage of the (arguably manufactured) taste for urban observation to arrange these larger, collective high-value publications.

While the examples of Ladvocat and Curmer have been studied at some length by other critics (such as Lauster, Cohen, and Taylor-Lerner), relatively little attention has been paid to de Kock's *La Grande Ville: Nouveau tableau de Paris*. It resembles the previous collections of "sketches" in physical composition and in the formats in which it was sold and marketed, but volume one of *La Grande Ville* differs from its predecessors by being produced by a single author. A second volume followed quickly in 1843, collecting the work of heavyweights such as Balzac and Alexandre Dumas *père*, in addition to popular writers and journalists such as Soulié and Edouard Ourliac.[83] While de Kock's work may have represented a less explicitly orchestrated editorial project, it nonetheless exemplified many of the characteristics of the large-scale urban panoramic texts. A close examination of de Kock's *La Grande Ville*, a work published after many of the other collected works but still during their popularity, shows the author honing in on and perfecting the qualities that had made his predecessors commercially successful while also revealing a distinctly literary approach to his subject. In this new era in which authors made their living from writing instead of being sponsored by wealthy patrons, *La Grande Ville* offers one example of the trend of the *tableaux de Paris* that dominated the contemporary marketplace.

The publisher's prospectus of de Kock's *La Grande Ville: Nouveau tableaux de Paris* touted this 1842 work as "un ouvrage d'une telle importance, écrit par le romancier le plus populaire de notre époque," specifying, "Ce n'est point un roman, ce ne sont pas non plus de simples tableaux: c'est une immense comédie à cent actes divers. . . . C'est Paris tel qu'il est, tel que Paul de Kock l'a vu, l'écrivain le plus vrai, le plus gai, le meilleur observateur de son temps."[84] This collection of short tableaux depicting different urban phenomena promised readers a sprawling representation of Paris that was both entertaining and faithful by one of the period's best-known writers. Taking advantage of the author's fame and reputation, this prospectus uses almost hyperbolically positive descriptions of his skills as an observant, faithful, and witty writer to hype the importance and originality of the work. Other promotional materials for this new work could be found throughout the press surrounding the time of its publication. In an August 30, 1842, issue of *Le Charivari*, the satirical journal's usual daily lithograph was replaced with images excerpted from *La Grande Ville* and a note on the preceding page explained, "Le *Tableau de la grande ville*, dont les vignettes remplacent aujourd'hui notre lithographie, est un amusant et fidèle panorama de Paris. Il parle à la fois aux yeux et à l'esprit:—aux yeux, par des dessins dus au crayon de nos plus spirituels artistes;—à l'esprit par un récit vif, piquant, animé, tel qu'on devait l'attendre de la plume de M. Paul de Kock."[85] Full of praise for *La Grande Ville*, this note—likely a paid advertisement—banks on readers' attraction to contemporary popular artists and to de Kock and repeats the same qualities found in the prospectus: this Parisian "panorama" is both "amusant et fidèle."[86]

De Kock's preface contextualizes the succeeding fifty-two chapters of *La Grande Ville* in relation to other works on the city, explaining that though many of his predecessors have attempted to make Paris known to their readers, his effort is different. Though he aims to produce a more "modern" depiction than Mercier, De Kock's narrator, like that of *Le Tableau de Paris*, will use walking and observing as a means of documenting nineteenth-century Paris, and he playfully invites the reader to accompany him through the streets of Paris, exclaiming, "Promenons-nous au hasard."[87] Assuming the role of *flâneur*, the narrator will not set up a preplanned itinerary around the city but rather will report on whatever he stumbles upon: a store where one can rent a bathtub, the ubiquitous stands selling *galettes* (cakes), the sidewalks themselves. The narrator uses a lighthearted tone but takes seriously a number of crucial themes surfacing in literary discourse of the period, ranging from the popularity and difficulty of depicting Paris in a literary work to the concept of realism, the status of the author within the literary text, and the relationship between history and modernity.[88] With this light yet richly intertextual preface, de Kock's narrator sets up *La Grande Ville* as a consciously literary work, acutely aware of its position in the literary tradition of the *tableau de Paris*. Although the subtitle of his work offers "comique" as the first adjective in describing the subsequent tableaux of *La Grande Ville*, the preface establishes its status as a "critique" as well.

La Grande Ville, a mixture of text and image, proves also to be a blend of genres in its structure and content. As noted earlier, "Ce n'est point un roman, ce ne sont pas non plus de simples tableaux: c'est une immense comédie à cent actes divers."[89] The work is made up of fifty-two chapters, a journey through the streets of Paris with an observant guide, depicting a blend of commercial, domestic, social, and recreational spaces, indoor, outdoor, and in-between. The form of each of the narrator's observations changes shape as often as the Parisian sites he reports on.[90] The chapter "Les Révérbères" (The Lampposts), for example, is a concise historical description of lampposts in Paris, from oil lamps to the *becs de gaz* (gaslights). "La Galette" (The Cake) is journalistic in tone and reports on the newest craze in Paris: where one can find a good *galette* stand, examples of fortunes earned by opening a *galette* stand, and how the *galette* is on par with, if not superior to, other modern inventions, such as the steamboat, the free press, and the moustache. "Les Bains à domicile" (Home-Delivered Baths) takes the form of a short story about a young *grisette* (young working-class woman) who, furious over her eviction, seeks revenge on her landlord by ordering six bathtubs and enough warm water to fill each of them to be delivered to his home at once. "Les faux-toupets" (The Toupees) instead of describing the advent of the toupee, presents a dialogue between two women—"Écoutez plutôt la conversation de deux jolies dames"—who critique a well-known society man for tricking them into admiring his false locks.[91] "Une soirée dans la petite propriété" is told as a moral lesson, a fable in the style of La Fontaine (whom the narrator quotes at the beginning of the piece), on how all people, desirous of what those in the higher classes have, attempt to imitate them at all costs. De Kock's guide to midcentury Parisian social life is thus a compilation of genres and discourses, from the theatrical scene to the short story, from history and journalism to the fable, all grouped together under the form of a comedy, as the publisher remarks in the preface (written the same year as Balzac's own preface to his *Comédie humaine*), but also as a sort of travel narrative of the city of Paris and an *étude de moeurs*.

In addition to the multiple literary genres that form this hybrid work, close textual readings of de Kock's social urban guide reveal the author's literary approach to his subject, in particular the relationship the narrator establishes with his interlocutor throughout this work. De Kock's debt to Mercier is obvious in his preface, yet he faults Mercier and other writers for including themselves in their prose. De Kock explains, "Il ne faut que décrire ou relater des faits; [le défaut des auteurs] c'est de venir toujours se poser entre le lecteur et le sujet qu'on traite, comme pour lui dire: 'A propos, n'oubliez pas que c'est moi qui écris cela.'"[92] To distinguish himself he almost fully absents himself from the text after the introduction, remarking wittily, "Qu'est-ce que tout cela fait au lecteur, qui s'inquiète fort peu de savoir comment vous est venue l'idée de faire tel ou tel ouvrage, mais qui veut seulement que cet ouvrage l'amuse, l'instruise ou l'intéresse?"[93] While the *je* of the introduction is certainly absent from the fifty-two chapter-length vignettes, one for each week of the year, that compose *La Grande Ville*, the pronoun *vous* seems to be the focal point of the guide. De Kock's narrator has created an extraordinarily varied interlocutor, using *vous* in a complex and inconsistent manner, even writing the fictitious interlocutor into each of his descriptions of Paris. In the first vignette, "Bureau des nourrices," *vous* is an observer of the scene, whose wife has just had a baby and who is unaware of how to procure a wet nurse. Clearly this *vous* is a bourgeois French male. Throughout the chapters, however, the interlocutor varies in gender, class, and nationality. In the vignette titled "Le Daguerréotype," the *vous* evoked by the narrator who climbs to the second floor of an *immeuble* (apartment building) to have his or her portrait taken is of ambiguous nationality, a fact evident when the narrator states at the beginning of this chapter, "Les Parisiens ne sont pas les seuls à se faire daguerréotyper: les étrangers qui sont venus visiter Paris ne veulent pas en partir sans avoir essayé de cette invention."[94] Here the *vous* may be a Frenchman from the country, a Parisian, or even a visitor from outside the Hexagon. In the chapter "Les Bains à Domicile" the *vous* begins as an impersonal pronoun but is soon referred to as "Madame," changing gender from the previous vignette. The female *vous* returns in the episode "Le Vent" when the narrator calls out to women in danger of having their skirts blown by the wind.

Throughout the vignettes colloquialisms and cultural facts are explained to interlocutors, as if some will comprehend certain aspects of Parisian life and others will not. In fact the narrator calls out explicitly to readers of different classes. For example, in "Chantier de Bois à Brûler," he declares, "Vous qui vous chauffez agréablement les pieds devant un bon feu . . . bon bourgeois, commis, hommes d'affairs, employés rentiers, vous tous qui sans avoir une assez grande fortune pour charger votre intendant ou vous domestiques des détails intérieurs de votre maison" and later, in "La Galette," "Vous qui, pour vous enrichir, croyez qu'il est nécessaire d'aventurer de nombreux capitaux."[95] De Kock's *vous* here thus seems to encompass all Parisian citizens and to invite each one to come to their own understanding of this nuanced city. The narrator addresses as wide an audience as possible and, by extension, makes the work as widely consumable as possible.

De Kock's almost frantic, ever-shifting interlocutor—changing genders, professions, classes, and even nationalities—can be seen from a noncommercial standpoint when one considers the context of its eighteenth-century predecessor. As Priscilla Ferguson points out, Mercier's text was radical for its democratic view of the majority of the city of Paris: "The consequent jumble of the text faithfully reproduces the disarray of the city. Both, in Mercier's aggressively egalitarian view, repudiate the hierarchy and chronology that implicitly or explicitly order the conventional guidebook."[96] If Mercier's guide is "radical" for reproducing the chaotic nature of the city with his short tableaux and for almost anticipating the Revolution with his writings on the poor Parisians as well as the rich, de Kock's guide reflects a more complex politics of class, equality, and inclusion concurrently being played out in the Paris of his time. Such an overtly all-inclusive narrator might also be seen from a commercial perspective as a way of targeting as broad an audience as possible (within the limits of those who could pay to purchase the text either in the fifty-two weekly installments or as a bound edition). This is the same sort of marketing from within that we saw with the *physiologies*. Despite this similarity, in its form and content de Kock's *La Grande Ville* is as emblematic of large-scale panoramic texts, whose hybridity stood in contrast with the more fixed *physiologie*.

CLASSIFYING PANORAMIC LITERATURE

An examination of the *Bibliographie de la France* and other midcentury literary bibliographies shows that at the moment of their publication and shortly after, the "panoramic literary" texts betrayed a generic instability, suggesting that the contemporary literary field had difficulty classifying the phenomenon with the tools available to it. Beginning in 1811, the *Bibliographie de la France* was the official, national bibliography in which all legally registered works were listed as a matter of practice; they were indexed by title, author, and genre, and the titles of these generic categories varied occasionally.[97] This literary database avant la lettre was administrative, but it was also, as its subtitle, *Journal général de l'imprimerie*, and its supplementary, *Feuilleton*, suggest, a professional tool for publishers. In addition to indexes of authors and titles, mid-nineteenth-century editions of the *Bibliographie* contained a section entitled "Table Systématique," under which works were classified, first under a more general rubric ("Sciences et Arts," "Théologie," and "Histoire," for example), and then under more specific subcategories ("Finances," "Liturgie," and "Histoire de France," for example). Both the *physiologies* and their larger, more expensive counterparts were most often found indexed under the general rubric of "Belles Lettres," a category that predictably contained subgenres like "Romans et Contes," "Poétique et Poésie," and "Théâtre." Under the heading "Belles Lettres," a vaguer category of "Philologie, Critique, Mélanges" existed for texts that could not easily be classified but still fell under the rubric of the literary. Between 1831 and 1848 the *physiologies* were one of the most prominently featured texts in the category of "Mélanges." With a few exceptions *physiologies* ranging from the infamous 1832 *Physiologie de la poire* to the 1834 edition of Balzac's *Physiologie du mariage* appeared in this "Mélanges" category, along with more than sixty of the *physiologies* published in 1841 and more than twenty published in 1842, at the height of their popularity.[98] The *physiologies* thus were reliably read by the publishers of France's official bibliography as belonging to no clear literary category, yet nonetheless as literary. Their uniform categorization as hybrid shows both an awareness of these texts as embodying a tension in the literary field on the part of the professionals who classified them (and, by extension, those who consulted this document in order to sell them) and, more generally, the instability of literary genres at this moment.

Lyon-Caen notes that the "*Bibliographie de la France* . . . range bien la littérature panoramique et les romans dans la section 'Belles Lettres' et les enquêtes sociales dans la rubrique 'Economique politique' de la section 'Sciences et arts,'" in her contention that though the panoramic literature and the "enquêtes sociales" share common practices and "brouille[ent] les frontières de genres et registres," these texts were seen as distinct at the time.[99] Yet aside from the *physiologies*, the larger collections in the category "panoramic literature" were classified and reclassified, suggesting confusion about their genre. Though the *Livre des cent-et-un* was, like the *physiologies*, classified as "Philologie, Critique, Mélanges" from 1831 to 1833 and again in 1835, it was also catalogued as "Encyclopédie, Philosophie, Logique, Metaphysique, Morale" in 1834, a category that did not even fall under the overarching rubric of "Belles Lettres" but rather "Sciences et Arts." *Les Français peints par eux-mêmes* was classified as "Encyclopédie, Philosophie, Logique, Metaphysique, Morale" in 1840 and 1842. While various 1833 and 1834 editions of *nouveaux tableaux de Paris* were also labeled under the "Encyclopédie" category, an 1835 *nouveau tableau de Paris* merited the label "Mélanges." Curiously de Kock's volume of *La Grande Ville* and the second volume, written in 1843 by Balzac, Dumas *père*, Soulié, and others, were placed in a third category: "Romans et contes." Aside from the possibility that those in charge of categorizing these texts did not read them to determine their proper genres, one further simple explanation for this classification is that the contributors to the work were themselves well known for their novels and short stories and thereby classified accordingly. Nonetheless that a book documenting everyday life in Paris, in a decidedly non-fictional literary tradition, whose publisher openly stated in its prospectus that it was *not* a novel, should be officially categorized as "Romans et contes" raises significant questions about the way these texts were understood (even by those who produced them). These disparate categorizations indicate a distinction in most cases made by the publishers of the *Bibliographie* between the *physiologie* series and the larger collections of urban writings. Though not all of the literary guidebooks were classified under the same rubric, and at times (albeit infrequently) were labeled "Mélanges," it is clear that they were not overwhelmingly read as generically identical to the *physiologies*.

These were France's and the book industry's "official" generic indexes of the panoramic texts, but other contemporaneous bibliographies and publications often replicated these categories when classifying the July Monarchy works. Mainstream publications such as the journal *Revue Critique des Livres*

Nouveaux tended to place the *physiologies* they reviewed under a section entitled "Mélanges" in their table of contents. Works like the 1841 *Physiologie de l'amour* and *Physiologie du parapluie* (this second text written, anonymously, by "two coachmen") were grouped under "Mélanges" in the table of contents. Their 1840 predecessors *Physiologie du théâtre* and *Physiologie du chant* were reviewed under the categories "Poésie, Art Dramatique" and "Arts Industriels, Beaux-Arts," respectively. The *Revue*'s headings reproduce the *Bibliographie de la France*'s method of generally defining the *physiologies* as literary but occasionally categorizing them by the subjects they studied.

Over twenty years after the phenomenon of the *physiologies* and the *tableaux* had peaked, Pierre Larousse's *Grand Dictionnaire Universel du XIXe Siècle* (published between the late 1860s and 1870s) also included a lengthy "Bibliographie générale" in its sixty-two-page entry on Paris (history, geography, culture, etc.) that replicates some of these generic categories and offers evidence of how this movement was viewed in the later half of the century. This particular bibliography, in which the author aims to detail "la série d'ouvrages de toutes sortes qui traitent de Paris à ses divers points de vue," is split up into several categories, including "Descriptions topographiques, guides, plans, estampes," "Moeurs et coutumes," and "Romans."[100] We would expect to find the majority of the literary guidebooks listed under "Moeurs et coutumes," defined by Larousse as "[où] l'on trouvera la liste de tous les ouvrages sérieux ou plaisants qui ont rapport à la physionomie de Paris et à la physiologie de ses habitants," and this is indeed the case.[101] Mercier's *Le Tableau de Paris* and subsequent *Nouveaux Tableaux de Paris* (1833, 1855), de Kock's *La Grande Ville* and *Paris au Kaléidoscope*, the multi-authored *Le diable à Paris* (1844–45), and other works are grouped under this category, as well as a small sampling of *physiologies*.[102] Exceptionally *Paris, ou le livre des cent-et-un* is listed here under "Romans," as de Kock's literary guidebook was in the *Bibliographie de la France*. This work, whose publisher labeled it a "drame à cent actes divers" and "une encyclopédie des idées contemporaines . . . l'album d'une littérature ingénieuse et puissante," and which was repeatedly categorized as "Mélanges" in the *Bibliographie de la France*, was situated, in other words, in a group with Hugo's *Les Misérables*, Flaubert's *L'éducation sentimentale*, Zola's *La Curée*, and a number of Balzac's urban novels.[103] Like de Kock's *La Grande Ville*, a book that also called attention to its nonnovel status but is nonetheless officially indexed as one in the *Bibliographie*, Janin's "heterogeneric" work, to borrow Cohen's phrase, was classified as a fiction (novels/short stories) by Larousse. These categorizations lead us to conclude that the hybrid form of the literary guidebooks transcended contemporary generic conventions, and in so doing fully embodied the moment of flux in literary history in which they were published.

In an attempt to establish a taxonomy of these panoramic works, themselves so focused on categorizing nineteenth-century culture, it has become clear that the nineteenth-century book industry resisted classifying these works in a uniform way, marking them as hybrid ("mélanges"), setting them apart from more clearly established categories, or inconstantly labeling them across generic categories ("sciences," "belles lettres") and subcategories ("tableau de moeurs," "roman").[104] While the *Bibliographie de la France* is surely the most influential of these archives given its official status and great prominence in the nineteenth-century literary market, these other documents serve to stress the "authorized" bibliography's fluctuating, varied classification of the literary guidebooks and its recurrent generic distinction between the *physiologies* and their larger counterparts. Pushed a step further, we might even posit that both the more fixed *physiologies* and the larger hybrid texts I have examined betray the instability of literary categories, the vagueness of all literary boundaries and genre even as they were being formed.

These panoramic works, which often incorporated references to commerciality and wide readerships into their form and content, explicitly staged the dynamism of the marketplace in which they were produced; not only their marketing but also their content served to promote the work. The publicity campaigns surrounding them developed as the phenomenon progressed, marking out clearly and in real time the new advances in the world of book advertising and the interconnected network of literature, advertising, and the press. Those authors linked to the phenomenon were often categorized as purely industrial writers, yet these texts also help to expose the blurring of boundaries between "high" and "low" authors. Balzac, as we will see, both contributed to and disparaged the trend of panoramic literature; de Kock— one of the major figures of this popular trend—more openly appropriated its typological tropes into his fictional works and, paradoxically, often received critical praise for just these passages. When reading the work of these two authors, and others, through the lens of this overtly commercial phenomenon, a more complex picture emerges of the hierarchies of the early to mid-nineteenth-century literary field.

Chapter Two

THE DE KOCK PARADOX

Nearly thirty years after paying 800 francs out of pocket to publish his first novel, *L'Enfant de ma femme*, Paul de Kock, now well into his career as a popular writer, found himself caricatured in the April 15, 1842, issue of *Le Charivari*, in the journal's "Panthéon Charivarique." A short poem satirizing the prolific novelist's work completed the image, which depicted de Kock as an enormous head with a beak atop a rooster's body and surrounded by his masses of readers:

> Vénéré des portières et chéri des grisettes
> Pour qui ses gais romans ont d'immenses attraites
> Paul de Kock est de plus admiré des Anglais
> Et cela se comprend car ses œuvres complètes
> Ne sont pas d'un très bon Français.[1]

This comical poem depicts, to a certain degree, the reality of de Kock's success among a working-class and bourgeois reading public in France and in Britain, where his works were cheaply translated and sold extensively. But it hardly represents the first or the last time the author would be caricatured or that literary journals would poke fun at his work. By the early July Monarchy, in fact, de Kock's name had been a fixture of the Parisian literary scene for over a decade, thanks to his inexhaustible production of vaudevilles, novels, songs, and occasional writings on Paris. Between *L'Enfant de ma femme* in 1811 and his death in 1871, the author composed his works "de façon industrielle ensuite un roman en un mois chaque année" even after the heyday of his career in the 1830s and 1840s.[2] Although known as the favored novelist of *grisettes* and *cuisinières* (female cooks), he occupied "une figure particulière dans le champ littéraire: celle de l'écrivain bourgeois."[3] If de Kock was the July Monarchy's bourgeois writer par excellence, by the 1830s his name carried a specific connotation: "Paul de Kock" signified "bad" literature, a sort of Bourdieusian marker of poor taste.[4] Other generations of writers certainly had their own straw men against whom they contrasted their work, yet the use of "Paul de Kock" as a brand name for "bad" style was so engrained in early July Monarchy culture that on October 11, 1835, *Le Charivari* entitled the unrelated report of a comical legal case a "Scène à la Paul de Kock."[5] And, as noted in the introduction, by the second half of the century Flaubert was using the name as a critically charged sign for lowbrow literature.

While no reputable author wished to "faire du Paul de Kock," the name also connoted market success, for, as his biographer Eugène de Mirecourt wrote, "le jour où l'on mettait en vente un roman de Paul de Kock, il y avait une véritable émeute en librairie."[6] In fact by the middle of the July Monarchy, de Kock, like Hugo, could reliably be counted upon to sell out a print run of 2,500 copies; in comparison Balzac and Sue (at least before the publication of *Les Mystères de Paris*) were likely to sell 1,500 copies.[7] Unlike Sue, few individual works of de Kock's stand out as exceptional best sellers; what is distinctive about him is the sheer number of works he published: in 1842 alone, no fewer than seventeen titles were registered under his name in the *Bibliographie de la France*.[8] This market success made him one of the more lucrative writers of the July Monarchy: his multiple hundreds of novels and plays afforded him "a comfortable, bourgeois standard of living in Paris."[9] He did command less per novel than some of his contemporaries, earning approximately 5,000 francs for each four-volume novel he produced between 1835 and 1840, whereas Sue earned 100,000 francs for *Le Juif errant* in 1844 and George Sand earned 10,000 for *Jeanne* in the same year.[10] Nevertheless de Kock's prolific novelistic output assured him a steady income, as did his vaudevilles and melodramas (works almost exclusively based on his novels) and other occasional writings. The author thus occupied the dual positions of commercial success and critical failure that Stiénon characterizes as a "succès initial de diffusion" and a "délégitimation d'une esthétique dépréciée pour sa facilité et sa grivoiserie."[11]

Not simply emblematic of "bad" writing or commercial success, de Kock was a complex figure who understood and capitalized on early mass-market culture. Literary and cultural historians, especially in the past twenty years, have evoked him and his novels with some frequency in studies on reading and publishing in the nineteenth century.[12] Most existing scholarship, however, rarely focuses on the content of the work or on de Kock as a singular literary figure. He and his work thus have become emblematic for critics of historical development or of a popular genre: in particular he is grouped, correctly, into the commercially successful category of fiction and panoramic literature that focused on "la description et [le] décryptage des mécanismes de la société contemporaine."[13] De Kock's novelistic representations of contemporary Paris can and should be seen as narrative tactics to appeal to his wide readership. But instead of focusing on de Kock as one of multiple popular decoders of July Monarchy Paris, this chapter offers literary readings of his work alongside its reception history to expose complexities that both nineteenth-century and current received ideas about de Kock overlook.

Analysis of his digressive style, in particular passages depicting urban phenomena, show de Kock cannily comprehending and responding in literary form to the interests of a public obsessed with reading about modern urban life. Examination of one of the author's better-known novels, *Mon voisin Raymond* (1823) demonstrates how he deployed humorous narratives of debauchery and moral castigation to appeal to his readers while simultaneously reassuring them of the values of the bourgeois classes who both populated and read his works. This reading nuances the critical commonplace that de Kock produced "vulgar," "immoral" fiction and shows at the level of form his comprehension of contemporary literary tastes.[14] Consideration of the reception of his first publications through the peak of his career in the July

Monarchy indicate that while "Paul de Kock" does come to embody anxiety over the influx of popular literature in the burgeoning literary market of the 1830s and 1840s, it actually held simultaneously distinct, and sometimes opposite, meanings—even within the same journal—depending on the historical moment and context. We are ultimately left with what we might call the "de Kock paradox": that the static definition of "Paul de Kock" as lowbrow literature, coupled with his often varied reception throughout the July Monarchy, betrays his more complicated relationship to the changing literary field. More than simply validating a bad/good binary of taste, these reviews evince contemporary critics' recognition of de Kock as having successfully mastered a formula for popular writing in the modern age of the *feuilleton* and of an increasingly larger reading public. A more nuanced understanding of this paradox questions rigid high/low literary paradigms twenty- and twenty-first-century critics still apply unproblematically to de Kock and also documents his command of a changing media environment.

URBAN DIGRESSIONS, OR "UN JOLI TABLEAU À FAIRE"

A reviewer of de Kock's 1837 novel, *Un Homme à marier*, in the *Revue Critique des livres nouveaux* praised the author's keen ability to paint the daily lives of the Parisian bourgeois, but also pointed to what he saw as de Kock's inability to sustain this representation over the course of an entire volume, writing, "Renfermé dans les étroites limites d'une scène de 5 ou 6 pages, [il] aurait pu être fort plaisant, parce que l'auteur excelle à peindre les ridicules et les travers de la bourgeoisie parisienne; mais délayé dans un volume, il perd tout son prix et n'est plus que trivial sans gaîté."[15] This critic replicates familiar tropes in nineteenth-century reviews of de Kock—tropes I examine in detail below—highlighting his observational skills but ultimately rejecting his style. Yet his point that the novel could be pared down considerably to a short "episode" is worthy of note. The central plotline of *Un Homme à marier* is actually quite brief: the failed courtship of Mademoiselle Augustine by the forty-nine-year-old bachelor Théophile Girardière. Girardière, who has decided it is time to be married, meets Augustine and her aunt at a restaurant, and the young woman appears to be attracted to him. After paying her many visits, however, Girardière is discouraged to hear her mention the name of another man (M. Frontin), and, suspicious and hurt, he abandons her for a month's time. He finally returns but learns that, while M. Frontin is actually the name of her cat, in his absence Mlle Augustine has become betrothed to another man, despite her initial fondness for Girardière. Distraught, he dies. This story line is extended into a nine-chapter work, which includes many anecdotes of Girardière's botched pursuits before meeting Mlle Augustine that provide background to the character but do little to advance the central narrative.

If the plot of *Un Homme à marier*, a work originally included as a literary supplement in *Le Figaro*, is Girardière's attempt to woo Mlle Augustine, then the account begins when he arrives at the restaurant where he will encounter her: "Il était près de cinq heures lorsque Girardière entre dans le salon du restaurant."[16] Readers might expect the plot to remain focused on the protagonist's experience in the café, but the narrator instead launches into a multichapter background narrative in the next sentence, taking us through Girardière's exploits and misfortunes while unsuccessfully wooing women. We see him rejected in chapters whose titles reflect the reasons for the series of rejections: "Trop Pauvre" ("Too Poor"), "Trop Laid" ("Too Ugly"), "Trop Vieux" ("Too Old"), "Trop Bête" ("Too Dumb"). Each is an anecdote recounting the lengths to which Girardière will go to marry. In fact only in the penultimate chapter does the narrator bring the reader back to Girardière's initial café setting: "Maintenant que vous connaissez suffisamment les précédents de M. Girardière, ayez la complaisance de revenir avec lui chez le traiteur."[17] In other words, though the text posits as its main, structuring plotline Girardière and Augustine's encounter and relationship, nearly two-thirds of it is made up of background anecdotes, narrative meanderings vaguely reminiscent of a Voltairian *conte* or even a picaresque novel but that, unlike the texts of de Kock's literary predecessors, do not necessarily build upon one another to create a more linear story line (the type that de Kock himself adopts in many of his other novels). Instead the bulk of the novel is a digression masked as essential background information on the protagonist, each chapter a movable (and removable) piece of text, with little bearing on the actual diegesis at the center of the novel.

Even more jarring is another prolonged digression inserted into the final third of the novel. Once we return to Girardière in the café, the narrator begins to describe his surroundings, in particular a bourgeois family of four who enter noisily. This family will occupy the thoughts of the narrator for the next several pages, as they ungracefully settle in, make inappropriate demands on the waiter, and leave without paying the bill in its entirety. This digression is different from the previous one, because, though the narration veers back to the protagonist as he briefly speaks with an acquaintance and, later, as he interacts with the newly arrived Mlle Augustine and her aunt, he is not the principal character in this scene. Paying limited attention to Girardière, the narrator returns unfailingly to the four he humorously calls "the respectable family" until they depart: "Et la respectable famille . . . s'éloigne, après avoir eu soin d'emporter tous les cure-dents qu'on a mis sur la table."[18] Girardière's interactions with Mlle Augustine are not affected by the presence and the actions of these characters; neither character takes note of or interacts with the family. When they leave, the narrator's next words betray no evidence that their existence as characters carries any weight within the broader context of the novel itself: "[La tante d'Augustine] et sa nièce avaient aussi achevé leur diner; elles paient, Girardière en fait autant, et ils sortent ensemble de chez le restaurateur."[19] The central plot unfolds as Girardière accompanies the women to a play. The family is never mentioned again, and the reader discovers that characters present for nearly one-tenth of the novella are structurally unnecessary or that they function as what we might call de Kock's attempt at a reality effect—details or description that merely reinforce the scene's "realism."

Un Homme à marier is written relatively early in de Kock's long career, yet it is a typical example of the author's digressive style. While it is somewhat unusual for his method to interrupt the narrative with such a lengthy, analeptic passage, passages that do not advance the plot and that depict scenes of everyday Parisian life are omnipresent in his writing. The misbehaving petit bourgeois family is only one of many descriptions of urban phenomena that pepper de Kock's works. This particular scene of the family can be read therefore as a comical *tableau de Paris*, unessential to the progression of the intrigue of *Un Homme à marier* but nonetheless providing trenchant observations on urban occurrences. These digressions, which, as Lyon-Caen notes, often openly gesture to an urban reader, indicate an attempt to target a specific reading public. Noting the connection between the panoramic literary texts of the 1830s and 1840s and de Kock's novels, Lyon-Caen writes that the author "ne s'adresse pas à la postérité, mais à un lectorat ancré dans le présent pour lequel il compose un guide Romanesque de la société contemporaine."[20] In these digressions, in other words, the author targets a specific audience and creates a space for his work in a market driven by literature that depicts contemporary society.

Published six years before *Un Homme à marier*, *Le Cocu* (1831) successfully sold an estimated fourteen thousand copies in its first years in print (for perspective, the same number of copies as Hugo's *Notre-Dame de Paris*). It tells the story, as the title suggests, of the adulterous marriage between M. Blémont, a lawyer and former playboy, and Eugénie.[21] Though the two eventually separate, the novel's moral lesson is the importance of fidelity, a good marriage, and forgiveness, and the text itself functions as a detailed study of one such marital case. *Le Cocu* is lengthier than its 1837 successor; it follows a more linear narrative, depicts characters that reoccur throughout the novel, and has fewer digressions, with the exception of the first chapter, "Un Cabinet de lecture." The mise-en-scène is a bustling reading room. The narrator is present and in fact establishes his own position vis-à-vis the other clients: "Moi, je suis debout à l'entrée du salon, où je fais rarement une longue station."[22] He will eventually pick up a newspaper, but rather than read it he prefers to watch the other characters: "Je tiens encore mon journal, mais je ne le lis plus. Je m'amuse à considérer toutes ces figures penchées sur ces feuilles de papier imprimé. Ce serait un joli tableau à faire pour un peintre de genre."[23] This aside from the narrator gives insight into the rest of the chapter, because he then dedicates his time to painting lively descriptions of the comings and goings of a large cast of characters within the *cabinet*. There is the fastidious reader for whom "il faut que la lampe soit juste devant lui, que ses pieds aient une chaise pour s'appuyer et que sa tabatière soit placée à côté de son journal."[24] There is the man known as the "épouvantail des cabinets de lecture" who routinely takes four hours to read the newspaper.[25] There is the sleepy client who reads in bed and who desires "quelque chose qui l'endorme tout de suite."[26] These three examples, among many others, form part of the panoramic representation inside the lending library, the "joli tableau" de Kock evokes.

Like many of the caricatures that illustrated de Kock's works, these characters are rather superficially drawn, and there is no attempt at further development. Once identified they receive no further mention, and the narrator presses on to depict the remaining clients. In fact the only thing linking the characters, besides their physical presence and activity at the *cabinet de lecture*, is the narrator himself. The narrator leaves his post as observer when his friend Bélan arrives, ending the chapter: "Et prenant M. Bélan sous le bras, je l'entraîne loin du cabinet de lecture."[27] The narrator never returns to the reading room or mentions those whom he observed there. From a structural standpoint, then, this chapter has no proper function within the narrative: it does nothing to advance the plot; it contains many characters but no character development; and it is never evoked in the remaining chapters. In theory the plot of *Le Cocu* would be the same, with or without this chapter.

A short passage from this chapter (a passage cut from later editions) underscores de Kock's larger tactical aims in beginning the novel with a seemingly unrelated digression. As the narrator observes his surroundings, he eavesdrops on a conversation between the owner of the reading room and a young client, expressing his agreement with this avid bibliophile's interests in "les tableaux de moeurs, les scènes contemporaines."[28] "Un roman qui a plus de vingt ans," explains the woman, "ne peut pas peindre les moeurs actuelles."[29] The narrator, like the client, prefers to read recent descriptions of modern life, and by evoking this popular literary trend described nearly two centuries later by Lyon-Caen, he situates his own text within this category. This metadiscourse on contemporary literature in the context of the first chapter invites the reader to understand it as a necessary depiction of modern Parisian life, whether or not connected to the main narrative. The novel is hybrid, blending fictional narrative with a modern *tableau de Paris*—similar to those beginning to gain traction by 1831, like *Paris, ou le livre des cent-et-un*—fulfilling the interests of the narrator and characters, and once again affirming de Kock's position among the successful writers of the July Monarchy who "inscrivent leur intrigue dans un décor contemporain."[30]

The list of these digressive passages describing contemporary urban phenomena found throughout de Kock's prolific novelistic oeuvre is a long one.
His 1840 *La Jolie fille du faubourg*, for example, contains a scene depicting
an evening of socializing and crafts in the home of a *grisette* during which
the protagonist, Alexis, quietly takes his place in the corner and observes the
entire evening with few interactions with the women: "Alexis va se placer
sur une chaise qui est contre un lit, à l'autre extrémité de la chambre. Au
bout d'un moment la conversation et les chants reprennent comme avant
l'arrivée de ces messieurs."[31] Cited by one reviewer as an example of the
"talent véritable de M. Paul de Kock,"[32] this *soirée des grisettes* is similar to
the scene in the *cabinet de lecture* in that Alexis, like Blémont, observes an
elaborate scene but does not necessarily participate. Instead he witnesses this
"réunion . . . composée de sept demoiselles y compris la maîtresse du logis,"
while "deux faisaient des fleurs comme mademoiselle Julienne, une brodait,
une autre faisait de la tapisserie, une autre des reprises dans un beau châle,
et enfin la septième tenait le patron d'un corsage de robe qu'elle tournait
et retournait sur ses genoux."[33] Additionally, before entering the *grisettes'*
apartment, Alexis's companion Durozel justifies his interest in frequenting
these women by stating, "C'est justement parce que je suis raisonnable que
j'aime à fréquenter les diverses classes de la société. Les gens qui ne veulent
en voir qu'une seule se privent de beaucoup de tableaux de mœurs curieux et
intéressants."[34] Once again a character's metacommentary helps to articulate
de Kock's own literary project in this citation. In *La Jolie fille du faubourg*
the author makes space for such "tableaux de moeurs curieux,"[35] this one
featuring the *grisettes*, an important demographic of his reading public. If,
as Lyon-Caen has argued, these urban novels, like the larger movement
of panoramic literature, functioned "à déchiffrer, à décrypter, à dévoiler, à
représenter le monde social comme un texte lisible, un paysage visible," then
de Kock's novelistic scenes can be said to serve in some sense as guides to
the city, guides through which his eager readers could comprehend their
urban surroundings.[36] De Kock's commercial acclaim stems in part from
his consistent inclusion of urban life, both as part of the central plot and in
these digressive passages.

Do such *tableaux de Paris* exist in the texts of de Kock not situated in his contemporary Paris? *Le Barbier de Paris*, for example, written in 1827 but set in 1632, contains no urban digressions. In this lengthy mystery about hidden identities and the overlapping and confusing of social classes, the historical distance seems to have inhibited de Kock's typical digressions on contemporary Parisian types and scenes of petit bourgeois life in Paris. If the narrator does pause frequently to remind readers that what they are reading is not set in nineteenth-century Paris, he nonetheless permits himself far fewer urban *tableaux* than in other novels.[37] The few existing prolonged digressions—the idle blathering of a gossipy maid, the drunken exploits of a comical knight—nonetheless consistently advance the plot or develop characters rather than serve as disconnected urban scenes, as in the other works I have presented. It seems, then, that by setting the novel in a previous century, de Kock allows himself to focus more fully on the plot, creating a tighter and more intricate narrative, and less on his tangential observations of everyday Parisian life. On the other hand, the absence of observations about contemporary Parisian life in *Le Barbier* underscores the author's otherwise omnipresent focus on studying and chronicling his own modern city.[38]

The novelist's shorter works of fiction—his *contes* found in *Moeurs parisiennes*, for example—show de Kock's ability to control these digressions and hone them into a single and connected narrative. In "Une Soirée bourgeoise," a tale of a botched dinner party, the narrator excels at depicting the guests and the individual mishaps that take place over the course of the evening. In "Une Partie de plaisir," the story of a man who is forced into spending a weekend in the country, the narrator recounts the hilarious frustration of the unfortunate friend on whom a getaway with a cast of excruciating characters is imposed. These short stories function too as studies of specific Parisian phenomena and exhibit how de Kock's narrative style actually lends itself to producing sharper short fiction than long fiction, a reading with which the author's contemporaries would agree. As the 1837 reviewer of this collection remarked, "*Mœurs Parisiennes*, renferme plusieurs morceaux … qui me semblent être ce que l'auteur a fait de mieux. Ce serait là, je crois, le véritable caractère de son talent, qui excelle à peindre certaines scènes grotesques de la vie commune."[39] Whether strategically inserted into longer works of fiction or as the focus of his shorter pieces, de Kock's depictions of everyday Parisian life appealed to readers and, at times, critics, explaining in part the commercial success of his work.[40]

At a time when sales of the novel boomed it is not surprising that the market-savvy de Kock, in conjunction with his publishers, published more novels than short stories and plays. Adding textual bulk to his short stories—and thereby turning them into novels—also earned de Kock more money. Many of his publishers paid him in advance for novels, and it is not unthinkable that many of the digressions I have described added not only length but monetary value to the texts. In this respect de Kock can be said to have benefited from something fundamental about the literary market during his lifetime, namely, that despite digressions from the plot, despite the introduction of characters who are left by the wayside once the narrative takes off, despite the hybridity of many of the novels he produced, his readers were willing and eager to purchase his works precisely because of his focus on contemporary urban life. De Kock's novels also almost universally evince the preservation of bourgeois morals, despite accusations of immorality and debauchery from his critics.

MON VOISIN RAYMOND: RESTRAINT AND EXCESS

De Kock's novels conform to a certain narrative formula, one Jacques Migozzi characterizes as a medley "de méprises, de surprises à fonction narrative ou ludique, de coïncidences, de quiproquos ou de mystifications," embellished with "épisodes burlesques et de grivoiseries."[41] Mostly situated in Paris and peppered with digressions on urban phenomena, they often conclude with moral, commonsense lessons.[42] Deemed "le roman typique du genre" by the *Grand dictionnaire universel* (1236), *Mon voisin Raymond* (1823) was the novel "everyone thought was [de Kock's] best."[43] *Raymond*'s central plotline focuses on the amorous quests of the protagonist, Dorsan, quests that are consistently thwarted by his meddling neighbor Raymond. Whether attempting to woo Dorsan's former love Agathe, sleeping with Dorsan's wife, Pélagie, or courting Dorsan's other lovers, Raymond unfailingly returns to pester Dorsan and anyone else he encounters. The two *rentiers*, Dorsan and Raymond, have an antagonistic relationship, a typical trope of de Kock's novels whose function is usually comedic.[44] While Raymond's "grotesque" excesses provide comic relief and extend the narrative of Dorsan's romantic life, these behaviors are consistently punished throughout the novel.

Dorsan, from whose perspective the novel is narrated, is himself not a particularly upstanding character. He too has romantic dalliances, yet, contrary to Raymond, he has an awareness of his actions and their consequences. For example, after spending an evening unabashedly flirting with uninterested flower sellers, Dorsan offers to accompany one named Nicette home, remarking, "Vous voyez, lecteur, j'ai du bon quelquefois."[45] When Nicette's mother refuses her entry into their home, Dorsan allows her to stay with him, but doggedly attempts to seduce her. Stung by Nicette's discomfort and rejections, Dorsan explains, "Elle m'a demandé l'hospitalité et j'allais profiter de cela pour la séduire! C'est fort mal."[46] Though at times his personal admonishments seem less than genuine, Dorsan's self-reflections distinguish him from Raymond, whose extravagant conduct betrays no inner moral compass.

As a first-person narrator, Dorsan polices his own behavior but is also the first to reprimand Raymond for his misconduct. He takes Raymond to task for stealing his ex-lover Agathe, for injuring a bystander, and for upsetting boxes and a display of colored glasses as he flees the scene. Dorsan first scolds his neighbor by making him aware of his careless deeds: "'L'homme que vous avez blessé est très mal; . . . les dégâts que vous avez commis dans le jardin sont considérables.'"[47] When Raymond tries to flee again, Dorsan tricks him by pretending to serve as his lookout, then leaves him waiting indefinitely: "Sa conduite de la veille méritait bien cette petite vengeance."[48] Bad behavior is, once again, punished.

One final example of the chastising of Raymond's excesses occurs on an outing in the countryside, where Raymond tries ineffectively to seduce a servant. She resists but mockingly indicates the direction of her bedroom, to which he proceeds despite Dorsan's warnings. The next morning Dorsan finds Raymond in a pantry "ayant une jambe prise dans un piège, et assis sur une pile de jambons sur laquelle il est endormi."[49] While Raymond makes "une grimace épouvantable" as he is removed from the trap, "la grosse fille rit aux larmes."[50] The antagonist's sexual appetite is left unfulfilled, and he is painfully injured and humiliated for his impropriety. In this case Dorsan does not reproach Raymond overtly, but the reader understands his disapproval:

"Je pourrais railler mon compagnon sur le guignon qui le poursuit dans ses bonnes fortunes, mais je suis généreux et je me tais."[51] Dorsan evinces more control over his behavior than Raymond does and extends kindness to his antagonist, even as he acknowledges his own faults.

The "good" and "bad" characters are clearly demarcated at the conclusion of the novel: Pélagie and Raymond's infidelities are discovered, Pélagie dies repentant, and Dorsan and Nicette are reunited. The two lovers travel to Switzerland to begin anew, but when they arrive at their *auberge* (inn), they learn that a traveler has fallen fatally ill from overeating eggs as a bet: "[Il] a pretendu qu'il était plus habile que personne, et qu'il avalerait six oeufs durs avant de déjeuner et mangerait encore plus vite que tout le monde."[52] The egg eater is, of course, Raymond, who "venait de mourir des suites de son pari," killed by his excesses, this time by his gluttonous appetite and competitive nature, without having learned from his previous castigations.[53]

The moral lessons of excess and restraint found in *Raymond* function comically, and not subtly, and arise in a large number of de Kock's works. Scenes of egregious adultery in *Un Mari dont on se moque* (1869), for example, are corrected when the unfaithful wife is killed off, and in *Le Cocu* the spouses separated by adultery forgive one another their faults. Ribald drunkenness in *Le Barbier de Paris* is remedied when the inebriated character is humiliated. The "excès," the "petits faits vulgaires," which for Legrand-Chabrier were the legacy of the author's works, are consistently reined in or offered in opposition to the basic bourgeois virtue of self-regulation.[54] Likewise Ellen Constans underscores the conservative morals in the author's works, noting that "bien des romans de Paul de Kock pourraient recevoir comme sous-titre 'Les épreuves et le triomphe du mérite.'"[55] While the subjects this bourgeois writer chose may have troubled some early to mid-nineteenth-century readers, his obvious emphasis on virtue belies the assessment of his works as "licentious tableaux." Close readings of his reception problematize received ideas about de Kock's immorality, both in the nineteenth century and in modern criticism.

CRITICALLY SITUATING DE KOCK

As Flaubert's worry that he might "tomber dans le Paul de Kock" exemplifies, by the mid-nineteenth century the name de Kock had become a critical

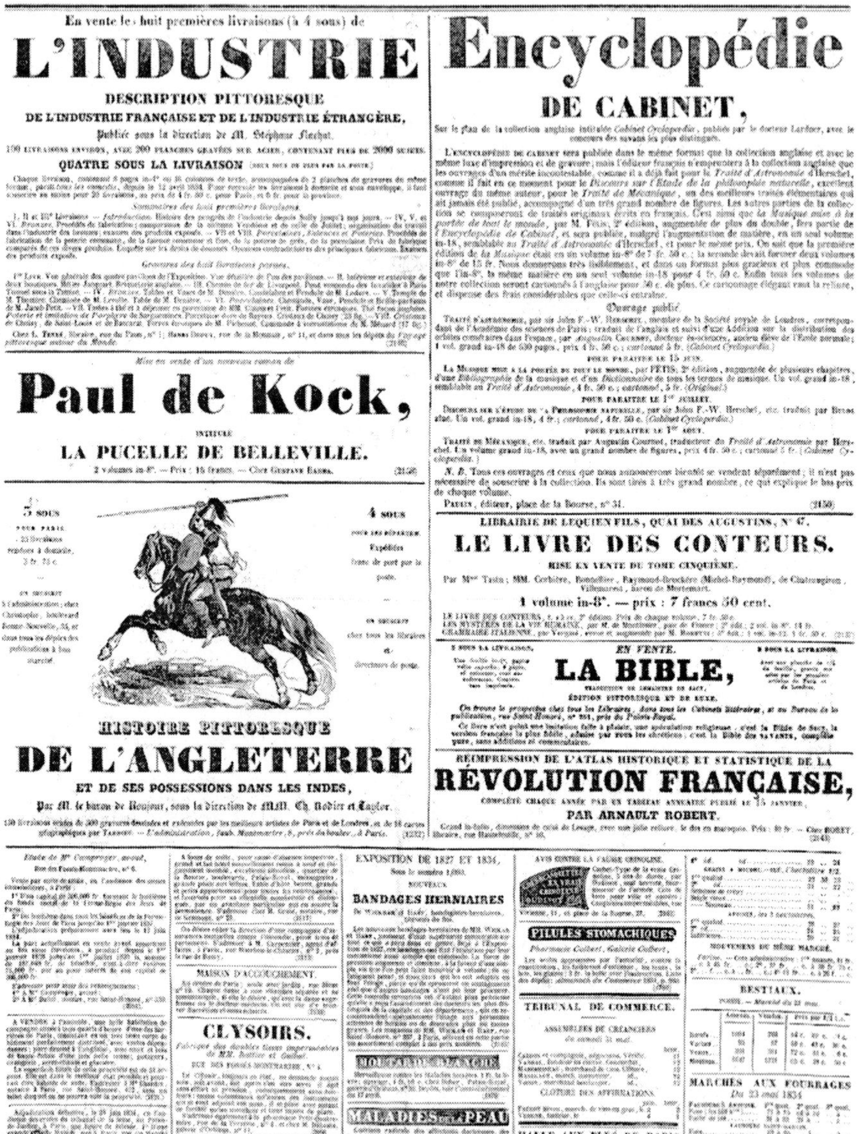

En vente les huit premières livraisons (à 4 sous) de

L'INDUSTRIE

DESCRIPTION PITTORESQUE

DE L'INDUSTRIE FRANÇAISE ET DE L'INDUSTRIE ÉTRANGÈRE,

QUATRE SOUS LA LIVRAISON

Encyclopédie

DE CABINET,

Paul de Kock,

LA PUCELLE DE BELLEVILLE.

LE LIVRE DES CONTEURS.

1 volume in-8°. — prix : 7 francs 50 cent.

LA BIBLE,

HISTOIRE PITTORESQUE

DE L'ANGLETERRE

ET DE SES POSSESSIONS DANS LES INDES,

RÉVOLUTION FRANÇAISE,

PAR ARNAULT ROBERT.

CLYSOIRS.

BANDAGES HERNIAIRES

PILULES STOMACHIQUES

MALADIES DE LA PEAU

TRIBUNAL DE COMMERCE.

HALLE AUX BLÉS DE PARIS

BESTIAUX.

MARCHÉS AUX FOURRAGES

FIG. 6. Back page of the *Journal des débats*, May 31, 1834, with ad for Paul de Kock novel. Bibliothèque Nationale de France.

doxa signifying "bad" literature, literature written for a popular audience.[56] A survey of journals from the beginning of de Kock's career through the July Monarchy reveals the early 1830s as the moment when this negative connotation solidified; few examples of the name "de Kock" as a synonym for lowbrow literature appear in the 1820s. By the July Monarchy, however, critics often evoked de Kock's name to critique other authors and as a negative marker of bourgeois taste, characteristic of the "taxinomie indigène, née de la lutte des classements dont le champ littéraire est le lieu."[57] For example, a review of Aubert du Bayet's "Les Nudzadelphines" in an 1836 issue of *La France littéraire* assessed the work as "presque du Paul de Kock en vers"— hardly praise for Bayet's poetic abilities.[58] The following year the same journal suggested that the title of Emile Souvestre's *La Maison Rouge* "annonçait tout au plus un roman à la manière de Paul de Kock."[59] These critics operated under the assumption that their readers understood "Paul de Kock" as philistine literature. Perhaps the most revealing example of de Kock's critically charged name is found earlier regarding his vaudeville *Un Raout chez M. Lupot*. In this one-line review the critic simply writes, "Je vous dis que la pièce est de—Mon-Sieur-Paul-de-Kock !"[60] Placing emphasis on each syllable of the name visually and textually reinforces its significance. One sentence suffices to describe the play's style and content: readers can judge it by its author. Appearing in 1835, this tongue-in-cheek review demonstrates that by the beginning of the July Monarchy de Kock's literary reputation had crystalized.

De Kock's name also, paradoxically, connoted that of a sought-after, profitable author; his name could be frequently found splashed across the back page of the very same *Journal des débats* in advertisements for his popular novels.[61] These ads in fact contained little more than the author's name in large print that often dwarfed the title of the new text; this was not an altogether uncommon advertising strategy at this moment. A May 31, 1834, ad for *La Pucelle de Belleville* boasted "Paul de Kock" in letters quadruple the size of the title, indicating that this newly released work was less significant than the fact that it was written by de Kock (fig. 6). Six weeks later an advertisement for *Les Oeuvres de Ch. Paul de Kock* graced the back page of the *Journal*: "Paul de Kock" was written once again in type so large that the only other word as prominent on the back cover was "Testament" in an ad for the Bible.

This marketing tactic appeared throughout the July Monarchy—in ads for a new edition of *Mon voisin Raymond* in 1835, in massive page-wide ads for de Kock's collected works in 1836 and in 1840, in an ad for a new edition of *Le Barbier de Paris* in 1842. In 1841 de Kock's publisher Gustave Barba used the name to sell the works of a newly popular British author: a March 27, 1841, ad in the *Journal* read "Nouveau roman du Paul de Kock Anglais (Charles Dickens) Oliver Twist."[62] Barba banked on de Kock's popularity to help him sell Dickens's work.[63] Here again we see "Paul de Kock" signifying something entirely different from its critical meaning; it is used as a publicity technique to attract potential readers rather than repel them from an inferior literary commodity. This double connotation is all the more powerful when we consider that within the same month or week, this name would have appeared twice in the same journal at cross-purposes. Sainte-Beuve's "De la littérature industrielle" identifies this phenomenon, asking critically, "Comment condamner à deux doigts de distance, qualifier détestable et funeste ce qui se proclamait et s'affichait deux doigts plus bas comme la merveille de l'époque?"[64] This double value of "Paul de Kock" in the July Monarchy literary market is an established phenomenon that nevertheless invites an in-depth analysis of reviews of his work and belies the idea that for all critics "Paul de Kock" had a single negative meaning.

De Kock's early critics generally exhibited more in-depth, nuanced analyses of his work than those in following decades. Despite mentions of the lightly immoral content of his work and his stylistic excesses, reviews of de Kock's works from the early 1820s give little indication that his name would become synonymous with lowbrow literature by the end of the decade. For example, in the first review of de Kock's work in the *Journal des débats*, a November 28, 1820, study of *Georgette*, the critic evokes the immodest subject matter yet elucidates the morality at the heart of the novel: "Le but de ce roman est moral; mais les détails ne sont pas toujours assez pudiques. . . . La mère en défendra la lecture à sa fille. Mais . . . la mère pourra bien s'en permettre la lecture, et la mère s'amusera."[65] Despite the caveats about the novel's content, this generally positive review praises de Kock's humor, guaranteeing that adult readers will enjoy themselves. Far from panning the novel's style and virtue, it defines de Kock's burgeoning literary method well: humorous prose peppered with lightly salacious details that seek nothing more than to uphold established morals.

Reviews of his nonnovelistic works appeared in the *Journal* soon after, and while an August 18, 1821, reviewer of de Kock's opéra-comique *Philosophe en voyage* criticized the staging and music, he was impressed by the play's prose: "La pièce de M. de Kock, renferme des situations comiques, une action vive, il y a de la gaîté dans le style et quelques mots heureux ont fait passer une foule d'invraisemblances."[66] Once again the playfulness of de Kock's style is noted, as are comic scenes that delight the audience. In these early reviews of the popular novelist, before his reputation as an author of the masses has crystalized, his style is appreciated rather than reproached as trite, immoral, or mediocre.

In the mid-1820s de Kock's name appeared numerous times in reviews of vaudeville plays based on his novels, which he authored or coauthored, a standard practice of the period.[67] An August 10, 1825, review of the opéra-comique *Enfants de Maître Pierre*, whose dialogue de Kock wrote, delves into a detailed analysis of his style, beginning with strong words of praise for the author who "y a réuni son double talent de romancier et de dramaturge."[68] Recognizing that de Kock often transformed his novels into plays, this reviewer actually encourages him to do the opposite: "Rien ne serait si facile que de tirer de son opéra un bon roman en quatre volumes."[69] Unlike many July Monarchy critics, who often lamented hearing de Kock's prose at the theater, this reviewer incites the author to remediate his works further and, despite some grievances about style, ultimately labels the work an "ouvrage estimable à beaucoup d'égards."[70] The author of a February 14, 1828, review of the novel *Jean* calls attention, as others would later do, to de Kock's monetary success. Yet he congratulates the author for having "présenté sous des formes nouvelles un sujet qui offre de si heureux développements... *Jean* est un des romans les plus gais qu'il ait composés jusqu'ici."[71] This assessment puts into question the notion that financial success somehow diminished de Kock's literary prestige. Such close attention to style suggests that in the late Restoration literary field the name de Kock had not yet attained its July Monarchy meaning. De Kock was less omnipresent then, but also less reproachable.

As the regime of Louis-Philippe began, reviews of and ads selling de Kock's work cropped up more consistently in the *Journal des débats*, as well as in newly established papers like *Le Charivari* (1832), *La France littéraire* (1832), and *Le Monde dramatique* (1835). While these frequent reviews were not universally negative, negativity toward and growing disdain for this popular author did increase. Because many of these critiques are well known, I have chosen to touch on only a few. Purely negative reviews were not as ubiquitous as the critical consensus seems to suggest, but given the author's ultimate reputation as the embodiment of lowbrow literature, their increased frequency under the July Monarchy merits attention.

One often criticized aspect of de Kock's writing was his tendency to turn a novel into a play, or vice versa, thereby proving for some his lack of originality. An April 17, 1834, review of his play *La Femme, le mari et l'amant* in *L'Indépendant* evoked this habit of reproducing material from one genre to another: "M. Paul de Kock n'a pas fait grands frais d'imagination pour bâcler cette prétendue folie-vaudeville; il a tout bonnement transcrit une partie de son roman."[72] The pejorative "bâcler" (to botch) immediately indicates the critic's appraisal of de Kock's literary talents. A month later another reviewer wrote of de Kock's lack of originality in *La Maison blanche*: "Il est convenu quand M. Paul de Kock fait une pièce quelconque, que c'est toujours avec un de ses romans.... Cela épargne à M. Paul de Kock la peine d'inventer, et à nous celle de parler de ses pièces."[73] Here his work is deemed uninspired, unworthy of serious consideration. The author's literary recycling contributed to the perceived absence of creativity in his work and required critics to double their efforts as they reviewed the same work in multiple formats. Representative reviews from this period make clear that, as the volume of de Kock's novelistic and theatrical production increased, so too did critical dismissal.

Another reproach often found in reviews of de Kock's works is of his style. A July 27, 1840, reviewer of the theatrical version of *La Jolie fille du faubourg* remarks, "Il écrit, il est vrai, comme un barbare, il n'invente rien, sa fable est commune, ses personnages sont d'une trivialité déporable." This play is "comme toutes les autres histoires du même auteur, un de ces mauvais contes qu'il improvise avec si peu de sans-gêne et tant de bonne humeur."[74]

We also find a number of instances that simply take de Kock's "barbaric style" for granted. A July 7, 1842, article in *L'Indépendant* announced, "Malgré la chaleur et la prose de M. Paul de Kock, les exercices périlleux et vraiment extraordinaires des *Marocains* attirent la foule."[75] Despite having drawn a crowd, *Les Marocains* suffers from de Kock's writing. A September 14, 1846, review in the *Journal* labels his *Place Ventadour* an "insipid joke," while a September 27, 1847, review calls *La Femme à deux maris* "une bouffonnerie que le théâtre du Palais-Royal n'aurait pas voulu en plein carnaval!"[76]

Much of this criticism either anticipates or articulates arguments found in "De la littérature industrielle," where, as we saw in the introduction, Sainte-Beuve complains of a literary field under attack by a coalition of untrained, untalented writers. Railing against the unoriginality and unfavorable style found in this flood of industrial literature, Sainte-Beuve sees the moment in which he is writing as the "height" of this "invasion," even though inferior literature has always existed. For him industrial literature emerged in the July Monarchy: "Lorsqu'il y a tout à l'heure dix ans, une brusque révolution vint rompre la série d'études et d'idées qui étaient en plein développement, une première et longue anarchie s'ensuivit. . . . Mais en voilà qu'en littérature, comme en politique, à mesure que les causes extérieures de perturbation ont cessé, les symptômes intérieurs et de désorganisation profonde se sont mieux laissé voir."[77] These negative reviews of de Kock seem perfectly in keeping with common anxieties about a broader "profound disorganization" in the literary culture of the 1830s and 1840s. It is also worth noting that reviewers who evaluated his work negatively were, on a certain level, positioning themselves hierarchically in this same literary field.

Despite these purely negative ones, a significant number of reviews throughout the July Monarchy took a less unilateral approach to de Kock's oeuvre; they tended instead to critique the novel or play in question for its style or content but then highlight a redemptive sense of wit.[78] An 1837 review of *Tourlourou* from *Le Monde Dramatique* cautions potential spectators, "Ne cherchez rien d'extradorinaire dans *Tourlourou*," but concludes that "il y a de la joyeuseté de cabaret, de bonnes bêtises de caserne, de la folie, de l'esprit de bas étage, et tout cela à pleine gorge. Aussi, a-t-on beaucoup ri sans se soucier du reste."[79] There are formal criticisms to be made but also conviction that humor redeems the work. This critical tendency to highlight stylistic flaws while extolling wit is exemplified in Jules Janin's assessment of *L'Agnès de Belleville* in August 31, 1835. Calling it "cet infect volume," Janin grapples with why readers are drawn to the "horrible plaisir" of de Kock's work: "C'est que dans ces sortes d'ouvrages, que repoussent également le goût, le bon sens, le style, l'imagination, tout ce qui fait les hommes raisonnables . . . l'auteur a délayé quelque chose à son insu, que rien ne remplace et qui remplace toutes choses, esprit, génie, invention et style. . . . Jugez après ce que c'est que cette grande puissance—la gaîté!"[80] The term *gaîté* (cheerfulness) punctuates this quotation, which considers de Kock's work both at odds with taste and style yet powerfully humorous; even in small doses this *gaîté* is capable of convincing readers to consume the author's works. In spite of twenty-first-century critics' assertions that, for example, "la lecture de la reception des adaptations théâtrales des romans de Paul de Kock montrent un auteur victime de sa popularité," we have seen, conversely, that despite what they perceive as formal shortcomings, July Monarchy critics still recognize literary and entertainment value in his oeuvre and, on the whole, did not universally dismiss the author as "bad."[81] On some level these critics seem aware that, despite their own assessments of the works' aesthetic qualities, the author has undeniably tapped into a popular market with the genre of work he produced.

Amid negative and mixed July Monarchy reviews of de Kock's novels and plays, there emerged yet another critical trend regarding his contributions to the genre of panoramic literature, a popular phenomenon to which he was a key contributor. Reviewers heaped praise on Pierre-François Ladvocat's enormous 1831 volume, *Paris, ou le livre des cent-et-un*, a work by 101 different writers in an attempt to relieve the éditeur of his financial distress. Of this "fidélité d'observations dans la variété des situations et des moeurs," one critic in the June 29, 1833, *Journal* signaled his appreciation of the collaboration of such a disparate list of authors: "M. Paul de Kock comme M. Charles Nodier sont également à l'aise dans ce champ d'imagination et du cœur, où l'art d'écrire ne rencontre d'autres règles et d'autres limites que le devoir de plaire ou d'attacher. Ces habiles écrivains ont si bien empreint leur travail du génie particulier que leurs autres productions nous avaient appris à connaître et à aimer."[82] Given this same journal's critique of de Kock's *Le Bon enfant* seven weeks later as "absurde, faux, fatigant et ennuyeux," it is surprising to see him called a "gifted writer" for his contribution to Ladvocat's volume.[83] It is worth pointing out that this first, more positive assessment might be a classic example of the *réclame*—what Marc Martin describes as "la publicité rédactionnelle, déguisée en article"—which was usually situated "à la page 3 ou 4 juste avant les annonces avec qui elle fonctionne souvent en binôme."[84] Nonetheless this positive critical treatment of de Kock's work in the texts that would eventually make up the corpus of panoramic literature is not unique and shows the availability of alternative readings of this author.

Over the next two decades, in particular during the boom of panoramic literature in the first few years of the 1840s, de Kock's ability to observe and document Parisian phenomena, his ability "to please and to connect," earned him critical capital. A September 25, 1841, passage in the *Journal* characterized his newly published *Physiologie de l'homme marié* as "un texte plein d'esprit et d'observation."[85] On February 13, 1842, a similar report on the publication of *Les Français peints par eux-mêmes* lists de Kock's contribution among other "remarkable articles."[86] For what was perhaps de Kock's most significant contribution to the movement of panoramic literature, his 1842 *La Grande Ville*, a *nouveau tableau de Paris*, the author received praise for having "répandu toute la gaîté, tout le naturel qui en ont fait le peintre de la bourgeoisie parisienne."[87] For July Monarchy critics, then, de Kock excelled at depictions of social life and urban phenomena in the panoramic genre; his textual *tableaux* attempting to understand Paris at its most modern moment represented some of his best work. Even if these positive treatments may be examples of ads disguised as articles, we see in them instances of a different image of de Kock disseminated to a wide reading public.

In addition to works that make up what is now recognized as the canon of panoramic literature, a number of de Kock's theatrical and novelistic efforts containing scenes or digressions on Parisian phenomena received critical acclaim for their realistic, comic depictions of urban life. In a September 14, 1845, *Charivari* review of *Place Ventadour*, the critic deems the idea behind the play to be very light but points to "ces petits tableaux de mœurs dans lesquels il excelle; il en a même trop mis.... Le tableau n'est pas

neuf, mais il est gai."[88] He chides the author for his excessive use of urban
tableaux but concedes that de Kock's talent lies in these pleasant paintings of
Parisian bourgeois life. It is helpful here to recall this simultaneous critique
of de Kock's style and praise for his panoramic observations in the 1840
review of the novelistic version of *La Jolie fille du faubourg*: "Il s'y trouve
trois ou quatre scènes qui sont, dans un genre un peu trivial sans doute, de
petits chefs-d'œuvre de vérité et d'observation ... [qui] méritent d'être citées
comme échantillons du talent véritable de M. Paul de Kock."[89] Here de
Kock's novelistic passages that mirror the panoramic literary texts in form
and content give evidence of his literary talent. The popular panoramic
genre, with Ladvocat's 1831 work as its precursor, exploded onto the literary
scene roughly between 1840 and 1844, years during which many of these
positive assessments of de Kock's work were written. Contrary to critical
commonplaces, then, during the boom of panoramic literature de Kock
actually gained cultural capital for his contributions to that genre. Even if
we keep in mind the personal and professional concerns of his critics—their
biases and self-positioning within the media environment of this period—a
more complex picture of de Kock emerges from analyses of their reviews.

RECYCLED LITERATURE

A final critique of de Kock, found in both the reviews of his day and in
scholarship of our own, charges the author with recycling his novels, essentially regurgitating the same plot throughout his oeuvre. A critic of his 1837
Moeurs parisiennes remarked, for example, "Quand on a lu un roman de Paul
de Kock, on peut dire qu'on connaît, non seulement tous ceux qu'il a faits,
mais encore tous ceux qu'il fera. Jamais imagination de romancier ne fut
moins féconde que la sienne."[90] In a more recent and perhaps more charitable
assessment, Lucien Minor's 1975 monograph on the nineteenth-century "hack
writer" claims that although de Kock produced hundreds of volumes in his
career, "ordinary mortals are reassured, if a bit disappointed, when they learn
that de Kock's novels are really just the same novel written and rewritten,
repeated endlessly with only small changes of décor and accessories."[91] The
1994 edition of the *Dictionnaire de biographie française* makes "official" this
concept of literary recycling, asserting that "Paul de Kock n'a jamais fait

qu'un seul roman, dont il a varié à l'infini le cadre et les détails accessoires, en y faisant mouvoir les mêmes physionomies, en racontant presque les mêmes aventures."[92] Rather than viewing this repetition as a purely negative aspect of de Kock's writing, one might instead attribute this strategy of reuse to his market-savvy production. He was, in other words, able to convince his public of the variety in his texts and create a type of writing for which there was a lucrative commercial demand, anticipating modern strategies of the publishing and entertainment industries. While the study of whether de Kock simply wrote one novel might not provide a productive entry into his oeuvre, it is nonetheless interesting to consider the actual literary recycling he conducted throughout his career.

It bears mentioning that, in the context of de Kock's theatrical works, these claims about the repetition of characters and plotlines are not only justified but are exemplary of common practices among producers of popular theater, vaudeville, and melodrama. On the source material for his plays, Marie-Pierre Rootering writes that "toute la majorité de ses oeuvres dramatiques sont des oeuvres dérivées de ses propres romans."[93] Attracted to the business of popular theater by "the potential for serious money," like so many of his peers, Terni explains, de Kock remediated his own works across genres.[94] In fact de Kock reworked an estimated eighteen of his novels into plays; on a few occasions he produced multiple versions of these plays; and he was also known to adapt the work of other writers, like Alexandre Dumas, for the stage, though he was nowhere as infamous as Dumas for collaborating with and appropriating the works of other authors.[95] These consistent theatrical contributions, in addition to (and perhaps aided by) his novelistic production, assured the author all the more revenue and fame by enabling him to find "le plus large public."[96] Like his novels, his plays also evince the interconnected nature of the cultural marketplace in which they were produced.[97]

One instance of de Kock's recycling will stand as an example of his ability to profit from a still developing and often unregulated literary marketplace. As we saw in chapter 1, de Kock published *La Grande Ville: Nouveau tableau de Paris, comique, critique et philosophique* in 1842, a comical pseudo-sociological study of July Monarchy Paris based on Mercier's *Tableau de Paris*. This fifty-two-chapter collection examining diverse Parisian phenomena was initially published in installments, and in its subtitle and preface it called attention to the specific literary tradition in which the work participated. Nonetheless, after its initial publication in 1842, de Kock republished and reworked versions of the same text for financial gain. A longer, theatrical version of the second chapter, "Les Bains à Domicile" (Home-Delivered Baths), was written and performed in 1845, another example of this theatrical remediation of his novels and short stories and, more generally, of the overlap of stock characters and plotlines in both genres. More curious, however, is the fact that the author essentially republished *La Grande Ville* three years after its initial publication under a different title. His 1845 *Paris au kaléidoscope*, which came out in two volumes from the publisher Dolin and sold for 15 francs, was a forty-eight-chapter book that contained, word for word but in a different sequence, forty-two of the same chapters with the same titles as *La Grande Ville*. Though de Kock opens *Paris au kaléidoscope* with a new chapter that is absent from his 1842 *tableaux*, "Un Bal dans le grand monde" (A High-Society Ball), the second chapter, "Les Bouges et les sorcières" (The Hovels and the Witches), is an exact reproduction of the twenty-sixth install-ment of *La Grande Ville*. The author continues this pattern of alternating new chapters with the old ones, offering the original "Le Conservatoire" (The Conservatory) before inserting the repeated "Les Floueurs" (The Swindlers), after which he places "Les Passages" (The Arcades), a chapter not seen in *La Grande Ville*. The succeeding eighteen chapters, however, which make up the remainder of the first volume, are all recycled from *La Grande Ville*, though in a different order. This new volume, in other words, offers three new short studies of Parisian phenomena and twenty chapters published three years previously under a different title, a pattern he follows in the second volume of *Paris au kaléidoscope* as well.

The new title of this now remediated work engenders questions about its genre: Is *Paris au kaleidoscope* also a modern rewriting of Mercier's *Tableau de Paris*? If the word *tableau* evokes an artistic and theatrical tradition, while the kaleidoscope (patented for the first time in 1817) was like panoramic literature itself, a popular phenomenon in early nineteenth-century Paris, then can *Paris au kaléidoscope* still be considered the "immense comédie à cent actes divers" de Kock refers to in his 1842 preface to *La Grande Ville*?[98] Do these disparate terms force the two publications into distinct genres? Or should we accept the conclusion of the *Bibliographie de la France*, which classified both works under the rubric "Romans et contes"? These generic concerns are eclipsed by a more pertinent commercial one, namely that de Kock published another two editions of a work entitled *La Grande Ville ou Paris il y a vingt-cinq ans* in 1867. As one might suspect, this version contains no original chapters on Paris but rather is made up of thirty-nine of the same chapters in a slightly different order than the 1842 version. In the preface to this 1867 version, published by both Degorce-Cadot and Sartorius, de Kock is not shy about copying nearly word for word the preface of the 1842 version. Acknowledging the fact that he is blatantly reproducing his earlier text, he writes, "Nous avons fait paraître cette espèce de tableau, en 1842. Nous le laissons aujourd'hui tel que nous l'avons écrit, il y a 25 ans, et nous n'y faisons aucun changement; persuadé que beaucoup de lecteurs pour lesquels on fait à chaque instant des Paris modernes, ne seront pas fâchés d'en connaître aussi un ancien. Du reste, pour ce qui est des mœurs, des ridicules et des sottises de la société, ils seront surpris de voir qu'il n'y a que fort peu de changement chez les Parisiens."[99] In this different commercial context, de Kock sees his retrospective of Paris as a relief to readers flooded with modern representations of the city, and he seems to contradict his previous thoughts on the ever-changing nature of the modern city by writing that Parisians actually change very little. With the exception of a few topical modifications, this work's preface even concludes with the same imperative—"Promenons-nous donc au hasard dans Paris"—without clarifying that in one instance Paris will be the city of the present day, 1867, and in the other the Paris of twenty-five years earlier, a city untouched by the radical transformations of Haussmann that were happening in the Paris wherein he republished this version. *La Grande Ville ou Paris il y a vingt-cinq ans*, unlike *Paris au Kaléidoscope*, calls attention to itself as a recycled text and even uses that description to promote itself.

While this literary repurposing may simply seem like a particularly disingenuous attempt by de Kock to make more money, we should also remember that such reissuing was not at all uncommon during the time period. Thérenty writes of the frequency in the July Monarchy, for example, of the "changement de titre qui permet de tenter de vendre deux fois le même recueil au même lecteur," and as I explained in the introduction, laws about authors' intellectual property rights, as well as the role of the *éditeur*, were very much undefined at the moment in which de Kock was publishing his urban studies.[100] This is a moment when, according to Haynes, "the average author dealt with thirteen publishers over the course of his career" and payment came in "the form of a lump sum, in exchange for which the publisher obtained the right to publish a limited edition of the work during a short period of time."[101] De Kock himself worked with a number of publishers throughout his career. Notably, however, he was involved in multiple and lengthy legal battles with his principal publisher, Gustave Barba, to whose father (Jean-Nicolas Barba) he had signed away early in his career the rights to his increasingly prolific novelistic production until the beginning of 1840, a deal that conferred great financial benefit on Barba. De Kock's biographer Eugène de Mirecourt tells of how Barba *père*, who had previously published some of de Kock's theatrical works, initially recommended that the author publish his second novel, *Georgette* (1821), with the *libraire-éditeur* Hubert instead of with him. De Kock followed Barba's advice. But Barba quickly changed his mind when he witnessed de Kock's success with his early novels and realized he could be sitting on a goldmine. According to Mirecourt, "il se mit à exploiter à lui seul le talent de Paul de Kock et à ne pas laisser aux autres le plus léger filon."[102] Barba locked de Kock into a multiyear contract in which he would be paid in advance approximately 2,000 francs per work for the exclusive rights to print and sell his novels, which would each be published in four volumes in the in-12 format. These payments, according to another of de Kock's biographers, Timothée Trimm, "n'étaient pas très-élevés. Mais encore valaient-ils mieux que la *Gratuité* de son premier ouvrage."[103] Barba thus foresaw de Kock's immense popularity and capitalized on it for his own profit, a commercial move de Kock's admittedly biased biographers readily describe as predatory.

De Kock tried valiantly and usually in vain to skirt the regulations of the contract, especially once his popularity grew, ultimately facing off against Gustave Barba in court multiple times.[104] Between 1831 and 1836 the two participated in numerous legal clashes over the rights to de Kock's collected works, which he had offered to another publishing house; de Kock also accused Barba of publishing his work in a format (in-8°) that was not stipulated by their contract. In another 1839 case, Barba, who (according to the contract) owned the exclusive rights to de Kock's novels, fought the author in court when he discovered that he had sold a short story ("nouvelle") to another publisher, who subsequently advertised the work as a novel ("roman"). Throughout this process at times the charges were dropped and at other times the decision was subsequently appealed; in some cases the author and publisher were required to pay damages and fines. Yet all of these legal cases are exemplary of de Kock's (and Barba's) attempt to capitalize on the novelist's popularity and exploit the market from every possible angle.[105] Despite any legal setbacks with Barba, then, the example of *La Grande Ville*'s reworkings reinforces de Kock's (and his future publisher's) grasp on the way this nascent literary market worked. De Kock shrewdly manipulated the forms and formats in which his work appeared and capitalized on the economic conditions of this transitional moment in nineteenth-century literary history and on a new demographic of readers.

"PAUL DE KOCK"

I want to return to the consumers of de Kock's novels: those for whom "Paul de Kock" signified someone whose work was worth purchasing, those for whom it connoted critical failure, and those who found themselves in between. Despite the cliché "On l'aime ou on le déteste," we have seen a more complex response to de Kock, whose name truly became emblematic of the anxiety over changes in the literary market developing in the early July Monarchy.[106] While critics around 1830 began to use his name synonymously with lowbrow literature, many of their reviews evinced an appreciation of some elements of his work and recognition of his successful command of the taste of modern readers. Simply put, "Paul de Kock" did not always signify "Paul de Kock."

Moreover his work, with *Raymond, Le Cocu,* and the other novels I examined as illustrative examples from his enormous oeuvre, demonstrates the author's keen understanding of his target readership. The repetition of moral lessons and scenes of bourgeois urban phenomena shows de Kock mastering a key formal element of market success. For Stiénon this clear "thématisation des valeurs de l'univers bourgeois urbain" is directed toward his target audience, for whom the author attempts to offer "une reception à court terme, pratique et divertissante, quitte à faire de son oeuvre une production de commande."[107] These values, coupled with the amusing, digestible plotlines, drew in and retained his readers. De Kock actually corroborates the readings of some twenty- and twenty-first-century critics in his preface to the 1842 edition of *Raymond*: "J'ai toujours cherché à montrer les suites de l'inconduite, à prouver où peuvent nous entraîner nos passions, à tourner le vice en ridicule. . . . Aux yeux de bien des gens je serai toujours coupable, mais je compte sur l'indulgence du plus grand nombre."[108] Bourdieu, writing over 150 years later of the author's novels, "qui flattent le public en lui renvoyant sa propre image sous la forme de héros à la psychologie directement transcrite de la vie quotidienne de la petite bourgeoisie," would certainly concur.[109] If analyses of de Kock's work and reception do not necessarily change his position as a representative of bourgeois art (in Bourdieu's words), such studies nonetheless complicate our understanding of his field of cultural production.

De Kock was acutely aware of his position in the contemporary literary market and aptly exemplifies the response of "minor literati to their new commercial context."[110] Consistently stigmatized as texts for the lower classes, de Kock's work was actually consumed by a much broader audience. Recent critics acknowledge a gap between those who read de Kock and those who admitted to reading him: "Si en réalité de Grégoire VI à Chateaubriand, tout le beau monde le lit, il est mal vu de se dire son lecteur."[111] If everyone read him but no one acknowledged it, then de Kock was mythological in the same sense as the bourgeois class itself, if we take seriously Sara Maza's argument that while late eighteenth- and early to mid-nineteenth-century politicians and intellectuals fought on behalf of the bourgeoisie, virtually no one claimed it as his or her own class.[112] De Kock truly was, then, the bourgeois author par excellence. On the one hand, he emblematizes the literary field of the mid-nineteenth century, when, for Bourdieu, high culture and commercial culture were newly pitted against one another. De Kock represents a particular moment in the early modern mass-media market and serves as a marker—often negative—of social positioning and taste. On the other hand, as my analysis of his works and reception demonstrates, within the framework of these established markers of taste, de Kock actually challenges the rigid binaries of the nascent nineteenth-century literary field. Though his literary production was less consistently successful than that of de Kock, Eugène Sue—an author often seen as emblematic of industrial literature thanks to his best seller, *Les Mystères de Paris*—also demonstrates a more nuanced engagement with this literary field, and, as such, his oeuvre too is worthy of reexamination.

Chapter Three

THE ADAPTABLE EUGÈNE SUE

"THE GREATEST BESTSELLER OF ALL TIME"

In an 1844 issue of the *Revue de Paris*, an advertisement from the publisher Charles Gosselin announced the latest edition of Eugène Sue's incredibly popular *Les Mystères de Paris*, as well as new editions of his previously published works (fig. 7). Capitalizing on the record success of this 1842–43 serial novel, the ad claims, "Le succès incontestable des *Mystères de Paris* ... ayant augmenté le nombre des lecteurs des précédents romans de M. Eugène Sue, plusieurs de ces romans ont été réimprimés. On voudra relire *Mathilde, Arthur, la Salamandre* et tous les romans de l'auteur qui ont précédé les *Mystères de Paris*."[1] In a calculated formal tactic designed to catch the eyes of insatiable readers and potential booksellers, "Les Mystères de Paris, 10 volumes in-8°" is printed in bold and centered above a list of all of Sue's other titles, which are not in boldface. The physical proportions of *Les Mystères* itself (10 volumes), in comparison to the other works, also make the novel stand out from and loom over its predecessors.[2] The layout and the copy of this ad clearly posit *Les Mystères* as Sue's most dominant publication. Although it attempts to entice new readers to purchase his previous works, this announcement nonetheless indicates readers' familiarity with these

FIG. 7. Ad for a collection of novels by Eugène Sue. *Revue de Paris* 1, no. 1 (1844): 518. Bibliothèque Nationale de France.

pre-*Mystères* texts. The success of *Les Mystères* may have increased Sue's readership, but the use of the term *relire* (reread) instead of *lire* (read) indicates that the ad is targeting an already established audience.

By positioning *Les Mystères de Paris* as the apex of Sue's career while also alluding to his extant readership, this advertisement stages a critical problem for nineteenth-century and modern critics alike: How do we understand Sue (already a popular author in 1842) as anything but the author of what Peter Brooks has called "the runaway bestseller of nineteenth-century France, possibly the greatest bestseller of all time"?[3] The publication of *Les Mystères*—a defining and pivotal moment in Sue's career to be sure—is the lens through which his oeuvre is still read, even though he was relatively well known when this blockbuster was released. Perhaps because no other works of Sue attained the same "étourdissant succès" before *Les Mystères* and perhaps too because he experienced breakthroughs and setbacks in his literary production, his decade-long career leading up to this best seller is often critically unexamined or noted merely as the natural precursor to the publication of *Les Mystères*.[4]

Though Emile de Girardin launched his lower-priced newspaper *La Presse* along with the first French serial novel, Balzac's *La Vieille Fille*, in 1836, the phenomenon of the serial novel did not truly take off until the publication of *Les Mystères de Paris*, according to Lise Queffélec.[5] The novel would later be released in illustrated and unillustrated editions.[6] Between 1842 and 1850 an unprecedented 60,000 readers purchased *Les Mystères* and as many as 800,000 consumed it, a range that Marie-Eve Thérenty deems possibly underestimated.[7] Immediately scores of plagiarized copies, translations, and adaptations (from *Les Mystères de Bruxelles* to *Les Mystères de la Nouvelle Orléans*) were produced in France and across the globe, making it a media phenomenon of international proportions.[8] Critics have attributed Sue's domestic success to different factors: the appealing intersection of urbanization and criminality (Thérenty); the popular movement of romanticism in tandem with the development of the reduced-priced press (Armand Lanoux); the desire to restore order to an increasingly unreadable society (Lyon-Caen); the exoticized representation of the underbelly of Paris (Queffélec).[9] Regardless of why it drew readers, it is hard to understate the novel's popularity and its status as an early if not the earliest example of a modern, global blockbuster.

An 1843 illustrated edition of *Les Mystères de Paris* offers insight into the author's keen understanding of market concerns. Included as prefatory material to the edition is a letter to Sue from the historian and author Jean-Baptiste Théodore Burette that addresses the trend of illustrating popular novels, a practice about which Sue claims to be skeptical.[10] Burette supports this fashion, writing, "La mode est là qui s'impose."[11] Already a follower of literary trends, Sue likely quotes Burette to lend gravitas to the project but also to justify his reasons for wanting to generate even more hype surrounding the novel. If Burette observes that Sue's newfound popularity overwhelms him—"Votre succès vous trouble"—this letter also makes plain that Sue is no stranger to fame and that since the publication of *Mathilde* (1841) he has already amassed a number of devoted women readers.[12] While the scale of his success with *Les Mystères* may have been new to the author, Sue, we see here, was already an author of renown who knew the rules of the game he was playing.

Burette's comment that "la mode est là qui s'impose" is applicable not only to the trend of illustrating novels but more generally to Sue's approach to his career. He was a savvy author who made multiple attempts at commercial success by exploiting his literary network and contributing to the established genres of maritime novels and *romans de moeurs* before attaining the unprecedented success of *Les Mystères de Paris*. Even when his novels were flops, his works charted changes in the tastes of his contemporaries. His serialized fiction became a phenomenon in part because of his previous literary and professional strategies; with few exceptions, however, scholarship on Sue tends to focus solely on *Les Mystères*.[13] His career is often described as the evolution of a dandy writing for fun and money to a politically engaged author with an enormous readership.[14] The beginning of his career is read, almost exclusively, in light of the end.

Moving away from this teleological reading of Sue's popularity, I argue that Sue made tactical, commercial moves in his choice of form and style before *Les Mystères de Paris* by analyzing three lesser-known (and critically underexamined) works—*Kernok le pirate* (1830), *Mathilde* (1841), and *Paula*

Monti (1842)—alongside their promotion and reception. Sue worked principally on established subgenres—maritime novels, *romans de moeurs*—a tactic that led critics to label him as either up-and-coming or trendy well before *Les Mystères* was published. Additionally he recycled and reworked tropes throughout these disparate works, modifying elements depending on the subgenre to which they belong. Plotlines, character types, and even language in these earlier novels are reworked in *Les Mystères*, calling into question received ideas about the exceptional nature of this text and linking the novelist's practices to those of other contemporary popular authors like Paul de Kock and to the producers of popular vaudeville and melodramas. By engaging with Sue's novels and the critical discourse surrounding them at the time of their publication, I seek to reconstruct Sue as an author who understood and capitalized on the developing literary field, as an adaptable author who picked up on trends and tailored elements of his existing work according to contemporary fashion. Even if works such as *Latréaumont* (1837) and *Paula Monti* (1842) were less critically and commercially acclaimed, his pirate fiction earned him multiple editions and critical praise, and *Mathilde* was a best-selling serial novel. Studying the pre-*Mystères* Sue and the literary recycling throughout his oeuvre reveals his strategic and profitable choices that, in turn, inform us about the tastes of his readers and the market for fiction in the dynamic literary marketplace of mid-nineteenth-century France.

KERNOK LE PIRATE AND SUE'S EARLY CELEBRITY

Sue made his literary debut in the early 1830s in the genre of maritime fiction, with which he achieved both commercial and critical success. This was already a popular genre due to the 1824 publication of *The Pilot* by James Fenimore Cooper. Six years later, when Sue made his own attempt to break into the literary field, he capitalized on Cooper's fame. He followed what Margaret Cohen, by way of Bourdieu, calls the model in which, "in order to validate a new practice, the newcomer places this practice under the aegis of established positions, which can be individuals, moments, groups, or poetic practices such as literary genres."[15] According to legend, "en 1830, un ancien camarade de l'artillerie dit à M. Eugène Sue: 'Les romans de Cooper ont mis l'Océan à la mode: tu devrais bien nous écrire tes souvenirs du bord et créer le roman maritime en France.' L'idée plut à notre auteur."[16] Sue openly expressed admiration for Cooper and hoped to re-create his work in the French context. He called attention to his desire to participate in the genre of maritime fiction in a letter to Cooper included in the preface of his 1831 maritime novel, *Atar-Gull*: "J'ai estimé qu'il était mieux de débuter modestement comme peintre de *genre*" (emphasis in the original).[17] Rather than developing a new literary practice, Sue adapts an established one for the French context.[18] His entrance onto the literary scene was thus tactical, an attempt to capitalize on a preexisting and commercially successful subgenre with whose subject he had some familiarity.

Sue was originally trained as a surgeon, his father's profession, and traveled extensively in his youth with the French naval forces. When he returned to Paris from his maritime adventures in 1829 at the age of twenty-five, he found that a literary fervor had taken hold of his acquaintances. Despite his naval background and the fact that until this point he had published only anonymous letters in *La Nouveauté* and other, smaller venues, Sue was intrigued enough to begin writing. "Que va faire Eugène?" writes his biographer Jean-Louis Bory. "Comme tout le monde: de la littérature. Un peu. Juste ce qu'il faut pour quelqu'un qui se veut de la bonne société."[19] These early forays included a few minor collaborative vaudeville projects and reviews in *La Mode* and had more to do with social obligation than the need to contribute meaningfully to the field.[20] The budding author frequented Paris's literati and was well connected among publishers, journalists, and authors. He would eventually use these connections to gain critical recognition.

Though Sue might not have considered these early ventures into the literary world serious, *Kernok le pirate*, his first significant publication, coincided with a major life change, the death of his father in April 1830, after which Sue officially abandoned medicine and the navy. After nearly six years in the Marine Royale, Sue was now free and had the financial means to maintain an extravagant social life. As his early reviews and correspondence show, the notorious dandy had developed an elaborate network of literary colleagues and quickly gained the friendship and respect of critics and authors alike.[21] *Kernok* and another maritime novella, *El Gitano*, were eventually published together under the title *Plik et Plok* (1831) by the well-known publisher Renduel (who would publish Hugo's *Notre-Dame de Paris* the following year), marking Sue's first commercial splash in the domain of maritime fiction. *Kernok* was followed by *Atar-Gull* (1831), *La Salamandre* (1832), and *La Vigie de Koat-Ven* (1833), among other titles, and many contemporary publishers and fellow authors took note. New editions and collections of these maritime novels attest to their consistent sales and an established readership. Sue's first major publication was thus the effective combination of his personal knowledge of the sea and his understanding of the existing taste for the seafaring subgenre.

Kernok's narrative is a rapid-fire succession of explosive plot points not uncommon to maritime fiction. This short novel replicates many of the existing tropes of pirate and maritime fiction and is filled with excess, violence, passion, plot twists, and a glimpse into life on the high seas, despite the fact that, as Francis Lacassin argues, "la mer et le navire ne font que servir de toile de fond à un drame farouche."[22] After the protagonist receives an ominous prediction from a Breton sorceress, during which it is exposed that Kernok has likely murdered his former captain, readers encounter the brutal whipping of a sailor (punished for arriving late to the boat's departure due to his mother's death), dramatic sea battles (the sailors load their cannons with stolen gold when they are out of ammunition and launch a spectacular hailstorm of coins), debauched celebrations, and, in what is perhaps the novel's most iconic scene, the unexpected murder of two Spanish lovers (Carlos and Anita) just as they are discussing their future together: "Elle ne put achever, car un boulet ramé, entrant en sifflant par la poupe, lui fracassa la tête, coupa Carlos en deux, et brisa les caisses de fleurs et la volière."[23] In a similar twist of fate, Kernok, responsible for the deaths of Carlos and Anita, loses his lover, Zéli, when her body blocks a bullet from an English vessel that otherwise would have sunk his ship. After losing Zéli, Kernok retires with his bounty and lives out a respectable, bourgeois existence on land. The popularity of the maritime novel established by Cooper coupled with the exciting narrative make clear why readers were attracted by Sue's debut.

In his preface to *Kernok*, Sue claims, "Un certificat de vie littéraire est donc toute l'ambition de l'auteur."[24] More than affording the author the simple validation to which he aspired, however, *Plik et Plok* attained moderate commercial success, and by the end of 1831 there were already three editions. The critical response too was on the whole positive, especially considering the author's more modest goals.[25] Reviewers tended to note both a lack of existing French maritime fiction (amid Cooper's popularity) and Sue's attempt to fill this void. The *Revue encyclopédique*'s January 1831 account claimed that with a few insignificant exceptions, "nulles scènes naturelles n'ont été moins exploitées chez nous que les incidents de la vie maritime," recommending Sue as a French Cooper.[26] Another review that month contended that the sea "n'a pas été exploité encore par notre littérature," that, until now, France did not have its own Cooper to challenge "la jeune partie de l'auteur du *Pilote* et du *Corsaire rouge*."[27] Jules Janin's March 1831 review of *Plik et Plok* maintained that Sue was not yet "marin comme Cooper" because he lacked "l'habitude de la mer et du ciel"[28]; these reviews nonetheless show the cultural capital critics associated with Cooper, the need for a French national maritime fiction, and the possibility that our author might be the one to create it. Sue excelled at this particular subgenre, gaining positive reviews and calls for more publications, evincing his already established acclaim in the decade leading up to *Les Mystères de Paris*.[29]

Critics of *Plik et Plok* almost unanimously praised its style in their 1831 reviews: "souple, clair, pittoresque"; "vif, coloré, brilliant"; "vif, pittoresque, ardent . . . le style hardi et animé."[30] These reviewers all found the book eminently readable, especially its colorful descriptions. In his February 5, 1831, review of *Plik et Plok* in *La Caricature*, Balzac offered little evaluation of the novella (he preferred not to "déflor[er] les sujets par une analyse critique"), except to say that Sue has "crayonné un admirable portrait de pirate" and that the work contains "quelques jolies marines, de délicieuses figures."[31] *Le Figaro*'s reviewer commends Sue for having intuited "toute la poésie" of the ocean and claims that this poetic rendering makes the novel worthy of recommendation; likewise a reviewer from the *Gazette des théâtres* called *Plik et Plok* "un livre tout d'art et de poésie."[32] Even a reviewer for the *Gazette littéraire* who was more harsh in his assessment, stating that Sue's novel lacks the seriousness found in the works of Cooper and Scott, nonetheless admits that the book is "bien executé" and that, with *Plik et Plok*, Sue indicates that "son talent a de l'avenir."[33] If this critic believes Sue's work shows future promise, others position Sue favorably within an existing body of work. *Le Figaro's* reviewer sees in this novel "l'école moderne dans toute sa fougue," and the reviewer in the *Gazette des théâtres* appreciates the secondary characters and plotlines in *Kernok* ("les accessoires"), concluding, "C'est du Cooper, c'est du Balzac, que sais-je?"[34] Similarly Janin views Sue's hero as an already established type: "Fait sur l'image des marins de lord Byron, bien plus que sur ceux de Cooper, Kernock est le héros du genre."[35] Reviewers—many of whom, it should be noted, were part of Sue's social circle and therefore not necessarily unbiased readers—understood the style of Sue's early novel in terms of an existing literary field and actively and positively compared him to his (commercially and critically) successful contemporaries.[36]

The *Gazette littéraire's* reviewer perhaps most aptly captured the dual nature of Sue's literary ambition and the contemporary commercialization of literature—elements of Sue's career usually attributed only to his serial fiction of a decade later—in his characterization of the success of *Plik et Plok* and in particular *Kernok*. With this tale of the high seas, foreign for many of his urban readers, the reviewer argues, Sue has certainly found "le secret plus rare de nous intéresser à ce récit."[37] If writing a page-turner was his goal, the reviewer continues, "il est clair que son but est atteint, que le livre à droit au succès et le nom de l'auteur à la reputation."[38] However, Sue had succeeded only in terms of pure commercial value. He had not achieved "un succès dans toute l'étendue du terme . . . un succès d'art et de public," because *Plik et Plok* lacked a more artistic or metaphysical quality that would allow it to be memorable. The reviewer goes on to speculate that perhaps Sue "ne l'ambitionnait-il pas?"[39] With *Plik et Plok*, two novellas that satisfy their readers but do not, according to this review, aspire toward conventions of literary greatness, Sue offers, at the onset of his career, an example of commercially viable literature that complicates the existing paradigms of literary value. He anticipates the debate about industrial literature that would later crystalize with the publication of his best-selling social novel.

Sue's correspondence during the early 1830s tells the story of an almost instantly successful author whom others—including those who would go on to form part of the French literary canon—predicted would ultimately have even more critical and commercial success. After the publication of Sue's pirate novel *Atar Gull*, Prosper Mérimée, author of *Carmen*, wrote on May 28, 1831, to congratulate him on this new contribution to the world of maritime fiction: "Monsieur, j'ai lu *Atar Gull*... qui m'a fait passer des moments bien agréables.... Peut-être que les prudes vous feront quelques reproches, mais soyez sûr que *tout* le monde vous lira."[40] Mérimée establishes a distinction here between the critical appreciation of the novel and its popularity and predicts a wide readership for Sue. Alphonse Lamartine too confirmed Sue's popularity. In a letter written after reading Sue's *La Salamandre*, the romantic poet affirmed his enthusiasm for the recent book: "Nous avons lieu d'être satisfait de ceux [sic] que l'avenir vous annonce car partout où nous lisons votre nom il est précédé ou suivi d'une épithète honorable ou bienveillante."[41] Lamartine repeats the prediction that Sue's future is a promising one and further substantiates this by reporting that Sue's name is already in circulation and widely understood to be favorable. A third contemporary literary figure, Balzac, announced Sue's inevitable success in *Le Voleur* on January 10, 1831, even before *Plik et Plok* had been released: "M. Eugène Sue a donné dans *La Mode* la ravissante marine de *Kernok*, et plus tard, *le Gitano*, révélant avec modestie un talent frais et gracieux qui grandira, car il est jeune, très jeune."[42] All of these statements in the future tense—*placera, lira, grandira* (will place, will read, will grow)—make it clear that Sue's contemporaries recognized his current reputation as a successful writer, while imagining an even more successful one to come. On some level, especially in the case of Balzac, we can see this delaying of Sue's success to a future moment as a way of forestalling any competition in the marketplace. Once Sue was more established, Balzac, as we will see in chapter 4, would consider him a rival.[43]

Kernok thus anticipated yet more prominence in the genre for Sue. In the early days of 1833, a *Charivari* review of the "Pléiade des conteurs" lamented the commercialization of literature in a way that predated Sainte-Beuve's "De la littérature industrielle" by six years, likening this collection to "ces carnets d'échantillons assortis que les tailleurs ont toujours dans leur poche."[44] Yet within this work, the critic is impressed with *Daja*, "une petite histoire pleine de charme et d'intérêt" penned by Sue, whom he calls "un second interprète" of "la littérature dite *maritime*" after the already well-known M. Jal.[45] Praising the short story's "contrastes, ingéniusement posés et développés avec art," the critic heralds this minor work as "l'une des plus remarquables choses qui soient sorties de la plume de M. Sue."[46] This critic calls the process by which literary works were then composed "une opération industrielle," thus demonstrating early critiques of mass-market literature at the same time that he lauds Sue's style and talent.[47] It is also noteworthy to consider Sue the "second interprète" of maritime fiction, as it is in keeping with the idea that he was not the instigator of a successful subgenre but rather someone who adopted already popular ones. Sue was thus not the most famous contributor to maritime fiction of the period nor the creator of the genre, but he was rising in the ranks, according to this critic, and deserved to be noticed.

Nearly half a year later, in a July 20, 1833, review of the newest volume of the *Livre des Conteurs*, a critic from *Le Charivari* spoke favorably of this publication, noting that the publisher, M. Allardin, had made "un appel à toutes les célébrités littéraires qui pouvaient concourir au succès de sa publication. MM. Charles Nodier, E. Sue, Jules Janin, A. Jal, Saintines, le comte de Peyronnet, Ancelot, Alexandre Dumas . . . ont su donner une variété, tout à la fois substantielle et attrayante à ce *pique-nique* de bonne société."[48] Sue is grouped here with other "célébrités littéraires" constituting this "bonne société," and it is noteworthy that he should appear second on this list—before Janin, Jal, and Dumas. In fact by 1833 Sue's celebrity status as an author of maritime fiction was firmly established, so much so that he received letters from readers, including one addressing his position as "un littérateur distingué, dont s'honore notre époque."[49] Sue's correspondence with his readers at the time of *Les Mystères de Paris*'s publication is well-known, but early letters like this one prove his visibility among and accessibility to a reading public at the early stages of his career.[50] In a September 1833 *Revue de Paris* article, Janin jokingly played off Balzac, whom he called "le chef de la catégorie des femmes" against Sue, whom he accused of favoring maritime fiction: "M. Eugène Sue est toujours sur un vaisseau, comme M. de Balzac est toujours dans un boudoir. C'est le même amour exagéré, c'est la même passion monotone, c'est toujours le même vaisseau ou la même femme. Corbleau! morbleu! sacre-bleu! Capitaine Sue, largues les voiles!"[51] This mocking tone underscores the familiarity Janin expects his readers to have with the work of both authors, and his own familiarity with their work. Sue's maritime tropes were by now familiar to this critic (which can be seen in Janin's repetition of *toujours* and *même*) and could be parodied and used to call out another celebrity author on his own tropes. Though Sue had not yet attained the mass readership his *Mystères* would eventually garner, these reviews indicate his distinction, at least among reviewers whose critiques promised, in theory, to sell more copies.

As Sue hit the apogee of his popularity as an author of maritime fiction, he abandoned this genre for a period of four years. In a personal letter to Janin written in 1833, the author, having just finished his latest maritime novel, *La Vigie de Koat-Ven*, hints that he would take a break from writing novels for the present. Sue ribs Janin for the "gracieuses méchancetés" he afforded him in the *Revue de Paris* article and threatens to return the favor in "la préface d'un gros et damné de roman, que j'ai (Dieu soit loué, ce sera le dernier), que j'ai terminé il y a quelques six semaines. Quatre gros volumes in-8°. J'ai voulu, comme on dit vulgairement, *vider mon sac* une bonne fois. Et c'est fini quant aux romans, oh ! bien fini ! Si j'ai du loisir de paresse, j'essaierai à faire quelques drames. C'est, en vérité, plus amusant (à faire)."[52] Sue's successful manipulation of the maritime fiction genre seems to have run its course, and he plans to move on to more amusing literary endeavors. This move actually anticipates the public's eventual dwindling interest in maritime fiction, pointing either to Sue's own fatigue with the genre or to his comprehension of shifts in taste. One critic wrote to describe how tired the trope of the sea had become: "La mer devint en littérature un accessoire . . . peu important."[53]

Sue dedicated the next three years to a nonfiction, multivolume study, *Histoire de la marine française*, based on official archival research. Regrettably this hard work paid off neither critically or commercially.[54] His ensuing attempt at historical fiction was also less than positively received, as was the case when he published *Latréaumont* in 1837 with Gosselin. This historical novel received prominent and harsh critiques by Balzac and Gustave Planche. Sue had attained fame and remuneration from his novels that conformed to the extant genre of pirate fiction, but once he strayed from this model, his work was less appreciated. Though unfortunate for the author, such a response indicated the public's desire for this recognizable genre; his reading public was uninterested in the historical fiction and nonfiction as adapted by Sue. He was thus not a consistently successful author, but even his professional mishaps help illustrate contemporary literary trends. Despite these less popular publications, Sue was far from being the one-hit wonder of *Les Mystères de Paris*. Attention to his early works and their critical reception shows an active and respected figure in the literary world of the 1830s, a well-connected author savvy about adapting his skills for marketable projects. If Sue considered his first forays into literature unserious, he nonetheless generated capital as a sellable author and honed tactics that he would develop over the course of his publishing career.

MATHILDE AND THE *ROMAN DE MOEURS*

Shortly after these professional setbacks, Sue had a personal one: he had depleted his inheritance and was desperately in need of revenue. Retiring to the country, he started a project that departed from his previous maritime fiction; as one reviewer in the *Charivari* humorously put it, "M. Eugène Sue a daigné toucher terre."[55] He turned to the customs and conventions of contemporary high society for his subject matter, straying into the fashionable genre of the *roman de moeurs* that Balzac, among others, had somewhat recently popularized. *Arthur, or Journal de l'inconnu*, part of which was published serially in *La Presse* and then in its entirety by Gosselin in 1838, was his first foray into the genre. Testifying to its good sales, multiple editions of the novel were issued, and Sue was back on the literary scene as a novelist of contemporary life who often, if not always, took advantage of the new serialized format. While he did produce a historical novel during this period (*Jean Cavalier*, 1839–40) and one that attempted to fuse the generic divide between maritime and historical fiction (*Le commandeur de Malte*, 1841), these now untrendy genres made little commercial or critical impact.[56] Despite such occasional incursions back into the maritime or historical novel, Sue seemed to understand, if somewhat inconsistently, that the public's taste was now for the *roman de moeurs*. Thus he published a number of such novels between 1839 and 1842: *Le Marquis de Létorière*, *Mathilde*, *Thérèse Dunoyer*, and *Paula Monti ou l'Hôtel Lambert, histoire contemporaine*.

I will focus briefly on *Mathilde* (Sue's best-known and best-selling *roman de moeurs*) and *Paula Monti* (a novel serialized almost contemporaneously with *Les Mystères de Paris* and somewhat eclipsed by its fame), as well as their reception, in order to showcase Sue's dramatic generic shift from pirate fiction to *roman de moeurs* and demonstrate its clear resonance with contemporary public taste.

Mathilde, serialized from 1840 to 1841 in *La Presse* and then published by Gosselin, is a lengthy and captivating novel with multiple subplots and a network of *mondain* (high society) characters. To summarize an elaborate plot rather swiftly, the novel, as its subtitle, *Mémoires d'une jeune femme* (Memories of a Young Woman), indicates, follows the orphaned Mathilde from her childhood, during which she is taken in by the cruel Madame de Maran alongside her cousin Ursule. She ill advisedly marries Gontran de Lancry, rejecting a certain M. de Rochegune, who nevertheless becomes a lifelong advocate for her. Mathilde and Gontran's initially happy marriage becomes corrupted by his reprehensible friend, Lugarto, who is in cahoots with Mme de Maran; Lugarto attempts to assault Mathilde and blackmail Gontran. Ursule, now married, has become a vindictive character and begins an extramarital affair with Gontran. After the deaths of both Ursule and Gontran, among many other plot twists, Mathilde ultimately marries Rochegune. All ends well, in other words, for those who have upheld proper values throughout the novel, in the same manner as in the majority of the novels of Paul de Kock.

If reviews of *Mathilde* have one thing in common, it is their repetition of the idea that the novel was a popular success. An 1840 reviewer from the fashion journal *La Sylphide*, for example, writing as the novel was still appearing in serialized form, referred to "la vogue éphémère et mondaine de *Mathilde*," describing it as "un des livres les plus à la mode en ce moment" and deeming it "rempli du plus vif intérêt."[57] Though likely a *réclame*, an article in the April 14, 1841, issue of the *Journal des débats* refers to *Mathilde* as a novel "qui excite vivement l'attention dans un certain monde" and speculates that *Mathilde* "obtiendra un grand succès ... [et] il méritera ce succès par le charme du style et tout l'intérêt du drame."[58] Even if this short text is a paid advertisement, its references to the existing and projected popularity of the novel are in keeping with other reviews. Though we might charge critics who reviewed *Mathilde* in the post-*Mystères* period with conflating its success with that of its successor, an 1843 review of the newly released illustrated version of *Mathilde* makes no mention of *Les Mystères de Paris*. It notes that the public had "dévoré l'oeuvre en feuilletons dans *La Presse*, . . . savouré à longs traits, et, pour ainsi dire, heure par heure, l'intérêt croissant toujours de ce long drame."[59] This later review from the *Revue Pittoresque* thus focuses on the success the novel enjoyed in serialization and the enthusiasm of its readers.

The novel's popularity is also evident in reviews of its eventual theatrical adaptation in 1842 by Sue and Félix Peyat. The October 2, 1842, issue of *Tribune dramatique* references the engaged readership of the novel in its assessment of the play: "C'est l'incarnation dramatique de cette fameuse *Mathilde* qui a ému, l'année dernière, toutes les femmes qui lisent, et soulevé tant de controverses littéraires chez les hommes qui écrivent."[60] The novel was thus both popular and provocative, assuring a large audience for the play: "Il est évident que tout Paris, qui a lu le roman de *Mathilde*, la province qui commence à le lire, et l'Etranger qui le traduit, se trouveront, pendant quatre mois, en présence au théâtre de la Porte-Saint-Martin."[61] The reviewer points to Parisian readers' familiarity with the novel but also gestures toward an increasing provincial and international audience—all potential theater spectators as well. In his September 26, 1842, review of the play *Mathilde* in the *Journal des débats*, Janin describes the public's recognition of the novel as a collective, national experience: "J'ai vu toute cette salle attentive qui s'amusait à se souvenir de sa lecture passé. J'ai entendu des hommes qui disaient tout haut—Voilà Mlle Ursule!—Des femmes qui disaient, en tout respect;—Voilà Monsieur de Rochegune! On eût dit une histoire nationale ou tout au moins un conte de fées qu'on était heureux d'entendre raconter une seconde fois. Ainsi a été poussé le succès de ce livre jusqu'à ses dernières conséquences!"[62] The shared recall of the characters and plot points of the novel called out in the theater indicate a universal popularity that critics today tend to associate only with *Les Mystères de Paris*.

Mathilde was evoked in criticism dealing with the question of industrial literature, even if it did not go on to emblematize the *roman-feuilleton* in quite the same way that *Les Mystères de Paris* did. An 1841 reviewer in the *Revue des Deux Mondes* focused principally on *Mathilde* in his lengthy study of the contemporary novel, calling it "l'exemple le plus frappant que nous puissions citer à l'appui de ce que nous avons dit contre le funeste mode de publication qu'ont adopté la plupart de nos romanciers"—a reference, naturally, to the mode of serialized publishing. The reviewer finds much at fault with the novel—"ses prétentions psychologiques, ses interminables longueurs, ses affectations un peu puériles d'élégance mondaine"—but nonetheless credits it with exciting the interest of readers and in fact finds "jusqu'à un certain point la curiosité dont il a été entouré" to be justified.[63] For this critic the novel is too long and unrealistic in its depiction of Rochegune, but its vivid imagery and focus are praiseworthy.[64] The most important fault this critic finds in the novel is Sue's tendency, like other industrial authors, to write hastily, a doubly upsetting critique for this author who finds Sue to be "bien loin d'avoir pour le style le dédain que semblent affecter plusieurs romanciers; il a très souvent au contraire des tendances vers ce qui exige le plus de soin et le plus de délicatesse dans l'art d'écrire."[65] Though the "influence du travail hâtif qu'impose la presse" is evident in Sue's style when compared to other serialized fictions, "il y a dans *Mathilde* des qualités éminentes et même, nous le maintenons, quelques parties entièrement louables"[66] Sue's novel is, for this reviewer, the victim of popular literary trends, but despite major stylistic flaws, it merits some of its popularity. All of these reviews, both positive and negative, indicate that the novel is on trend and point to Sue's regained sense of mastery of his reading public.

Still eager to continue working on contemporary high society, Sue began to serialize yet another *roman de moeurs*, *Paula Monti ou l'Hôtel Lambert*, as he prepared and published *Les Mystères de Paris*. Even though an editorial note in *La Presse* claimed the novel had "excité le plus vif intérêt," it is safe to say that *Paula Monti* was not the literary phenomenon that was *Les Mystères*.[67] Few advertisements for this novel appeared at the time of its publication, and when they did, the title was generally listed in ads for *Les Mystères* or other collected works of Sue and usually written in a much smaller type than the title of its popular successor. Though both novels take the urban metropolis as their principal setting, *Paula Monti* focuses exclusively on the upper echelon of Parisian society, in contrast to the *bas-fonds* in Sue's social novel published almost concurrently. Though the novels might seem opposed at the outset, an October 1842 reviewer in the *Revue Critique des Livres Nouveaux* does speculate about an overlapping theme: "Il nous a paru que sous ces dehors brillants se cachaient des moeurs et des penchants qui ne sont guère plus nobles que ceux des habitués du *tapis-franc*."[68] The nobles of *Paula Monti* might be just as "immoral" as those in *Les Mystères*; if some of Sue's lower-class criminals, such as Le Chourineur, repent and reform, many noble characters in *Paula Monti* meet their end due to adultery, murder, or suicide, clearly punished for their abhorrent behavior.

Paula Monti recounts the story of the Princesse de Hansfeld (Paula Monti) and M. de Morville, who is in love with the princess but whom she rejects because of a ruinous secret from the past that resulted in her marriage to Prince Albert de Hansfeld. Multiple plotlines ensue and ultimately begin to intertwine. They involve Iris, the princess's orphaned and devious ward; M. de Brévannes, with whom others have accused Paula of having an affair; Albert, who becomes close to the father of Brévannes's wife, Berthe; and Berthe herself. For example, Albert believes that Paula is trying to kill him, yet the reader ultimately learns that it is Iris who has plotted his demise. The culmination of the plot takes place on M. de Brévannes's hunting terrain, where, mostly due to Iris's handiwork, all of the characters converge. Brévannes mistakenly murders the princess, thinking she is his wife; he and Iris commit suicide; only Berthe, her father, and Albert escape unscathed.

Despite its close publication date to *Les Mystères de Paris* and, as we will see, some overlapping tropes in the two novels, *Paula Monti* by no means calls into question contemporary social issues. If, as the above reviewer correctly indicates, the narrator critiques the extravagant behavior of the upper classes, there are nevertheless no characters whose reform speaks to the need for societal intervention. Even those who are somewhat virtuous—Berthe, her father, and Albert—do not act for the greater good of society.[69] Berthe teaches piano to children, but does so for money, and Albert and Pierre save one another's lives, but make no attempt to save others. Nowhere to be found are characters like *Les Mystères*'s virtuous Fleur de Marie or Clémence d'Harville, who volunteers to visit women in prison. The moody Albert is not the same benevolent philanthropist as his German counterpart Rodolphe.

There is some class mobility (Berthe quickly ascends the social ladder by first marrying de Brévannes and, later, the prince) and some mild class commentary (Pierre is a vocal opponent of nobility because of his daughter's cruel husband but reforms his thinking after becoming close with Albert). Sue does not, in other words, exploit the space of this novel to think through the social questions of his period.

Similarly Sue does not depict a wide range of characters across classes with divergent moral tendencies, as he does in *Les Mystères de Paris*. While in the later work the lower and upper classes are populated with characters who commit immoral acts with no compunction (members of the Martial family, La Chouette, Jacques Ferrand, Sarah MacGregor) and those who come to see the errors in their ways (Le Chourineur, La Louve, Fleur de Marie), Sue offers a less varied view of July Monarchy society in the earlier work. With the exception of Berthe, Pierre, and Iris, all characters are nobles. This lack of diversity is partly explained by the fact that there are simply fewer characters in this novel; it does not aim to depict a wide urban network. But the lessons about virtue and redemption that Sue imparts in *Les Mystères* are not the same here, even if he writes the novels within months of one another.

As the second subtitle of the novel—*Histoire contemporaine*—suggests, Sue situates the novel in the recent past—the July Monarchy Paris of 1837. While most of the novel takes place behind the closed doors of the eponymous *Hôtel Lambert* or in the homes and hunting properties of the main characters, a number of scenes stand out as belonging to the contemporary trend of describing urban society more generally. Take, for example, the depiction of the premiere of a play at the Comédie-Française that incorporates the Parisian social scene and represents a significant shift in the novel's narrative style. Before recounting this theatrical event attended by the majority of the protagonists (Berthe, Paula, Morville, Brévannes, and the prince), the narrator inserts a short introductory chapter in which he announces the manner in which he will present this sequence to his readers: "Nous conduirons le lecteur dans quelques loges différentes, où il rencontrera plusieurs personnages de cette histoire que la curiosité générale avait attirés à cette *solennité dramatique*."[70] Using space as an organizing principle, the subsequent chapters are named for the theater boxes in which the characters can be found—"Premières Loges N°7," "Loge de Premières, N°29"—and these chapters alternate between recounting the interactions between the couples sitting in the theater boxes and the humorous story (reminiscent of de Kock's work) of a woman who, having been duped into wearing an absurd coiffure, is duly mocked by onlookers. A third-person narrator adjudicates these "loges" chapters, yet Sue interrupts this narrative with a purely dialogue-based chapter entitled "Les Stalles d'amis." This short chapter takes the form of a discussion among friends about the play and, above all, about members of the audience. Their dialogue does gesture toward elements of the plot: Morville is told, for example, that the Princesse de Hansfeld is sitting with his aunt, and the interlocutors comment on Mme de Brévannes's beauty. This playful conversation, whose theatrical nature is strategically chosen for its setting, is also reminiscent of the urban digressions à la de Kock that I examined in chapter 2. Sue's lively *tableaux contemporains* may depict the opposite end of the social spectrum from his contemporary de Kock, but he is nonetheless relying on popular tropes and adhering faithfully to the genre of the *roman de moeurs*.

Paula Monti and *Les Mystères de Paris*, overlapping for a few months in their serial publication and promoted together in the same advertisements, provide a curious generic contrast. Despite the reference to the public's great interest in the *feuilleton*, we know that *Paula Monti* clearly did not excite the public in the same way that *Les Mystères* did and led, at least in part, to Sue's waning interest in the genre of the *roman de moeurs*. This lack of popularity when compared with *Les Mystères* is perhaps why a *réclame* in a September 7, 1842, issue of the *Journal des débats* announces that, in addition to the release of the first volume of *Les Mystères* with Gosselin, the first volume of *Paula Monti* is also being published: "Cet ouvrage est un tableau de moeurs contemporaines et vient se placer avec avantage à côté de *Mathilde* et de *Thérèse Dunoyer*."[71] In this sense, then, the promotional materials tell us that *Paula Monti* is not a novel to be compared to *Les Mystères*; it is instead in the tradition of the author's previous novels *Mathilde* and *Thérèse Dunoyer* and should be read as such. Reading *Paula Monti* as *Mathilde*'s and *Thérèse*'s successor casts it in a favorable light, and this promotional strategy attempts to showcase Sue's strengths as an author of multiple genres. We can consider

Sue as someone who experimented with multiple genres—maritime fiction, historical fiction and nonfiction, *roman de moeurs*, and ultimately the social novel—genres often already well established and critically and commercially popular at the time he chose to write them. Yet while Sue was versatile, if strategic in his generic choices, he also adapted characters, plotlines, and tropes across these distinct subgenres. Such a tactic was perhaps more subtle in Sue's oeuvre than in that of de Kock, whose stock characters and plotlines were overtly repurposed within his many humorous novels and plays, a common practice especially in the domain of popular theater of the period. Sue's work in multiple genres nonetheless gives evidence of literary recycling throughout his maritime fiction, *romans de moeurs*, and social novels.

SUE'S LITERARY RECYCLING

The opening scene of *Kernok le pirate* (1830) begins on a "nuit de novembre, sombre et froide," on the coast of Brittany.[72] A dilapidated shack, "de misérable apparence," is rendered all the more "horrible et *infect*" by the "multitude d'os, de cadavres de chevaux et de chiens, de peaux ensanglantées, et d'autres débris" that surround it, the handiwork of the shack's owner, a skinner (my emphasis).[73] As the narrator shifts to the inside of the home, the grotesque nature of its inhabitants is brought into focus: in addition to a sorceress, whose cape covers everything but her "figure jaune et ridée," we meet a boy, Pen-Ouët, playing with a heap of bones as though they were children's toys.[74] The scene, which begins with a Breton proverb and is peppered with references to local folklore, quickly turns violent, as the boy's mother, the sorceress, throws him against the wall so hard that his head begins to bleed: he begins to laugh "aux éclats, d'un rire stupide et convulsif, essuya sa blessure avec ses longs cheveux noirs, et fut se blottir sous le manteau d'une vaste cheminée."[75] Tension remains in the room between the sorceress and the skinner; as the young boy laughs in the background, the two adults threaten each other with weapons. In a twist of fate, before either one can be harmed, "heureusement, on frappe à la porte de la cabane"; it is Kernok the pirate who has come at his mistress's behest to have his fortune read and who has interrupted the domestic dispute.[76]

If the structure of the first chapter of *Kernok* sounds familiar, that is because it is arguably the same structure as the well-known first chapter of *Les Mystères de Paris*. After the narrator of *Les Mystères* sketches out his project to study the urban "barbares" in the manner of Cooper and warns readers of the repulsive scenes to follow, the plot then begins on "le 13 décembre 1838, par une soirée pleuvieuse et *froide*" (my emphasis).[77] The buildings of the dismal Cité are described as having "quelques rare fenêtres aux chassis, vermoulus et presque sans carreaux," and the narrator evokes "de noires, *d'infectes* allées [qui] conduisaient à des escaliers plus noirs, plus *infects* encore" (my emphasis).[78] A scuffle unfolds in this setting between a man (le Chourineur) and a young prostitute (la Goualeuse) unable to pay off her debts. She scratches him with scissors; he follows her into a dark alley and is about to harm her when, out of nowhere, the hand of an unknown party seizes the Chourineur's neck. It is the beneficent yet unflinchingly just Prince Rodolphe. A battle between these two men ensues during which the Chourineur is soundly beaten. The three characters—Rodolphe, the Chourineur, and the Goualeuse—then proceed to the local watering hole (the *tapis-franc*) to dine. Much like the first scene in *Kernok*, then, after the establishment of a rainy winter evening (akin to the now-cliched "dark and stormy night") in a particularly rundown space, tension rises between two individuals until a third party enters into the narrative to disrupt the violence. From his earliest example of maritime fiction to his newest iteration in the social novel, Sue is employing similar narrative structures despite the significant difference in subgenre.

In addition to these two opening scenes, other repetitions between *Kernok le pirate* and *Les Mystères de Paris* abound. Though Sue's descriptions of the clients of the *tapis-franc* (whose "physiognomies étaient féroces ou abruties" and who demonstrate a "gaieté grossière ou licensieuse") do not appear until the following chapter, they are nonetheless reminiscent of the grotesque rendering of Pen-Ouët and his family.[79] So too are the descriptions of the subjects that, Sue announces in the first chapter of *Les Mystères*, will populate his novel: "des types hideux, effrayants [qui] fourmilleront dans ces cloaques impurs comme les reptiles dans les marais."[80] Both narratives thus begin with unseemly, almost animal-like characters depicted in hyperbolically negative language. Kernok himself, like Rodolphe, is initially figured with both hypermasculine traits as well as more feminine ones. The pirate is described as having a "taille large et carrée, qui promettait une vigueur athlétique, ... traits basanés ... larges favoris [qui] lui donnaient un air dur et sauvage," but also possesses a face that might have passed for "assez belle, sans la mobilité extraordinaire de ses épais sourcils."[81] The prince is of a "taille moyenne, svelte, parfaitement proportionnée" and may be, the narrator speculates, "trop beau peut-être pour un homme"; despite these softer traits, one can detect "la fermeté des contours de sa bouche, son port de tête quelquefois impérieux et hardi, [qui] décelaient alors l'homme d'action dont la force physique, dont l'audace, exercent toujours sur la foule un irrésistible ascendant."[82] If Kernok is a rough character with hints at a softer side, this masculine profile takes on a similar if more complex shape in Sue's best seller eleven years later. Finally, while there are, of course, no references to Breton culture in this first chapter of Sue's urban novel, *Les Mystères* is famously punctuated with Parisian street argot that the author italicizes and glosses. For one of many examples, the Chourineur admits that his "linge est lavé" when he is vanquished by Rodolphe.[83] *Kernok* and Sue's other examples of sea fiction are filled with sailors' slang from the moment the *Épervier*, Kernok's brig, is introduced: "Vrai Dieu! Mordieu! Cordieu! C'est un brave brick que le brick *L'Épervier!*"[84] Whether in maritime slang (common in the genre of pirate fiction, including Sue's contributions), regional details from Brittany, or criminals' vernacular, Sue flaunts his mastery of specific vocabularies in both novels and helps initiate his reader into each milieu.

Literary taste and the marketplace for popular fiction, more generally, changed significantly over the twelve years between the publication of *Kernok* and that of *Les Mystères de Paris*, a trajectory borne out in Sue's own career. The violence at the beginning of the maritime novella can be attributed, Emilie Pézard argues, to the vogue in the early 1830s of "la représentation de sujets horribles": "La mode," claims Pézard, "est au noir."[85] As Lyon-Caen does, we might assign Sue's fascination with the urban masses in the 1840s to the more widespread trend of scrutinizing social groups and types. Analysis of these two novelistic beginnings—one from 1830, at the very start of Sue's career; one from 1842 that would earn him the title of "le roi du roman populaire"— shows Sue recycling key elements of *Kernok* (the plot, the descriptions, the

mise-en-scène, even certain specific words) in *Les Mystères* at the same time
that he adapts these tropes for a different genre.[86] In fact this recycling is consistent throughout Sue's varied oeuvre leading up to *Les Mystères*. Though he
published novels across subgenres, he tended to reuse material from his previous works, modifying it slightly for his needs depending on the text. Critics
have also noted that Sue appropriates tropes from contemporary trends as
well as more specific character traits and plot points from his fellow novelists,
though was perhaps less notorious than an author like Alexandre Dumas for
doing so.[87] In fact, Alice Killen links both Sue and Dumas in their narrative
reliance on what she calls "tout l'appareil qui avait fait, à ses débuts, la fortune
du roman populaire: souterrains, voix sourdes, mystères et reconnaissances,
innocents victimes persécutées, spectres (au moins dans l'imagination des
acteurs), éclairs et coups de tonnerre."[88] By borrowing from himself and others, Sue replicates the writing patterns of his prolific peers producing industrial
literature—regurgitating words, tropes, and plotlines out of the necessity to
quickly turn over work—but also demonstrates an in-depth understanding of
the market as he modifies these tropes for new texts and for the new readers
the serialized form engendered.

On a micro level Sue repeats minor narrative tactics throughout his novels to incite suspense in his reader; in a certain sense he is merely following
genre conventions here. We see cliffhangers at the end of each chapter of his
serialized fiction, as well as the interweaving of multiple layers of plot.[89] For
one specific and rather obvious example, Sue's narrator often makes references
to a mysterious and specific date, that is then cited throughout the novel in
order to generate intrigue. In the opening chapters of *Les Mystères de Paris*,
Rodolphe's longtime squire, Murph, attempting to bring Rodolphe back to
his senses during a heated discussion, cries out, "Monseigneur, monseigneur,
souvenez-vous du 13 janvier!"[90] The date is repeated throughout the novel
and in the epilogue and is ultimately revealed as that on which Rodolphe
threatened the life of his father. In the opening scenes of *Paula Monti*, the
eponymous protagonist, in reference to her terrible secret, exclaims to Morville, "'Il n'y a au monde qu'Osorio ou M. de Brévannes qui ait pu vous dire
ce qui s'était passé à Venise, il y a trois ans, dans la nuit du 13 avril!'"[91] Rather
than draw out this mystery, however, the Princess divulges four chapters

later that she is referring to a duel that resulted in the death of her former fiancé, Raphaël. While *Mathilde* does not contain a mysterious date whose secret is stretched out over multiple chapters, the author nonetheless produces intrigue about dates he will subsequently explain.[92] For instance, in the chapter in which Gontran proposes to Mathilde, she sets up the scene in the following way: "Le 15 février, je me rappelle de ce jour, cette date, ces circonstances, comme si tout s'était passé hier," repeating "le 15 février" once again before describing the circumstances.[93] Even if these tactics are not new to readers of serialized fiction, these three examples show Sue reusing the same strategy to pique and sustain the interest of his reader, whether in the context of a high-society *roman de moeurs* or a social novel.

While repetition of these narrative tactics is not uncommon in serialized fiction, Sue's reuse of characters—in particular a type of threatening and marginalized secondary female character spanning his maritime fiction to his urban, social *mystères*—reveals a more sophisticated repetition of types. With the rise of commercial literature, as we have seen, the recycling of tropes became commonplace. Yet Sue seems particularly keen at adapting these tropes across subgenres. For example, in the first chapter of *Kernok* the menacing sorceress Ivonne, with a "figure jaune et ridée" and "sourire hideux," abuses her son; scares her husband, who believes she has conjured spirits in their home; and makes even the powerful Kernok tremble, stammer, and ultimately lose consciousness.[94] This sorceress, who resides on the edge of the water in Pempoul, one of the westernmost French coastal towns, adds an almost supernatural quality to the text, underscores Breton folklore, and, most important, serves as a warning to the protagonist that his days as a pirate and his lover Melie's days are numbered. This "vieille chouette," to whose "griffe" and "cuir" Kernok makes reference, is the first in a series of animal-like women that Sue will develop throughout his oeuvre.[95] Ivonne fits squarely within the conventions of maritime fiction, even if she is somewhat limited in her role in the novel. As the author moves on from this subgenre to the *roman de moeurs* and ultimately to the social novel, this violent female secondary figure returns, though modified, to play an important role in his other works.

In *Mathilde* the eponymous character's impoverished cousin Ursule is a full-fledged *femme fatale*. Here Sue is drawing on an already established type. Ursule is transformed from the sweet and tender childhood friend of the protagonist into a vicious rival who has an affair with her friend's husband. When she is introduced, she is depicted as virtuous and, physically, in a generally positive light: "On ne pouvait imaginer une physionomie plus intéressante, un sourire plus doux et plus amiable."[96] When Ursule reappears after both girls are married, she has become a stunning beauty but also begins to inspire fear in Mathilde: "La ruse, l'habileté de ma cousine m'effrayèrent."[97] While she does not threaten physical violence like Ivonne, nonetheless Ursule is described in terms that reference her dangerous, animal-like qualities. Her double nature is fully on display in the second half of the novel. She is called "belle . . . oh, bien belle ainsi . . . de cette beauté sensuelle qui a, dit-on, tant d'empire sur les hommes."[98] At the same time, as Sue does with his other female villains, she is cast as a dangerous beast ("vautour féroce," "panthère") and an evil force ("cette femme diabolique," "cette diablesse d'Ursule").[99] As with his description of Ivonne's "claws" and sorcery, the narrator employs both animal and supernatural terms to characterize this "depraved" seductress, although, unlike Ivonne, her physical beauty is also highlighted, ultimately making her a *femme fatale*. Alongside the cruel Maran and the evil male antagonist Lugarto, Ursule contributes to Sue's indictment of July Monarchy high society in *Mathilde*. Mathilde's observation that the new Ursule has finally found her "véritable *milieu*" in the high society she has come to embrace allows readers to see the perversity of Ursule's character as Mathilde's critique of the society in which she blossoms. It is important to note that, though Ursule and Ivonne are ultimately described in similar terms, each character is adapted to the conventions of the subgenre in which they are featured.

Paula Monti too contains a female character depicted as duplicitous and depraved and who is revealed to be the source of much of the novel's immoral behavior. This is Iris, the orphaned ward of Paula Monti and a dark-skinned "bohémienne ou maure."[100] She is described, as Ursule is initially, as having "traits assez réguliers" and masculine qualities: the narrator mentions that she has "quelque chose de viril" about her and that "cette fille avait pu passer pour un homme," underscoring a lack of feminine sexuality.[101] Unlike Ursule, who ultimately becomes a sexualized *femme fatale*, Iris's youthfulness conceals her dangerous nature. She is labeled "cette jeune fille" on several occasions, as well as an "enfant abandonée"; "Iris sortait à peine de l'enfance."[102] This youthful innocence is contrasted with her animal-like, savage qualities, manifested in her attachment to Mme de Hansfeld: "C'était un de ces attachements aveugles, sauvages, on dirait presque impitoyables, tant ils sont exclusifs."[103] Like a gruesome version of animal imprinting or an attachment "particulier à la race canine," Iris's "funeste exagération de son attachement" has led her to desire bad things for her *marraine* (godmother) so that she will be able to comfort her and to develop a hatred of anyone who poses a threat to their attachment.[104] She possesses an "égare[ment] par une jalousie féroce."[105] Iris hides her danger below the surface: "elle s'entourait d'une impénétrable dissimulation" and was capable of "exaltation sauvage" because of her "jalousie féroce."[106] Now sensitive to the double nature of Iris's personality, the reader is not at all surprised to learn that she singlehandedly sets into motion the majority of the violent acts in the novel. *Paula Monti*'s critique of July Monarchy society is less vicious than that of *Mathilde* since so many of the novel's "diabolical" crimes can be attributed not to the debauched nobles but to Iris, who is an abandoned gypsy child living outside of July Monarchy society.[107] Iris differs from Ursule and Ivonne in her lack of sexuality and supernatural qualities, respectfully; unlike the other two, her bohemian background endows her with a sort of exoticism. Still she is characterized by many of the same tropes and vocabulary.

The most famous of Sue's duplicitous and threatening female characters is Cecily, a Creole woman from *Les Mystères de Paris*. Rodolphe enlists the help of this "audacieuse métisse," imprisoned in Germany for her adulterous behavior, to bring down his nemesis, the evil notary Jacques Ferrand.[108] The narrator presents the two contradictory sides of this woman, calling her "aussi belle que pervertie, aussi enchanteresse que dangereuse."[109] Ample space is dedicated to describing her physical traits—"d'une stature haute et svelte"; "cou élégant et potelé"; "cheveux noirs"; "des paupières frangées de longs cils, la transparence bleuâtre du globe de l'œil"; "bouche, insolente et amoureuse . . . d'un pourpre vif"—before the narrator admits that he is describing an existing type: "Disons-le, cette grande créole, à la fois svelte et charnue, vigoureuse et souple comme une panthère, était le type incarné de la sensualité brutale qui ne s'allume qu'aux feux des tropiques. Tout le monde a entendu parler de ces filles de couleur pour ainsi dire mortelles aux Européens, de ces vampires enchanteurs qui, enivrant leur victime de séductions terribles, pompent jusqu'à sa dernière goutte d'or et de sang. . . . Telle est Cecily."[110]

Cecily replicates existing types: the exoticized female other, the dangerous seductress, the *femme fatale.* Yet not only does Sue borrow this type from the work of his contemporaries like Mérimée's *Carmen,* he also repeats the same supernatural ("vampire enchanteur") and animalistic ("souple comme une panthère") terms he used elsewhere to describe Ursule, Iris, and Ivonne. Once Cecily has begun her seduction of Ferrand, the narrator paints her as a "dangereuse créature," who returns to her "premier instinct" and makes an "action soudaine."[111] If these descriptions of her movements are not enough to underscore her animal-like qualities, the narrator reiterates that she makes a bounding motion and is "souple comme une panthère" as she seduces Ferrand.[112] Once again recycling tropes about beautiful, erotic, and dangerous women, the narrator mixes the now familiar animal and supernatural imagery to emphasize the brutality of Cecily. Once she has given Ferrand "un spectacle bouleversant de volupté, [elle] s'enfuit sans s'être laissée toucher."[113] The reader is not surprised to learn that Ferrand eventually dies, both from lust for Cecily and of fear, for she has stolen proof of all of his crimes. Though there are many criminals in *Les Mystères de Paris* and many "immoral" acts committed therein, it is notable that Sue has, once again, chosen a striking yet "diabolical" and animal-like female character as the only character "aussi pervertie" to be able to take down Jacques Ferrand.[114] If the plots, settings, and underlying critiques differ from *Kernok,* the author of these texts mines his own repertoire of tropes and characters, modifying them according to the genre in which he wrote. *Les Mystères* may have stood out thus as a unique event in Sue's career given its unprecedented sales and readership, yet many of its formal elements had already appeared throughout his oeuvre. The singular nature of *Les Mystères* as a media phenomenon may explain why it has become commonplace to study Sue purely in the context of this popular serial novel.

LES MYSTÈRES AND SELLING SUE

Upon its serialization *Les Mystères de Paris* became the period's ultimate literary commodity. The novel engaged unparalleled numbers of readers; despite the fact that its subscription rate was set at 80 francs—double that of *La Presse*—subscriptions to the *Journal des débats* "increased by many thousands in the early months of publication."[115] Additionally the back pages of daily newspapers boasted numerous advertisements for the 1842–43 bound editions produced by Gosselin. Promotional materials from the period show Gosselin taking advantage of the multiple publicity techniques available to promote his product. *Les Mystères* is publicized throughout *La Presse, Le Constitutionnel, Le Siècle,* and the *Journal des débats,* among other periodicals, using the "annonce-affiche," which could be a small or large advertisement; the "annonce anglaise"; and even *réclames.*[116] These ads positioned Sue next to more established writers; they described the material qualities of the illustrated volumes; they used coordinated but not always evenly executed publicity efforts; and they varied the visual presentation of the ads.[117]

Gosselin often used a header that both called attention to the name of his series, Bibliothèque d'Elite (a name in stark contrast with a great percentage of Sue's alleged readers), and to the names of well-known authors he published: Scott, Cooper, Chateaubriand, and Lamartine.[118] On the one hand, by associating Sue with such well-established romantic writers, Gosselin's ads conferred on him the cultural capital linked to those names. On the other, by grouping Sue with best-selling authors, the header links him to other profitable literary commodities.[119] The *réclames* produced to sell *Les Mystères de Paris* were replete with hyperbolic praise for the novel, such as "Le succès de cet ouvrage a été immense," and with accounts of how many volumes had sold.[120] One reported, "Le succès de cet ouvrage est tel que les éditions publiées jusqu'ici ont été rapidement enlevées, quoique tirées à grand nombre."[121] This tactic encouraged interested readers to get their copies while they still could, since, despite large print runs, these wildly popular volumes were quickly sold out. What was being sold was thus not so much the content of the narrative as the phenomenon of the *Mystères* itself.

FIG. 8. Ad for *Les Mystères du grand monde* in *Le Constitutionnel*,
October 31, 1843. Bibliothèque nationale de France.

Once the commercial success of *Les Mystères de Paris* was established,
promotional materials banked on the novel's value to sell works by other
authors. Two weeks after the serial publication of *Les Mystères* had come to an
end in the *Journal des débats*, *Le Constitutionnel* published an ad on October
31, 1843, announcing, "En vente chez tous les librairies commissionnaires. *Les
Mystères du Grand Monde*. M. Eugène Sue a peint les vices du Peuple, Nous
allons révéler les crimes du Grand Monde."[122] The composition of this ad is
striking. The large block print of the book's title is aligned to appear above
Sue's name such that, at first glance, the reader might believe it to be an ad
for *Les Mystères de Paris*. It is only when one reads the fine print that one
realizes the author of this different book (who remains anonymous here)
or its publishers count on readers' recognition of Sue's work to sell this new
product (fig. 8). The effort to ride the coattails of Sue's success was even more
flagrant in a November 14, 1843, *réclame* in *Le Siècle* for the *Almanach des*

Mystères de Paris, a book not authored by Sue but whose similarities were likely not coincidental.[123] At the top of the back page of the issue the words "L'Almanach des Mystères de Paris!" are in boldface followed by an exclamation mark and set apart from the rest of the text. This excerpt does not hide its reliance on Sue's work, even calling attention to the "grand" success of that novel—success to which these authors clearly aspire as well, as they preemptively announce here a print run of 200,000 copies. These effective if somewhat fraudulent and entirely typical marketing tactics, coupled with that of the *réclame*, whose position outside of the designated advertising section allowed readers to mistake it for an article, make it clear why contemporaries were suspicious of advertising.[124]

These ads clearly demonstrate the scope of the mediatized response to the publication of *Les Mystères de Paris*. With its multiple translations and international adaptations, this novel transcended the level of mere domestic best seller to be the first iteration of the global blockbuster. *Les Mystères*, the social novel that exposed the injustices suffered by Paris's poor through the depiction of the urban *bas-fonds*, came to emblematize the concept of the literary phenomenon. Seizing on this success, Sue quickly produced another social novel in 1844, *Le Juif errant*, for which he was paid one of the highest sums an author had received before 1850 for a book contract: 100,000 francs.[125] For some perspective, Balzac, at this point a well-established author, received 20,000 for *Modeste Mignon* that same year.[126] *Le Juif errant* was serialized by *Le Constitutionnel*, read by huge audiences, and republished in numerous illustrated and unillustrated editions. Martyn Lyons estimates the print run of that novel to be between 32,000 and 40,000 copies, but such numbers are often rough approximations.[127] In other words, following *Les Mystères*, Sue elected to focus once again on the serialized social novel and, unsurprisingly, achieved yet more commercial success. Sue followed up with *Martin, l'enfant trouvé* (1846–47) and *Les Mystères du peuple* (1849–56), though they were not the best sellers that *Les Mystères* and *Le Juif errant* were. Ultimately he fused his political fiction with his real-life practice when he was elected as a socialist representative to the Assemblée Nationale after the 1848 Revolution.[128] Lyons notes, however, that starting in the early 1850s, there was a slowing down of new editions of Sue's social novels, due in part to the trend toward depolitizing the novel under the Second Empire.[129] Once again Sue had been savvy enough to produce work in a genre at the height of its popularity, and the diminution of his popularity reflected the waning and changing tastes of the literary field.

Sue's biographer Bory wrote, "Ce sont *Les Mystères de Paris* qui ont créé leur auteur. Ou plutôt le succès des *Mystères de Paris*—mais tout cela est indissociable."[130] As we can see from the advertisements and from both Sue's contemporaries and critics of our own time, his career is indeed conflated with the publication of *Les Mystères*, its international, record-breaking success, and its symbolization of the development of industrial literature. Yet even before the sensation of *Les Mystères*, Sue was already a well-known, at times even best-selling author. His forays into different popular subgenres reflected the changing tastes of contemporary readers and the author's own understanding of, or at the very least willingness to comply with, such tastes. From the beginning of his career as the author of maritime fiction to his *romans de moeurs* depicting Paris's high society along the lines of those produced by Balzac and, finally, his sweeping social novels replete with political commentary, these deliberate choices show Sue adapting himself to contemporary trends. In terms of the form (style, tropes, characters) and content of these works, we see him adjusting elements to suit the subgenre in which he is working. We might infer from this that, despite the outward desire for variety in fiction, readers responded well to a certain amount of repetition. Even Sue's literary missteps, such as his historical fiction and nonfiction and his maritime and social novels and *romans de moeurs*, published when the trends were waning, still inform us about contemporary tastes.

Ultimately it is not merely *Les Mystères de Paris* but Sue's oeuvre taken as a whole, with its mega–best sellers, its moderate-selling but well-received works, and its failures, that best illustrates the way authors adapted to the changing marketplace of the early to mid-nineteenth century. Sue's attempts at success demonstrate more flexibility and variability than his contemporary de Kock, whose inexhaustible comical *roman de moeurs* depicting the urban petit bourgeois found a smaller but more consistent readership; unlike de Kock's works, each of Sue's seemed to sustain his audience only for a short time before he was compelled to move on to another subgenre. If the sales of Sue's best sellers dwarfed those of de Kock's prolific novels, both authors evince calculated if disparate formal strategies for success in the early nineteenth-century popular book trade. They also represented, for Balzac, the type of literature against which he positioned himself (a commercial, plot-driven literature that appealed to a broad audience, as opposed to one with more aesthetic pretenses), even though he adopted many of the same tropes and professional strategies.

Chapter Four

BALZAC, HIGH AND LOW

In 1844, in a letter written to his future wife, Madame Hanska, Balzac employed the name of Paul de Kock, who connoted "bad" literature, to insult a competitor: the now extremely famous and lucrative writer Eugène Sue. As we have seen, he referred to Sue first as "ce Paul de Kock en satin et à paillettes" and later suggested that he was jealous of neither Sue's fame nor money because "Paul de Kock ne fait pas envie à Victor Hugo."[1] Balzac used this well-known signifier of commercial literature, in other words, to disdain the market success of the author of *Les Mystères de Paris* and to distinguish himself in the hierarchy of the contemporary literary field.[2] Sue's commercial successes were particularly vexing to Balzac. Before Sue's serial novels made him a major figure of contemporary popular literature, Balzac and Sue had been friends and had even collaborated on projects in the early years of the July Monarchy. Later, especially after *Les Mystères* became a runaway hit, Sue's success turned him into a rival: "Balzac ne va cesser de lutter contre lui, persuadé qu'on le persécute, porté par le sentiment d'une immense injustice, matérielle (les gains mirobolants de Sue l'obsèdent) et surtout littéraire, contraint à un immense effort."[3] Balzac envied the triumph of his popular rival and worked hard to distinguish himself from Sue and other commercial writers of the period. Despite this disdain Balzac engaged in many of the same practices as his more popular peers: recycling work across publications, publishing his work in serial format, participating in the genre of panoramic literature, and even incorporating tropes from this commercial subgenre into his novels. This ambivalence is evident in a number of Balzac's works of fiction. Analysis of this complicated relationship to popular literature in novels from different points in his career (the *Histoire des Treize* trilogy of 1833–35 and his 1844 *Les Employés*), in which he appropriates and adapts the prevalent practices and tropes from this very literature, shows the author staging tensions engendered by the demands of the developing marketplace.

COMMERCIAL AND COUNTERCOMMERCIAL

De Kock and Sue exemplified different yet largely successful methods of adapting their works to the popular tastes of their readers. Even as Balzac operated within the same literary marketplace, he attempted to differentiate himself from it.[4] At the beginning of his career he produced several pieces of commercial writing, including *codes* (effectively popular conduct manuals), novels, plays, journal articles, and literary reviews—published either anonymously or under a pseudonym. He also participated in a number of business ventures, most of which failed.[5] These early publications manifested his burgeoning intellectual interests as well as his need for money. In fact his first two major publications, both from the year 1829, emblematize the author's ongoing struggles between literary and commercial value. That year Balzac published a historical novel, *Les Chouans* (first published as *Le Dernier Chouan*), with Urbain Canel; it was the first novel to which he would sign his name (as Honoré Balzac, without the *de*). Popularized initially by Walter Scott, the historical novel was almost guaranteed to secure his successful entry into the literary scene.[6] For *Le Dernier Chouan*, Balzac received an advance of 1,000 francs, and 1,000 copies of the novel were printed. Despite a number of positive reviews (some of which, admittedly, were written by his close friend and coeditor Henri de Latouche), not even half of the copies sold.[7] *Les Chouans* garnered neither the critical nor the commercial renown the author had hoped for, though it would later be considered a novel of key critical import for the project of *La Comédie humaine*.

Mere months later, however, Balzac's luck turned when the éditeur Lavasseur approached him about the reimbursement of a debt. The author offered him a piece he had drafted and then shelved at an early point in his career, when he had written a number of the trendy *codes*.[8] Lavasseur agreed to publish this work, *Physiologie du mariage*, in hopes of capitalizing "on what little prestige the author had acquired through *Les Chouans*."[9] Whether it was luck or foresight about contemporary market trends, *Physiologie du mariage* sold considerably better than *Les Chouans*, and according to a number of his biographers, Balzac found himself an overnight success.[10] Catherine Nesci suggests this was the moment that transformed "le jeune écrivain en auteur à la mode, coqueluche des dames et des directeurs de revue."[11] According to Sharon Marcus, "He soon began to receive numerous responses from a largely female readership," and Noel Gerson writes, "Suddenly everybody who was anybody wanted to meet him, and every important door in Paris was opened to him."[12] The ultimate print run of this nonfiction work—20,000 copies sold and seven French editions issued before 1850—made it one of the biggest best sellers of Balzac's career.[13] While this was many fewer copies than his peers Sue and Dumas would go on to sell, initial sales of *Physiologie du mariage* did reinvigorate those of *Les Chouans*, even if, according to Graham Robb, these two works "failed even to pay the rent."[14] Now recognizable as a popular and especially a witty author, Balzac had staked a claim for himself in the literary field—not initially through the established genre of historical fiction but through what had been and what would continue to be a popular nonfiction genre. Shortly thereafter his first fictional "grand succès de librairie," *La Peau de Chagrin* from 1831, would establish his critical legitimacy and would also garner impressive sales figures.[15] The author's first major publications from this short three-year period thus demonstrate his attempts at self-positioning in the developing literary marketplace.

Balzac famously critiqued the contemporary literary field and the production of commercial literature, the press, and the profession of publishing. He did so in his novels (*Illusions Perdues* is the most obvious example), in his nonfiction (*Monographie de la presse parisienne*), and in his correspondence.[16]

To give just one of many examples, he deplored the commercialization of literature though the *cabinet de lecture*, writing in 1834 of the "milliers de misérables cabinets littéraires qui tuent notre littérature."[17] He claimed he was incapable of producing "bad" literature: "Il y a en moi je ne sais quoi qui m'empêche de faire consciencieusement mal. Il s'agit de donner de l'avenir au livre, d'en faire un torche-cul ou un ouvrage de bibliothèque."[18] Balzac, a self-styled elite author, faced the dilemma of wanting to produce writing with high aesthetic aims—works replete with figurative language and metaphysical import as opposed to the plot-driven works of his popular peers whose goals were to sell copies—but he also needed to pay the bills, and at times his turn to nonnovelistic writing was a means of solving this problem. As Roland Chollet puts it in his study of Balzac's early journalistic work, "Le système de la publication en revue a apporté à Balzac une solution littéraire et commerciale au problème qui s'était posé à lui en terme d'urgence quotidienne et de fatalité économique au lendemain de la *Physiologie du mariage*: comment survivre sans cesser d'être romancier?"[19] However, these two facets of his production should be viewed in tandem, for, as Chollet has argued, it is important to consider the impact of his nonliterary writing on his fiction and vice versa: "Dans le cadre même de *La Comédie humaine*, des œuvres importantes apparues dans *la Mode*, la *Revue de Paris*, la *Revue des Deux Mondes*, gardent les stigmates de leur naissance journalistique. En outre, Balzac journaliste a exercé dès 1830 une influence considérable sur le développement de la presse littéraire au XIXe siècle."[20]

In spite of his engagement in the popular literary market of the July Monarchy, Balzac is still typically read as separate from it. To distinguish him from that ubiquitous marker of popular literature, for example, Chollet and Stéphane Vachon write that, some professional overlap aside, "Paul de Kock, il est vrai, c'est un autre monde, un monde que Balzac a refusé"; they contend further that within the context of the contemporary literary field, if Balzac worked within "les contraintes idéologiques et commerciales de son temps . . . il est parvenu à les dépasser."[21] Balzac is thought by biographers and critics alike to have outshone his popular peers, a reading with which the author himself no doubt would agree. He nonetheless engaged in, borrowed from, and actively positioned himself within their world throughout his career. In addition to the numerous articles, codes, and anonymous fiction and nonfiction works he produced for merely financial reasons at the onset of his career, many of his novels reveal the staging of his complicated and ultimately ambivalent relationship to the emerging mass marketplace. More specifically his involvement in the so-called panoramic literary movement—a subgenre with self-consciously commercial aims—and its formal effects on his novels attest to his active reflection on these questions of high and low literature engendered by the new market conditions.

BALZAC AND PANORAMIC LITERATURE

As I noted in chapters 1 and 2, under the July Monarchy (1830–45), particularly between 1840 and 1842, a so-called panoramic literature exploded onto the market. This included a series of short, comical, and inexpensively printed pseudo-scientific tracts called *physiologies* portraying and typologizing popular Parisian phenomena. The corresponding *tableaux de Paris* were larger collections of descriptions of Parisian phenomena that cost more and tended to be more hybrid in their form and content. De Kock appropriated the descriptive techniques and *tableaux* into his popular novels, tropes that on the whole were received positively by his critics. Never absent from the list of authors and publishers involved in this explicitly commercial phenomenon is Balzac, the author of *Physiologie de l'employé* (1841), the coauthor of *Physiologie du rentier de Paris et de province* (1841), the anonymous author of *Physiologie du cigare* (1831), and the contributor of chapters to the collections *Nouveaux Tableaux de Paris* (1834), *Les Français peints par eux-mêmes* (1840–42), and *La Grande Ville: Nouveau Tableau de Paris*, volume 2 (1842–43).[22] Moreover Balzac is often credited with giving birth to the *physiologie* phenomenon because, although Brillat-Savarin's 1826 *Physiologie du goût* preceded the *Physiologie du mariage*, some see Balzac's work as "the direct model for the genre."[23]

Yet although he contributed frequently to the *physiologie* series and no doubt profited from their sales, Balzac also was critical of the movement. In his *Monographie de la presse parisienne*, he charts the term *physiologie* as it evolved from a serious scientific endeavor to a comical, frivolous one. Here Balzac humorously sketches a type called the Bravo who, "s'il n'est pas compté parmi les faiseurs d'une entreprise quelconque, il attaque l'entreprise," offering the anecdote of the rejection of this Bravo's *physiologie* by a publisher.[24] In this "raccourci railleur," Balzac's Bravo retaliates against the publisher, writing, "Aujourd'hui, la Physiologie est l'art de parler et d'écrire incorrectement de n'importe quoi, sous la forme d'un petit livre bleu ou jaune qui soutire vingt sous au passant, sous prétexte de le faire rire, et qui lui décroche les mâchoires."[25] The series are depicted as inaccurate, banal, and made exclusively for profit. Even after the Bravo's *physiologie* is accepted by the same *libraire*, however, this temperamental writer continues to poke fun at the movement, writing, "Les Physiologies sont comme les moutons de Panurge, elles courent les unes après les autres," implying their lack of variation.[26] Balzac nevertheless humorously praises their wit: "Ces petits livres sont écrits par les gens les plus spirituels de notre époque."[27] Regardless of whether Bravo, whose contested *physiologie* bears the same name as one of Balzac's own works (*Physiologie du cigare*), is meant to be the novelist's *porte-parole*, this comical but mostly negative treatment of the phenomenon of the *physiologies* shows a devaluing of and even critique of the popular series. Balzac, as we have seen, also often critiqued the quality of the work of his more popular peers and positioned himself as a writer belonging to a different category.

Critics' tendency to see Balzac's work as distinct from the *physiologie* series replicates the author's own preoccupations with cultural value in the emerging midcentury literary marketplace. In one of the foundational essays on the *physiologies*, Andrée Lhéritier underscores the significance of Balzac and Brillat-Savarin, "[qui] ont donné sous le nom de 'physiologies' des études sérieuses, traitées sur un ton qui voulait être badin, pittoresque et plaisant."[28] While their tone may be playful, Lhéritier considers them serious and thus distinct from the series established by Philipon. Similarly Lyon-Caen insists on the complexity of Balzac's fictional types, claiming that even if "on peut lire la *Comédie humaine* comme une grande galerie de types ancrés dans l'histoire contemporaine," "les relations entre types et personnages chez Balzac sont néanmoins plus complexes, chaque personnage tendant à la fois à incarner, à créer, et à dépasser le type."[29] This cultural historian too indicates overlaps between the two genres of a "disposition typisante" but, like Lhéritier, characterizes Balzac's novelistic types as multifaceted—and therefore better.[30] Richard Sieburth draws the most explicit high/low distinction when he counsels against making connections between Balzac's project in the *Comédie humaine* and that of the physiologies: "Although it is certainly no mere coincidence that the 'Avant-Propos' to the *Comédie humaine*, which contains Balzac's most ambitious statements on the novelist as taxonomist of 'les espèces sociales,' was composed at the very height of the physiologie vogue (1840–1842), and although Balzac himself contributed … to the series, it would be misleading to equate Balzac's 'scientific' theory of the novel with the taxonomic project of the physiologies."[31] Sieburth warns against conflating the pseudo-scientific project of the *physiologies* and Balzac's own, more laudably metaphysical project of writing an *histoire des mœurs*. While some critics assert that Balzac's *Comédie humaine* is more complex than the humorous *physiologies*, and though his contributions to the series might be explained away as side projects separate from his more serious novels, *Histoire des Treize* and *Les Employés* show Balzac himself exploring the question of his works' relationship to panoramic literature and to commercial literature more generally.

TABLEAUX IN THE *TREIZE*

In his *Histoire des Treize*, a trilogy composed of *Ferragus* (1833), *La Duchesse de Langeais* (1834), and *La Fille aux yeux d'or* (1835), Balzac openly borrows from the trendy urban tropes of the *tableaux de Paris* but also destabilizes the subgenre, exposing contemporary tensions relating to literary value and exposing the precarious position of his own oeuvre. These three short novels contain macabre and even occultist plots—stories, the narrator of their preface explains, that were confided to him by a member of the underground band of thirteen men known as the *Treize*—and all transpire in predominantly interior, intimate spaces. Nonetheless it is not surprising that Balzac chose to classify these novels among the *Scènes de la vie parisienne* because they are replete with descriptions of Parisian culture, people and phenomena alongside their more obscure underground plots. In some cases Balzac inserts typological descriptions of contemporary social and urban phenomena so fashionable in contemporary popular literature, at times even recycling this work from previous nonfiction publications. As well as blending tropes from these more openly commercial texts into his fiction, he also opens each novella with a detailed and yet progressively more figurative *tableau de Paris*, exposing his own complicated relationship to commercial literature.

The second of the three novels in this trilogy, *La Duchesse de Langeais*, contains an arguably standard *tableau de Paris*. This lengthy digression depicts the moral, political, social, and physical aspects of a noble milieu, the Faubourg Saint-Germain, and is one of many examples of Balzac's incorporation of this popular trope into his fiction. A novel often linked to Balzac's own romantic life, *La Duchesse de Langeais* recounts the love affair between the Marquis de Montriveau and Antoinette de Langeais in a "Gothic melodrama of sexual frustration, thwarted ambitions, domination and revenge."[32] Deeply rooted in the historical context of the Bourbon Restoration, it begins in a sea-swept Andalusian Carmelite convent with the illicit meeting between Montriveau and the duchesse (here Soeur Thérèse), before the narrator whisks the reader back to Restoration Paris to explain how this encounter came about. The novel revolves around Montriveau's passion for the duchesse, her flirtation but consistent refusal to consummate their love, and the ultimate intervention of the violent fraternity of the *Treize*. But before delving into the backstory between these Platonic lovers, the narrator launches into a lengthy explanation and denunciation of the aristocracy under the Restoration or, as he calls it, the *faubourg Saint Germain*. He begins by establishing the *faubourg Saint Germain* as the locus of upper-class Parisian life, clarifying that the proper noun Faubourg Saint-Germain can connote an aristocratic lifestyle outside of the geographical confines of the *faubourg* itself:

> Ce que l'on nomme en France le faubourg Saint-Germain n'est ni un quartier, ni une secte, ni une institution, ni rien qui se puisse nettement exprimer. La place Royale, le faubourg Saint-Honoré, la Chaussée d'Antin possèdent également des hôtels où se respire l'air du faubourg Saint-Germain. Ainsi, déjà tout le faubourg n'est pas dans le faubourg. . . . Les manières, le parler, en un mot la tradition faubourg Saint-Germain est à Paris, depuis environ quarante ans, ce que la Cour y était jadis, ce qu'était l'hôtel Saint-Paul dans le quatorzième siècle. . . . Cette singularité périodique offre une

ample matière aux réflexions de ceux qui veulent observer ou peindre les différentes zones sociales.[33]

Moving from this almost topographical commentary on the *quartier* and its customs, the narrator goes next into a prolonged digression on the social and moral shortcomings of those who inhabit the Faubourg Saint-Germain and on the existing geographical separation between classes in Paris. Critics have traditionally read this passage not as a *tableau de Paris* but as a political excursus.[34] Yet the narrator, who characterizes the passage as an "aperçu semi-politique," also notes that the particularities of the nobility offer much on which to reflect for "ceux qui veulent observer ou peindre les différentes zones sociales."[35] In this sense the narrator, like authors of the popular panoramic texts or even de Kock, cues his readers into the scene or tableau of this geographical and social urban space that he is about to paint.

The portrait of Saint-Germain contains some (albeit infrequent) physical descriptions of this section of the city: "Pour premier trait caractéristique, le faubourg Saint-Germain a la splendeur de ses hôtels, ses grands jardins, leur silence jadis en harmonie avec la magnificence de ses fortunes territoriales."[36] Later the narrator returns to this depiction of luxury, enumerating the "châteaux et des palais aristocratiques, le luxe de leurs détails, la somptuosité constante des ameublements, l'*aire* dans laquelle s'y meut sans gêne, et sans éprouver de froissement, l'heureux propriétaire, riche avant de naître."[37] The narrator eschews proper nouns (street names, names of *hôtels particuliers*, landmarks) and extensive detailing of the physical space but offers the traits, if nonspecific, of the area amid a treatise on the postrevolutionary flaws of the aristocracy.[38] Similarly, in a section dealing with the individuals living in the Faubourg Saint-Germain, the narrator explains, "Çà et là, dans le faubourg Saint-Germain, se rencontrent de beaux caractères, exceptions qui prouvent contre l'égoïsme général qui a causé la perte de ce monde à part."[39] He does not evoke as many details of a particular phenomenon as he will in his typologies from, for example, *Ferragus*, but this passage nonetheless offers a general description of the geographical space and population of the *faubourg* amid the narrator's otherwise political critique. Reminiscent of de Kock's panoramic digressions in this sense, the passage openly references the observation and painting of social life (*observer* [to observe], *peindre* [to paint]) even if its moral, political, and historical descriptions serve ultimately to explain the passionate and violent narrative of the duchesse, who is firmly entrenched in aristocratic Restoration social norms, and Montriveau, a relic of Napoleon's empire.

If the description of the *faubourg* has until now not been explicitly linked to the typologies so central to the tradition of the *tableau de Paris* and the *physiologies*, the first scene of the first novel in the *Histoire des Treize* trilogy certainly has. The opening pages of *Ferragus* have consistently been read as a typology of Parisian streets: "Il est dans Paris certaines rues déshonorées... rues nobles... rues simplement honnêtes."[40] The narrator effectively draws up a sociocartographic representation of the streets of Paris as an introduction to the plot, meandering until he happens upon one of the novel's protagonists. This character, Auguste de Maulincour, who also wanders about these same streets, is surprised to espy Clémence Desmarets, one of Paris's most beautiful and virtuous women—"une chaste et délicieuse personne de laquelle il était en secret passionnément amoureux"—in a dark and narrow street infamous for criminal activity.[41] The chance encounter provides the catalyst for the narrative, which is itself composed of Parisian typologies and chance encounters possible only, according to the narrator, in the French capital. The plot will revolve around Auguste's quest to discover Clémence's secret—that her father is the convict Ferragus—which will lead to Auguste's untimely death.

In this passage the author begins with a detailed study of specific Parisian streets and their sociocultural connotations, but ultimately he elaborates a figurative reading. The narrator initially personifies Paris's streets as possessing "des qualités humaines, et nous impriment par leur physionomie certaines idées contre lesquelles nous sommes sans défense."[42] Moving on from this general comment to the particular streets themselves, he notes the physical and social characteristics of several of them: "Quelques rues, ainsi que la rue Montmartre, ont une belle tête et finissent en queue de poisson.... La place de la Bourse est babillarde, active, prostituée; elle n'est belle que par un clair de lune, à deux heures du matin."[43] Because of the geographical positioning of certain "rues étroites exposées au nord," the narrator explains, the lack of sun leads to such criminal activity that "la Justice d'aujourd'hui ne s'en mêle pas."[44] He specifies, in other words, traits of the city's streets: their location, physical characteristics, and social subtext.

Noting that his observations will be "incompréhensibles au-delà de Paris," the narrator then turns from cataloguing the streets and their associations to painting the city in figurative terms, thus moving away from the more general descriptive *tableaux* of de Kock's fiction and panoramic literature.[45] The narrator uses the physical elements of the city to compose the body parts of what he calls the "plus délicieux des monstres" that is Paris: "ses greniers, espèces de tête pleine de sciences et de génie, ses premiers étages, estomacs heureux; ses boutiques, véritables pieds."[46] This monster's movements, he writes, are "invisiblement manoeuvrées par trente mille hommes ou femmes, dont chacune ou chacun vit dans dix pieds carrés," and he describes these movements using animal-like terms: "Il rugit, puis ses mille pattes s'agitent."[47] The narrator then partially abandons this metaphor for another with which to figure the city: "Chaque homme, chaque fraction de maison est un lobe du tissu cellulaire de cette grande courtisane de laquelle ils connaissent parfaitement la tête ... cette mouvante reine des cités."[48] This layering of metaphors indicates that the descriptive *tableau* has shifted in register, becoming more overtly figurative. Yet the narrator will not linger too long on Paris as monster, courtesan, or queen. Mere sentences later he picks up his previous train of thought, "Oui donc, il est des rues," recalling his earlier argument on the connotations of the streets and returning to a more literal discussion on the social ramification of frequenting suspicious streets.[49] The passage, which comes to an end quickly thereafter when we encounter Maulincour, departs thus from its descriptions of geographic and social conditions of Paris's streets to render the vision of Paris more allegorical; the figuration, however, is bookended by more traditional descriptive passages. Balzac published parts of *Ferragus* in the *Revue de Paris* in early 1833, just one month before the first chapters of *La Duchesse de Langeais* appeared in *L'Echo de la Jeune France*.[50] Both novels' introductory *tableaux* show the author engaging with the popular trope of the *tableau* while also beginning to incorporate literary figures more overtly, subtly manipulating the *tableau*'s conventions and thereby separating himself from practitioners of the more commercialized genre.

As with the other two texts in the *Histoire des Treize* trilogy, *La fille aux yeux d'or* begins with a lengthy passage on contemporary Parisian life, which David Bell has called a "veritable treatise on the class structure of Parisian (and French) society."[51] It describes "l'aspect général de la population parisienne" and is part of the novel's first section, "Physionomies Parisiennes."[52] In fact this excerpt has appeared in critical readings of Balzac more than the other introductory passages I have discussed and is often linked by critics to the tradition of the *tableaux de Paris*.[53] Despite such critical association with the tradition of the *tableaux*, the passage most clearly exposes Balzac's complication of the model of this subgenre. Especially in comparison with the other *tableaux* of the trilogy, the narrator moves still further from a depiction of the physical and social traits of an urban space to a more openly figurative study of the city, one whose almost hyperbolically formal qualities call attention to themselves as distinct from the genre of the *tableaux*. This passage evinces, in other words, aesthetic qualities that would have been valued as highbrow at the time, distinct from the *tableaux*'s more descriptive renderings of Parisian phenomena.

This last novel of the trilogy concerns the dandy Henri de Marsay, an exquisitely handsome man with strikingly feminine qualities who enjoys a lascivious lifestyle. On a walk in the Tuileries he is drawn to Paquita Valdès, an exotic, catlike woman with piercing golden eyes. Though the two are clearly attracted to and become intimate with one another, Paquita makes it clear that their time together will be brief and dangerous; she is, in other words, a *femme fatale*. After she calls him by the wrong name during a sexual encounter, de Marsay plots to murder her and returns a week later with three colleagues (including Ferragus) to finish the job. They are too late. Paquita's lesbian lover, whom Henri discovers is his sister, has already stabbed her to death.

La Duchesse de Langeais's introductory *tableau* offers a social, political, and physical description of the Faubourg Saint-Germain. *Ferragus*'s introductory *tableau de Paris* is focused principally on the geographic and physical aspects of Paris but also contains a passage representing Paris metaphorically as a monster, a courtesan, and a queen. The introductory *tableau* of this third and final novella represents an even more overtly figurative rendering of the city. In *La Fille aux yeux d'or*, Balzac's narrator provides almost no concrete physical description or tangible social typology but rather weaves together metaphor and allegory to paint what we might call a moral thesis about the city. While the introductory typology of Parisian streets in *Ferragus* certainly ascribes moral values to the streets and that of *La Duchesse* forms ethical judgments based on the physical and social descriptions of the *faubourg Saint Germain*, the initial *tableau* of *La Fille aux yeux d'or* concentrates more on the spectacle of the Parisian social scene, focusing entirely on the general rather than the particular.[54] The narrator begins by offering "quelques observations sur l'âme de Paris [qui] peuvent expliquer les causes de sa physionomie cadavéreuse."[55] Yet these observations come less in the form of an urban typology and more as a totalizing vision of Paris, what Christopher Prendergast has called "Paris as a 'total' system."[56] Beginning with the *ouvrier* (worker) and touching on the *commerçant* (storekeeper), the *haute bourgeoisie* (upper middle class), the artists, and the nobles, the narrator mixes the analogy of the "sphères parisiennes" with that of the Parisian apartment building to show that, regardless of class, only one thing matters in Paris: "l'or et le plaisir."[57] He does enter into some detail about the daily lives of these various classes of people—the worker who returns to his conjugal bed at midnight after attending a play; the petit-bourgeois couple who pay for only one cook but who give their daughter 150,000 francs for a dowry; the businessmen obliged to attend the opera and lavish balls in order to find clients. Yet at no point is the reader treated to a developed typology of any of these figures. The description serves instead to prove the narrator's original thesis: money and pleasure are the cause of every class's actions. This overarching vision of Paris therefore differs from the smaller, fragmented *tableaux*, which treat individual phenomena and, only when put into a larger collection, such as the *Nouveaux Tableaux de Paris*, form a more comprehensive vision of the city.

The narrator's heavy reliance on metaphor also takes this passage out of the traditional realm of the *tableau de Paris*, especially considering that the metaphors deal with Paris as a whole entity rather than a particular aspect of the city. As Prendergast and David Harvey have noted, this introduction to the novel is almost entirely constructed of metaphor and analogy; Harvey in particular cites the passage's "rapidly shift[ing] metaphors."[58] While the narrator does at times cite particular examples from the level of the urban quotidian, as we saw earlier, most of the passage is composed of literary tropes and maintained at a figurative level.[59] Within the first few pages the narrator says, "Ce n'est pas seulement par plaisanterie que Paris a été nommé un enfer," labeling the city "cette grande cage de plâtre, cette ruche à ruisseaux noirs."[60] This overlapping of metaphor continues for multiple pages until we are at last introduced to de Marsay. The effect of this almost hyperbolic reliance on metaphor to describe the entire city—one image on top of the next—only underscores the mythical, all-inclusive characteristics of Balzac's treatment of Paris, so different from the smaller, more fragmentary urban *tableaux* or *physiologies*. Here, by moving away from the more descriptive typological texts, ones that the author had previously composed and continued to write in addition to his novels, Balzac offers a new model for capturing Paris more synoptically.

The self-conscious literariness of this passage stands in stark contrast to that of the works in the *Physiologie* series whose blatant commercialism would become commonplace less than a decade after Balzac published this trilogy. The figures are almost excessive in nature and there is little continuity among the images evoked in a passage.[61] Prendergast acknowledges the text's "prodigious figural input," explains that its "metaphor is eclectically chosen and promiscuously mixed," and calls the passage more generally "frenzied," "intense."[62] Still further, the somewhat disjunctive nature of this series of metaphors is employed in conjunction with sentences composed chiefly of enumeration, for example, "Là [à Paris] tout fume, tout brûle, tout brille, tout bouillonne, tout flambe, s'évapore, s'éteint, se rallume, étincelle, pétille et se consume."[63] The metaphors used to describe the city expand, one upon the next, once again moving the description further and further past mere factual observation.[64] The repetition of the words "l'or et le plaisir," words that return not only to remind the reader of the narrator's argument on Paris but also to serve as a poetic refrain, create lyric continuity to this otherwise rather unwieldy text. Finally the narrator goes as far as justifying the absence of urban physical description in this passage, implying that the moral description suffices to explain the topographical description of the city: "Cette vue de Paris moral prouve que le Paris physique ne saurait être autrement qu'il n'est."[65] These tropes call attention to the explicitly literary nature of the passage and distinguish it from the traditional *tableau* and even the *tableaux* found in the two preceding novellas of the *Histoire des Treize* trilogy. The text's more figurative treatment of the city, in place of a descriptive observation of a Parisian phenomenon, indicates a shift toward the more totalizing method of examining society Balzac defines in the *avant-propos* to the *Comédie humaine*.[66] This is a methodological move, we might think, that plays on popular commercial tropes with the goal of more clearly distinguishing the author on the level of form from those more popular writers.[67]

In these introductory *tableaux* Balzac engages with and destabilizes the trope by rendering his passages more explicitly figurative. At the same time he incorporates other, more traditional typological passages into this trilogy that present contemporary Parisian phenomena. At times these passages are copied directly from other, nonliterary publications. Balzac's involvement in what Schor calls the nineteenth century's "obsession to submit the entire social body to exhaustive scrutiny and record" is well known.[68] Shor herself links Balzac's fictional cataloguing of modern Paris to that found in so-called panoramic literature, writing that "these inventories take the form of the famous *physiologies*, the equally famous *guides* . . . [and] much of Honoré de Balzac's *Comédie humaine* and Émile Zola's *Rougon-Macquart*."[69] While Balzac's fiction certainly participates in this trend of categorizing modern Paris, the more explicit typologies of contemporary phenomena incorporated into the *Histoire des Treize*, especially when compared to the more figurative introductory *tableau*, stage Balzac's own liminal position in the contemporary literary field and the tensions surrounding commercial and "high-quality" literature more generally.

Among its many typologies, *Ferragus* contains, for example, a lengthy description of a *porte cochère* (carriage entrance) in the second chapter to set up the chance encounter that will enable Auguste to get closer to the mystery of Clémence.[70] While Maulincour is out in the streets of the city, a heavy rain begins, and walkers, including Auguste, are forced to take refuge as they can: under an umbrella, in a café, or under a nearby awning. Before Maulincour arrives on the scene, the narrator takes the opportunity to expound upon existing Parisian customs when it comes to shielding oneself from the rain:

Un fantassin de Paris est alors obligé de s'arrêter tout court, de se réfu-
gier dans une boutique ou dans un café s'il est assez riche pour y payer
son hospitalité forcée; ou, selon l'urgence, sous une porte cochère, asile
des gens pauvres ou mal mis. Comment aucun de nos peintres n'a-t-il
pas encore essayé de reproduire la physionomie d'un essaim de Parisiens
groupés, par un temps d'orage, sous le porche humide d'une maison?
Où rencontrer un plus riche tableau? . . . Selon son caractère, chaque
membre de cette société fortuite contemple le ciel, s'en va sautillant pour
ne pas se crotter, ou parce qu'il est pressé ou parce qu'il voit des citoyens
marchant malgré vent et marée, ou parce que la cour de la maison étant
humide et catarrhalement mortelle, la lisière, dit un proverbe, est pire que
le drap. Chacun a ses motifs. Il ne reste que le piéton prudent, l'homme
qui, pour se remettre en route, épie quelques espaces bleus à travers les
nuages crevassés.[71]

We are immediately alerted to the engagement of this passage with the
subgenre of the *tableau de Paris* by the narrator, who, surprised that no other
painter of Parisian life has chosen to depict this phenomenon, sets up his own
passage as a rich tableau. The nouns *peintres* and *physionomie* reinforce the idea
that the narrator is creating an urban portrait and underscore the language of
cataloguing social types. The narrator does not merely engage in a physical
description of the urban landscape, "le fond grisâtre de l'atmosphère" or "les
capricieux dégorgements des tuyaux pétillants."[72] He addresses urban types
as well: "le piéton causeur qui se plaint et converse avec la portière quand elle
se pose sur son balai comme un grenadier sur son fusil"; "le piéton industriel,
armé d'une sacoche ou muni d'un paquet, traduisant la pluie par profits et
pertes"; and "le vrai bourgeois de Paris, homme à parapluie."[73] Balzac's narrator
effectively weaves together a physical description of the city, typologies of
social categories, and a characterization of urban customs, as well as setting
a scene pregnant with potential for an aleatory encounter. Unlike de Kock's
tableaux, this passage is inextricably linked to the narrative—the *porte-cochère*
is where Maulincour will retrieve a letter that will lead him to Ferragus—yet
it also points to Balzac's engagement with these popular forms of nonfiction
writing and his incorporation of them into his fiction.

In addition to this *tableau* and that which opens the novel, *Ferragus* contains a third socio-urban portrait, that of Ida, the woman enamored of Ferragus. This portrait is found later in the novel, after mysterious accidents begin to befall Auguste and after Mme Jules's husband becomes suspicious of her outings. During a particularly tense moment between the two spouses, Ida bursts into their home. "Cette *demoiselle* était le type d'une femme qui ne se rencontre qu'à Paris," explains the narrator, before commencing a page-long physical and social description of this individual. Ida falls under the category of the *grisette de Paris* and, for this narrator, "la grisette dans toute sa splendeur."[74] This working woman's portrait, which prefigures Huart's 1841 *Physiologie de la grisette*, interrupts an intimate confession between Mme Jules and her husband and exposes the class imbalance at the heart of Mme Jules's mystery. In addition, as with the *porte cochère*, the narrator is once again in dialogue with the tradition of panoramic literature, as he comments on the inability of the urban artist to capture and appreciate fully the nature of this Parisian creature: "Vingt fois saisie par le crayon du peintre, par le pinceau du caricaturiste, par la plombagine du dessinateur, elle échappe à toutes les analyses, parce qu'elle est insaisissable dans tous ses modes, comme l'est la nature, comme l'est ce fantasque Paris."[75] This is one in a series of Parisian typologies in the tradition of the *tableaux de Paris* and which, far from serving as mere description, play an integral role in the establishment of character and the development of plot in *Ferragus*.[76] We might say that Balzac, like his contemporaries, relies on these tropes he knew to be popular among contemporary readers, while simultaneously undermining and critiquing them, a method he will use less than a decade later in *Les Employés* and in which he stages contemporary tensions about value in the marketplace.

What is more, whether Balzac exposes his resistance to or adaptation of the now commercialized *tableau* genre in certain passages of the *Histoire des Treize*, he also recycles typological urban writing from other publications into these same novels. He inserts for example a description of the young Parisian man into *La Fille aux yeux d'or*, a passage he would concurrently publish in the 1834 *Nouveaux Tableaux de Paris*. After de Marsay has been introduced, Balzac writes, "En effet, les jeunes gens de Paris ne ressemblent aux jeunes gens d'aucune autre ville. Ils se divisent en deux classes: le jeune homme qui a quelque chose, et le jeune homme qui n'a rien; ou le jeune homme qui pense et celui qui dépense." [77] The reader is then treated to a more general explication of the divisions among the moneyed youth, both educated and mediocre, and to a description of the relationships that exist among the different divisions. The novelistic description serves to explain further de Marsay's relationship with his friend Paul de Manerville and, as was the case of the typology of the *grisette* in *Ferragus*, to provide a broad representation of a particular character. With the exception of a few minor word changes, the majority of the passage from this novel is recycled into the distinct nonfiction publication. Balzac removes, for example, specific reference to de Marsay in his *Nouveaux Tableaux de Paris* contribution, writing simply, "Donc, au premier coup d'œil, il est naturel de croire très distinctes les deux espèces de jeunes gens qui mènent une vie élégante." [78] He elects not to include the phrase "aimable corporation à laquelle appartenait Henri de Marsay," as he does in *La Fille aux yeux d'or*. [79] Yet if he excludes the depiction of de Marsay in this version, he still cites Henri's friend de Manerville when describing the tendency of young men to elevate their social status by referring to what he calls "un tel" (so and so): "Un beau jour, si vous demandiez à UN TEL s'il connaît M. Paul de Manerville, l'héritier débarqué, UN TEL le définirait ainsi: 'Vous me demandez ce que c'est que Paul? Mais Paul ... c'est Paul de Manerville.'"[80] Balzac's contribution to the *Nouveaux Tableaux de Paris* collection (whose other contributors included the maritime novelist Auguste Jal, the popular writer Frédéric Soulié, and de Kock, among others) does go on in a more officious way to set up categories among the young men of the period: "Le Négateur est celui qui, ne sachant rien, nie tout pour en finir avec toute espèce de chose"; "Les Séctateurs sont une secte qui s'est formée pour contrecarrer les négateurs."[81] Nevertheless the majority of this text has been repurposed from the original novelistic context to a nonnovelistic one. This recycling testifies not only to Balzac's active involvement in the commercialized genre of panoramic literature but also, read alongside the introductory *tableaux* of the trilogy, exposes an ambivalence toward the practices of the contemporary marketplace. An even more explicit instance of his literary recycling from panoramic text to novel is found in *Physiologie de l'employé* and his novel *Les Employés*. His remediation of the nonfiction study of the bureaucrat into fiction exposes, this time even more explicitly than in the case of the *Histoire des Treize*, the author's ambivalence toward this particular brand of commercial literature at the height of the phenomenon of the *physiologies*.

RECYCLING *PHYSIOLOGIE DE L'EMPLOYÉ*

Balzac's understudied *Les Employés* actively stages his complex relationship with the *physiologies* series and, more generally, with the contemporary tensions of the literary field. Originally published as *La Femme supérieure* in 1837, the novel that would become *Les Employés* underwent drastic revision after the appearance of Balzac's *Physiologie de l'employé* (1841). The author's approach to the *physiologie* series takes a dual form, and his somewhat fraught relationship to this popular form is revealed throughout this multistaged literary project. In *Les Employés*, as in many of his other novels, Balzac consistently codifies his characters in the manner of the *physiologie* series and repurposes typological passages from his own *Physiologie* into the final edition of the novel. However, numerous passages in *Les Employés* show his resistance to the very goals of the typological method. Analysis of this contradictory stance toward typology in *Les Employés*—on the one hand a desire to classify and define types, on the other an acknowledgment of the ultimate impossibility of defining types—displays both Balzac's appropriation of and friction with the midcentury media phenomenon of the *physiologies*.[82] Furthermore these generic tensions, which play out on the level of plot and style in the multiple formats of *Les Employés*, mirror tensions between high and low literature that were being formed and debated in the nascent literary field in which Balzac and his contemporaries published.

First published as a *feuilleton* in *La Presse* in July 1837 as *La Femme supérieure* and later collected into a two-volume edition by Werdet, *Les Employés* was greatly altered before the definitive edition was published in book form as *Les Employés ou la Femme supérieure* in 1844 by Furne. Balzac was soon dissatisfied with the 1837 version, writing on October 12, 1837, "J'ai une préface à coudre, en forme de collerette, à *la Femme supérieure*, et une quatrième partie en forme de tournure, car les soixante-quinze colonnes de *la Presse* n'ont fourni qu'un petit volume."[83] Six years later he expanded these seventy-five columns and shifted the resulting novel's main focus from the tale of a woman attempting to secure her husband a ministerial position to a sociological study of the world of bureaucrats under the Restoration.[84] Balzac addressed his desire for a change of narrative focus in the preface to the 1838 edition, stating that for him *La Femme supérieure* was a title "qui n'exprime plus le sujet de cette étude où l'héroïne, si tant est qu'elle soit supérieure, n'est plus qu'une figure accessoire au lieu de s'y trouver la principale."[85] Elaborating on the disparity between the subject matter and the title, he explains, "Si vous trouvez ici beaucoup d'employés et peu de femmes supérieures, cette faute est explicable par les raisons sus-énoncées: les employés étaient prêts, accommodés, finis, et la femme supérieure est encore à peindre."[86] The immediate need to depict these bureaucrats, then, takes precedence over the narrative dedicated to the *femme supérieure*. In this sense Balzac's 1838 preface places his work in the tradition of panoramic literature in its pressing desire to represent a contemporary Parisian phenomenon.[87] As Karlheinz Stierle explains in his study of panoramic literature, and in particular the *tableau de Paris*, "each tableau was conceived as outdoing all preceding tableaux by representing the most modern aspect of Paris."[88] In his preface written six years before the publication of *Les Employés*, Balzac already renders his novel more modern and more relevant.[89]

Despite the title change a large portion of *Les Employés* remains dedicated to the narrative of a *femme supérieure*, Madame Célestine Rabourdin, wife of Xavier Rabourdin, an office manager. Central to the intrigue is the death of Monsieur de La Billardière, which has left a vacancy in the ministry for the position of *chef de division*. Rabourdin, who worked his way up the bureaucratic ladder, is the obvious choice for this position, a promotion that would allow his wife to realize her dream of joining high society. At the same time Elizabeth Baudoyer, wife of another office manager, schemes to have her inept husband, Isidore, selected. Both wives become the driving forces behind plans to advance their husband's career. Célestine is aided by the minister's secretary general, le comte des Lupeaulx, who loves her. Her husband's cause is damaged, however, by the discovery that he has been planning a major overhaul of the administrative system that would eliminate hundreds of unnecessary positions to compensate the remaining employees more handsomely. Baudoyer ultimately wins the position. Rabourdin resigns, promising his wife a better future despite their debts, and the incompetent Baudoyer is demoted shortly after achieving the coveted post.[90]

At the level of plot and character, *Les Employés* and the preceding version, *La Femme supérieure*, tend, like the *physiologies*, to group together, describe, and classify social types, but at the same time they focus on individual characters. The narrator's association of specific characters with a more general social type can be seen each time a major figure is presented to the reader. This juxtaposition appears as early as the first sentence of *Les Employés*, in which the narrator evokes the prevalence of characters like the protagonist Rabourdin: "A Paris, où les hommes d'étude et de pensée ont quelques analogies en vivant dans le même milieu, vous avez dû rencontrer plusieurs figures semblables à celle de M. Rabourdin."[91] This *chef de bureau* (office manager) should be familiar to Balzac's mid-nineteenth-century readers: he is a type. Though a more intricate portrait of Rabourdin's own physical traits and personal and professional background follows this opening sentence, the reader, now made sensitive to the question of typology, views Rabourdin not as a unique individual but rather as one of "plusieurs figures semblables."[92]

This juxtaposition of the individual and the type is not a unique phenomenon in either version of the novel (nor unique to this particular novel of Balzac), for the narrator regularly precedes character descriptions by the expression "un(e) de ces" (one of those) to underscore the notion that his protagonists are representative of a more general group. In the chapter "Monsieur des Lupeaulx," the eponymous *secrétaire général* (administrative officer) is introduced as "un de ces personnages que le flot des événements politiques met en saillie pendant quelques années."[93] He is not a man uniquely favored by the tides of politics; he is one of many. Later in the novel, as des Lupeaulx becomes even further enmeshed in the story of Baudoyer and Rabourdin's rivalry, the narrator remarks, "Des Lupeaulx était un de *ces* hommes qui, pour satisfaire une passion, savent mettre leur vengeance dans un coin de leur coeur."[94] As the narrator moves from the Rabourdin to the Baudoyer family, he once again typologizes one of the novel's protagonists, characterizing

Célestine Rabourdin's rivals as "une de ces figures qui se dérobent au pinceau par leur vulgarité même, et qui néanmoins doivent être esquissées; car elles offrent une expression de cette petite bourgeoisie parisienne, placée au-dessus des riches artisans et au-dessous de la haute classe."[95] Elisabeth is rendered all the more archetypal, for the narrator notes that she stands in for the Parisian petite bourgeoisie. Termed an "exophore mémorielle" by Eric Bordas, the phrase "un(e) de ces ... qui" is, he explains, a typical "stylème" that dominated "le récit français entre 1830 et 1890 environ" and that effects the "passage idéal du particulier au général."[96] In *Les Employés* the "exophore mémorielle" works in exactly this way. Further, the narrator's creation of general types out of his particular characters is reminiscent of the *physiologie* series and their tendency to codify social types; this minor trope engages with those of more commercial trends.

"A Paris, presque tous les bureaux se ressemblent" is a fitting opening line to the second book of *Les Employés*, for it announces that the narrator will continue to liken the novel's subjects to other Parisian phenomena, that is, to demonstrate the tension between the general and the particular.[97] "En quelque ministère que vous erriez pour solliciter le moindre redressement de torts ou la plus légère faveur," writes the narrator, "vous trouverez des corridors obscurs, des dégagements peu éclairés, des portes percées, comme les loges au théâtre."[98] There is little variation among departments, divisions, ministries. Thus we are told, "Peut-être suffira-t-il de peindre la division de M. de la Billardière, pour que les étrangers et les gens qui vivent en province aient des idées exactes sur les mœurs intimes des bureaux, car ces traits principaux sont sans doute communs à toutes les administrations européennes."[99] Because La Billardière's division is illustrative of almost all Parisian bureaucracy, the narrative that follows provides a typology of this entire social group. The introduction of La Billardière's office, as well as the narrator's consistent choice to present his protagonists with the phrases "un(e) de ces" or "semblable à," display a tendency toward the techniques of typologizing also found in the *physiologies*.

Both *La Femme supérieure* and *Les Employés* contain the same descriptive passages analyzed above; nevertheless, in addition to its new title, dozens of minor and major changes were made to the 1844 novel. Many (date changes, pauses in dialogue, grammatical changes), identified in Mary Scott's scrupulous comparison, simply create a more fluid and engaging narrative. However, these smaller changes pale in comparison to those "intended to enlarge the scope of the novel as a study of a class," including a large number of passages "inserted to develop the sociological study of the genus government clerk."[100] Both Scott and Anne-Marie Meininger credit Balzac's *Physiologie de l'employé* with provoking the most significant changes to the novel. Published by La Maison Aubert, this text, like others in the *physiologie* series, breaks down the category of *employé* (bureaucrat: a term I use here in concordance with the only recent translation of the novel), examining its history, culture, and subtypes. The work is divided into short chapters whose titles are "significatifs de cette méthode descriptive des différentes 'espèces sociales,'" which end for the most part with an *axiome* about the type.[101] Balzac draws on descriptive passages from *La Femme supérieure* in the *Physiologie* and, more important, adapts and recycles passages from the *Physiologie* in *Les Employés*, effectively shifting the focus and the genre of the work, a shift evident in the work's title change. "Il accroît tant l'importance des employés," argues Meininger, "qu'ils ravissent le rôle premier à *La Femme supérieure*."[102] Indeed with the addition of passages from the *Physiologie*, the novel becomes a hybrid text, a "sociological" study as well as the fictional narrative of the struggle for one bureaucratic position. This recycling also shows Balzac adapting his novel to fit the current tastes of readers living during the height of the *physiologie* trend.

Typological, descriptive passages explaining people and phenomena in the world of the bureaucrats originate in *La Femme supérieure*. Yet in the post-*Physiologie* version of *Les Employés*, the narrator expands upon and actively calls attention to these passages, stressing his own reliance on the *physiologie* genre. The typological *va-et-vient* between the various editions of the novel and the *Physiologie* is perhaps most notable in a passage introducing the office supernumerary, Sébastien, a passage that, with considerable variation, appears in all three versions. At one of Madame Rabourdin's Wednesday receptions, the narrator of *La Femme supérieure* writes of the supernumerary with whom Rabourdin speaks, "Il n'y a que deux variétés de surnuméraire: les surnuméraires riches et les surnuméraires pauvres."[103] Briefly explaining the differences between the two classes of supernumeraries, the narrator writes,

"Le jeune homme à qui parlait Rabourdin était un surnuméraire pauvre nommé Sébastien de la Roche."[104] The short description of this social type is thus diegetic; it is contained within the narrative of Célestine's *soirée*. Parts of this fictional description are revived and expanded on in the *Physiologie* in a chapter entitled "Le surnuméraire," whose focus is principally the poor supernumerary: "Le surnuméraire pauvre est donc le vrai, le seul surnuméraire."[105] More lengthy than the original passage, this chapter describes the social habits of this type: his living arrangements ("presque toujours logé dans un quartier où les loyers ne sont pas chers") and his eating habits (his mother slips him bread "afin qu'il puisse . . . franchir les neuf heures qui séparent son déjeuner de son dîner").[106] Fictional description of Sébastien has become pseudo-scientific taxonomy of one genus of bureaucrat.

The 1844 novel incorporates the section "Le surnuméraire" nearly word for word from the *Physiologie*, maintaining its taxonomic structure. A short elaboration on rich young men's role in the *surnumérariat* is added to the chapter from the *Physiologie*, for example, while the comical concluding sentences of the *Physiologie*'s chapter are clipped, perhaps in keeping with the "code implicite de la physiologie [qui] doit s'en tenir à la surface des choses" and whose tone is one of "badinage sans consequence."[107] Aside from these minor differences, however, the passages are nearly identical. What is more, after repeating the sentence establishing Rabourdin's conversation with Sébastien from *La Femme supérieure*, the narrator of *Les Employés* highlights the ensuing typology of the supernumerary with an extradiegetic phrase: "Ici, peut-être doit-on expliquer, autant pour les étrangers que pour nos neveux, ce qu'est à Paris un surnuméraire."[108] The diegesis is explicitly interrupted in order for the narrator to codify this Parisian phenomenon for readers unaccustomed to this type. While the text ultimately returns to the narrative focused on Célestine Rabourdin's *soirée* through the same transition cited earlier—"Le jeune homme à qui parlait Raboudin était un surnuméraire pauvre nommé Sébastien de La Roche"—the fact that this typology is deliberately set apart from the diegesis underscores both the author's repurposing of text from his *Physiologie* and his exploitation of tropes of the *physiologie* series.[109] The comparison among the three formats of the supernumerary passage shows the author becoming more dependent on the style of the *physiologie* in his novel over its several versions, not surprisingly as the short texts became more commercially viable.[110]

One final example of typological description from *Les Employés* further demonstrates Balzac's reliance on the *Physiologie*. Toward the beginning of the chapter "Quelques Employés vus de trois-quarts," the narrator alerts us to the great distinctions between Parisian and provincial bureaucrats: "Distinguez surtout l'employé de Paris de l'employé de province. En province, l'employé se trouve heureux: il est logé spacieusement . . . il boit de bon vin, à bon marché, ne consomme pas de filet de cheval. . . . Enfin, l'employé de province est *quelque chose*, tandis que l'employé de Paris est à peine *quelqu'un*."[111] This abridged typology acknowledges the existence of bureaucrats outside of Paris in a predominantly Parisian study. As in the supernumerary passage, this section sketches the quotidian details of the country bureaucrat, whose life, as opposed to that of his Parisian counterpart, is quite comfortable.

The preceding typology is entirely absent from the corresponding section in *La Femme supérieure*. Both novels contain, with minor differences, the sentence beginning "Avant d'entrer dans le drame, il est nécessaire de peindre ici la silhouette des principaux acteurs de la division La Billardière."[112] But where the 1837–38 edition launches directly into a description of the different characters who make up the office, the 1844 edition prolongs this sentence with a clause claiming this sketch of La Billardière's workplace will justify "encore le titre de cette Étude, essentiellement parisienne."[113] This final clause added to *Les Employés* underscores the generic shift in the novel: it has explicitly become a study of bureaucracy and one, like the *physiologies*, principally focused on Parisian phenomena. It should not come as a surprise, then, that the typology of the "employé de province" (provincial bureaucrat) has its origins in the *Physiologie*. In a short chapter entitled "Distinction," the *Physiologie*'s narrator explains, "Nous distinguons l'employé de Paris de l'employé de province. Cette Physiologie nie complètement l'employé de province."[114] The chapter goes on in detail greater than that found in *Les Employés* to describe the social habits of this type, his lodging, and the food he eats, and concludes by restating this text's particular focus on the Parisian bureaucrat: "L'employé de cette Physiologie est donc exclusivement l'employé de Paris." It establishes an *axiome*: "L'employé de province est *quelqu'un*,

tandis que l'employé de Paris est *quelque chose*" (emphasis in the original).[115]
These two examples of the development and recycling of typological studies
from the *Physiologie* to *Les Employés* demonstrate Balzac's explicit reliance
on the *physiologie* series in his avowedly fictional study of the bureaucrat.
They also further underscore his engagement with the popular literary trend
both in and outside of his fictional works and thus his keen knowledge of
this particular aspect of the contemporary literary field.

THE "NEED" TO DEFINE, THE "DANGER" OF CONFUSION

Balzac's effort to crystalize a typology of the bureaucrat is evident not only
in the generic shift of his text from novel to a hybrid novelistic–sociological
study of the bureaucrat but also in his insistence on language that renders
his individual characters into types. Yet *Les Employés* also reveals a desire to
subvert the project of typology in general and thus to distinguish the novel
from the popular literary tropes on which it relies so heavily. Throughout the
text characters insist on knowing the definition of a bureaucrat, a question
that theoretically subtends both Balzac's novel and the *Physiologie*. However,
in every case the question is deferred, ignored, or mocked. Balzac's first eva-
sion occurs in "Quelques Employés vus de trois-quarts," when Antoine, the
"plus vieux garçon du ministère," lectures his nephew and office boy, Gabriel,
about how much harder previous bureaucrats worked.[116] Gabriel asks, "Père
Antoine . . . puisque vous êtes causeur ce matin, quelle idée, là, vous faites-vous
de l'employé?"[117] With great seriousness, Antoine responds, "Un homme qui
écrit assis dans un bureau. Qu'est-ce que je dis donc là? Sans les employés,
que serions-nous? . . . Allez donc voir à vos poêles et ne parlez jamais en
mal des employés, vous autres!"[118] Gabriel's desire to define the bureaucrat
mirrors what, until this point, has been the desire of the narrator, who has
taken us painstakingly through this study that would enable the uninitiated
to have "idées exactes sur les mœurs intimes des bureaux."[119] At first Antoine
responds confidently: "Un homme qui écrit assis dans un bureau." Yet he
immediately throws into question this concrete definition by asking "Qu'est-ce
que je dis donc là?" Is the bureaucrat not, then, a man who sits at his desk?
Antoine seems unsure. Furthermore he poses the rhetorical question "Sans
les employés, que serions-nous?," offering no additional information about

the nature of the bureaucrat and rendering the first definition all the more hazy. What, then, is a bureaucrat? And who are these "nous," when the two office workers involved in the conversation are themselves demonstrably examples of the bureaucrat? Like Gabriel, the reader is sent away without achieving a precise understanding of this term. Antoine's foggy description is intensified by the almost panoramic vantage point he enjoys in the office. As the narrator explains it, directly following this exchange between uncle and nephew, "Antoine se plaça sur le palier, à un endroit d'où il pouvait voir déboucher les employés de dessous la porte cochère; il connaissait tous ceux du ministère et les observait dans leur allure, en remarquant les différences que présentaient leurs mises."[120] The "vieux garçon's" implied omniscience about the division, on the tails of his inability to answer Gabriel's question, leaves the reader questioning whether definitive understanding of the type is actually attainable.

At the end of *Les Employés*, as the characters debate the aftermath of Baudoyer's appointment, the narrator once again exposes his skepticism about mastery of typology. As Poiret, the highly regimented individual about to retire after thirty years of work, struggles to understand Baudoyer's nomination and Rabourdin's resignation, Bixiou, the office prankster, attempts to extract from Poiret a definition of bureaucrat:

BIXIOU: Avant de vous en aller d'ici, peut-être serez-vous bien aise de savoir qui vous êtes. . . . De définir, d'expliquer, de pénétrer, d'analyser ce que c'est qu'un employé . . . le savez-vous?

POIRET: . . . C'est un homme payé par le gouvernement pour faire un travail.

BIXIOU: Evidemment, alors un soldat est un employé.

POIRET : . . . Mais non.

BIXIOU: Cependant il est payé par l'État pour monter la garde et passer des revues. . . .

POIRET : . . . Eh! bien, monsieur, un employé serait plus logiquement un homme qui pour vivre a besoin de son traitement et qui n'est pas libre de quitter sa place, ne sachant faire autre chose qu'expédier.

BIXIOU : Ah! nous arrivons à une solution. . . . Ainsi le Bureau est la

coque de l'employé. Pas d'employé sans bureau, pas de bureau sans
employé. Que faisons-nous alors du douanier.... Où cesse l'employé?
Question grave! Un préfet est-il un employé?

POIRET : ... C'est un fonctionnaire.

BIXIOU : Ah! vous arrivez à ce contre-sens qu'un fonctionnaire ne serait
pas un employé! ... Je voulais vous prouver, monsieur, que rien n'est
simple, mais surtout ... je veux faire voir que: A côté du besoin de
définir, se trouve le danger de s'embrouiller.[121]

After spending his career in the bureaucracy, Poiret is unable to produce
a cogent definition of a bureaucrat, and Bixiou chides his colleague for
underestimating the complexity of the term. This interaction between the
two men asserts not only the comical idea that a man could spend thirty
years dedicated to a profession that he cannot define but also exposes the
precarious nature of the very study that attempts to come to a definition of
the bureaucrat. Bixiou's initial request to Poiret, "De définir, d'expliquer, de
pénétrer, d'analyser ce que c'est qu'un employé," is in essence the task that
Balzac has set himself in this novel, especially in the 1844 version. Yet by the
end of this exchange, in addition to leaving Poiret thoroughly befuddled,
Bixiou has also proven that any study attempting a definition risks ending
in confusion. By playing the role of comical contrarian, Bixiou demonstrates
that one can never arrive at a fixed definition of a bureaucrat, that regardless
of one's level of expertise, there will always be exceptions and contradictions.
It is certainly not by accident that this incident is situated fewer than ten
pages before the end of Balzac's novelistic sociological study.

Neither scene that evades defining the bureaucrat is found in *La Femme
supérieure*, reaffirming Balzac's simultaneous reliance on and rejection of the
project of the *physiologies* over the course of the publication of these various
works. In the first instance, the père Antoine of *La Femme supérieure* is never
asked "Quelle idée, là, vous faites-vous de l'employé?" Rather in the novel's
corresponding scene, Antoine rants to a different coworker, Laurent, about
the office's "tas de faignians," after which he asks the rhetorical question from
Les Employés, "Qu'est-ce que je dis donc là? Allez donc voir à vos poêles."[122]
A definition of bureaucrat is thus neither sought nor refused in the 1837–38

version. Similarly, contrary to the conclusion of *Les Employés*, which, after Bixiou's interrogation of Poiret, ends with Rabourdin's return to the office several years later, *La Femme supérieure* closes quickly after Rabourdin's resignation and a brief conversation among colleagues. It contains no part of the dialogue in which Bixiou presses Poiret for a definition. These additions to *Les Employés* demonstrate an evolution in Balzac's relationship to the typological project of the *physiologies*.

The *Physiologie*'s inclusion of definitive statements about the nature of the bureaucrat, however, also shows Balzac's nuancing of typology across genres, as well as his full participation in the popular genre of the *physiologie* and his manipulation of it in his literary fiction. The author begins his nonfiction study of the bureaucrat with a chapter entitled "Définition," whose first line is "Qu'est-ce qu'un employé?," and shortly after responds, "La meilleure définition de l'employé serait donc celle-ci: Un homme qui pour vivre a besoin de son traitement et qui n'est pas libre de quitter sa place, ne sachant faire autre chose que paperasser!"[123] He then gives lucid responses to the questions that Poiret will be unable to answer in *Les Employés*: "Evidemment le roi des Français ne peut pas être un employé. . . . Évidemment encore, un soldat n'est pas un employé: il souhaite trop quitter sa place. . . . D'après cette glose, un employé doit être un homme qui écrit, assis dans un bureau. Pas d'employé sans bureau, pas de bureau sans employé. . . . Où cesse l'employé? Question grave! Un préfet est-il un employé? Cette Physiologie ne le pense pas."[124] After these decisive statements defining who should and should not be included under the rubric of bureaucrat, the chapter continues by establishing the first and second *axiomes* about the bureaucrat: "1er Axiome. Où finit l'employé, commence l'homme d'état"; "2e Axiome. Au-dessus de vingt mille francs d'appointements, il n'y a plus d'employés."[125] Balzac's amusing maxims illuminating the definition of the bureaucrat in the *Physiologie* differ greatly from the haziness found in his novelistic treatment of the same topic three years later. Although the third and final *axiome*, "A côté du besoin de définir, se trouve le danger de s'embrouiller," will be repeated in *Les Employés* to warn readers of the precarious nature of defining types, here it appears after the extensive definition and the narrator's exclamation "Cessons de définir!" and functions as a comical conclusion to the otherwise complete classification.[126]

This different interpretation of the same statement is made all the more evident by the comments that precede the *axiome* in both editions. The *Physiologie*'s narrator states, "Pour parodier le fameux mot de Louis XVIII, posons cet axiome" and thus establishes its witty purpose.[127] Bixiou, himself a comic character, asks his audience to permit him "de retourner un mot de Louis XVIII."[128] The *Physiologie*'s *axiome*, if we are to follow the narrator, is meant in jest. Finally, to confirm further the *Physiologie*'s desire to establish a fixed definition of the bureaucrat, the text's second chapter refers to the thoroughness of the classificatory job performed in the first, declaring "la matière ainsi vannée, épluchée, divisée," before going on to question "A quoi servent les employés?"[129] Unlike its novelistic counterpart, Balzac's *Physiologie* does not question the limits of typology. Rather it celebrates, comically to be sure, its thoroughness in defining the bureaucrat. Anne-Marie Bijaoui-Baron warns against taking these definitions at their word: "Les physiologies se présentent comme des études de mœurs auxquelles une armature scientifique donne une apparence de sérieux; mais leur but réel est d'amuser le public par la désinvolture de leurs définitions."[130] They nonetheless highlight Balzac's more cautious method of establishing types in *Les Employés*. The generic conventions of these pseudo-sociological tracts dictate that authors offer a clear (if parodic) classification of social types or phenomena, but Balzac rejects this practice in his novelistic treatment of the same milieu.

In *Les Employés* Balzac is at odds with the typological project of the *physiologie* series. On the one hand, he has recycled and developed typologies from the *Physiologie de l'employé* and placed them prominently in his narrative, a narrative that already in its 1837–38 form used classificatory techniques to establish its characters. On the other, while he provides a decisive if comical typology of the bureaucrat and its various genera in his *Physiologie*, he resists a general definition of the bureaucrat in his novel, itself an increasingly visible social category in the postrevolutionary period. Far from replicating the simple high/low distinctions that critics have typically drawn, *Les Employés* elucidates the productive ambivalence of the author's relationship to the *physiologie* series. This ambivalence is mirrored in the novel's representation of Rabourdin's contested bureaucratic reform project, a project Franc Schuerewegen argues is "un peu *La Comédie humaine* en petit."[131] An elaborate critique and revision of current bureaucratic methods, Rabourdin's proposal is actually "'un déclassement' . . . 'une nouvelle nomenclature,' c'est à dire . . . une sorte de taxinomie."[132] Rabourdin has worked tirelessly on this controversial project that effectively catalogues the existing bureaucrats and proposes breaking down and restructuring the current system: a new typology. Yet like the definitions of the bureaucrat that his characters evade, Balzac allows his readers only glimpses of Rabourdin's plan, the evidence of which is ultimately destroyed by the protagonist. Balzac himself breaks down and declassifies his own hybrid study of the bureaucrat, perhaps not incidentally in the historical moment in which the craze of the *physiologies* itself fizzled out. The author's dual appropriation and rejection of this popular literary phenomenon in *Les Employés* reveals, on a larger scale, his conscious self-positioning within the developing literary marketplace of the mid-nineteenth century.

Although Balzac's sales figures were lower than those of Sue's major best sellers, less consistent than those of de Kock, and less marketable than the small and large examples of panoramic literature, his fiction nonetheless ultimately gained critical acceptance: these now canonical works, of course, connote cultural capital. Yet Balzac was actively involved throughout his career in this marketplace of commercial literature, the same one he would pan in *Illusions Perdues* and work to position himself against. He recirculated tropes that appealed to popular tastes, notably the typologizing tactics of the *tableau* and *physiologie*, into his fiction, thus evincing engagement with and understanding of the formal elements that made his contemporaries successful. He both openly and anonymously contributed to the movement of panoramic literature even if he critiqued it and even if he (and contemporary critics) viewed his participation in the movement as distinct. In the novelistic instances I have presented, Balzac blends a direct appropriation of the popular tropes with a highly figurative rendering of these same tropes to reenact on the level of form the tensions between high and low, commercial and noncommercial, "good" and "bad." Like his former friend Sue, Balzac had an extensive network. He may have disdained their work, but he published with and benefited from the major players of the world of popular literature under the late Restoration and the July Monarchy. Reading Balzac in the context of his popular contemporaries allows us to reimagine his work as being in close dialogue with those with whom he vied for sales, at the same time as he made overt and formal attempts to distinguish his work from theirs. He may not have developed reliable formal strategies for attracting the numbers of readers that de Kock and, especially, Sue did at the height of his career. Yet Balzac nonetheless sold notably more than some of his critically accepted peers. Alfred de Musset and Théophile Gautier reached a maximum print run of 900 and 600 copies, respectively, while Balzac's relatively moderate prints runs topped 1,500 during the height of his career.[133] Balzac's professional practices and formal experiments, many of which he addresses in his novel on the book trade, *Illusions Perdues*, embody and illustrate this very developing book trade of the early to mid-nineteenth century. They also offer a more complicated view of what is commonly accepted as a starkly binary literary field.

CONCLUSION

THE "PHÉNOMÈNE MURIEL BARBERY"

Throughout this study readers may have noticed striking connections between the dynamism of the literary environment studied here and our own moment. Changes in the material, social, technological, political, economic, and cultural conditions of the early to mid-nineteenth century fostered what we might now recognize as the origins of the modern mass-media marketplace. This marketplace for culture in France would become more fully established by the end of the nineteenth century with near universal literacy, educational reforms, and an increasingly mature capitalist economy.[1] In addition to these and other material changes in the marketplace, both minor and major authors adapted strategies within their literary productions—negotiations on the level of plot, style, character, and other formal elements—to respond to (or question) popular tastes.

It is no secret that the late twentieth and early twenty-first centuries have also seen great shifts in the way books are conceived, written, published, marketed, sold, and read. The Internet has facilitated the mass dissemination and democratization of information, and of literature as well. Massive online booksellers like Amazon and digital advertising have changed our way of purchasing books; e-readers, tablets, and Google Books have changed the format in which we consume literature; social cataloguing platforms such as Good Reads have enabled new ways of networking and sharing information with other readers. While their fully globalized scale means these changes in the material conditions of literature can seem more epochal than those experienced by readers, writers, and book professionals in the early to mid-nineteenth century, contemporary studies of the publishing world echo their early nineteenth-century predecessors in citing "une crise majeure": the "bouleversement global de la lecture en France."[2]

If the nineteenth century saw the development of the individual entrepreneurial publisher into the creation of the publishing house, the establishment of major publishing conglomerates has been a more recent site of upheaval in the industry. As of 2016, Hachette Livre was the main distributor of books in France. Throughout the twentieth century it acquired many smaller publishing houses, including Hetzel in 1914 and Grasset in 1954, before becoming Hachette SA (*société anonyme*) in 1977.[3] It was then acquired in 1981 by Jean-Luc Lagardère of the Matra group (originally in aeronautics, automobiles, and telecommunications), now called the Lagardère Group. A subsidiary of this major media conglomerate, the firm now named Hachette Livre, continues to expand: it acquired Time Warner Book Group in 2006 and established the subsidiary company Hachette Book Group USA, now Hachette Book Group. The second largest publishing group, Editis, was created in 2004 from a percentage of assets of Vivendi Universal Publishing and owns major publishing brands like La Découverte as well as educational and reference books.[4] Amid these giants, smaller publishing houses continue to thrive in France: Gallimard and Éditions du Seuil are just two of them. Yet the larger shift from small publishing companies to major media groups has, unsurprisingly, had an effect on the book trade, altering practices such as the management of companies and the promotion of products. As Frédéric Dorel and Christine Evain put it, "La concentration rapide des structures éditoriales et des outils de commercialisation ainsi que les méthodes de gestion mises aux normes des grands marchés, ont donc provoqué nombre de bouleversements, en particulier l'émergence nouvelle d'un vaste marketing éditorial."[5]

In the face of these trends toward corporatization and synthesis, however, France's book professionals and government officials have attempted to maintain the notion that the status of a book differs from that of other commodities.[6] In 1981 France adopted the Loi relative au prix du livre or the "Loi Lang" (after Minister of Culture Jack Lang), which imposed fixed pricing on books in an effort to uphold the traditional bookstore as a vibrant part of local commerce. According to this law, prices of books—new, not used—are determined by the publisher and printed on the book's cover, and retailers are given only a small margin of flexibility in pricing (no more than 5 percent), thus preventing competition between large and small retailers.[7] This was viewed, in part, as a response to the book discounts at the retail chain FNAC (Fédération Nationale d'Achats des Cadres), founded in 1954, that had expanded quickly over the following decades.[8] Recent debates about the relative rights of large and local retailers resulted in the 2014 implementation of the so-called "Anti-Amazon" law in France, which prohibited the online bookstore from offering the free shipping and discounts that, critics argued, were undercutting sales of local booksellers. "Qu'à cela ne tienne," as Enguérand Renault of *Le Figaro* put it. Amazon's response was to charge one centime for shipping. The company also stymied sales of works published with Hachette by, among other tactics, disenabling quick shipping and certain ordering preferences.[9] In early 2015, however, a tentative peace was brokered; Amazon and Hachette were projected to "resume normal trading" with "Hachette books . . . prominently featured in promotions."[10] These legal proceedings show France's commitment to books and the difficulty of maintaining those commitments in the face of changing marketplaces.

Nowhere is the tension between cultural value and commercialism more clear than in the case of Gallimard, that bastion of literary prestige that Bourdieu has called the paradigm of "les grandes entreprises anciennes qui culmulent toutes les espèces de capital, économique, commercial et symbolique."[11] Because of competition with the larger publishing conglomerates, Gallimard depends for revenue on the "phénomène des best-sellers," blurring at times established notions of cultural and commercial capital.[12] In particular Gallimard's prominent Collection Blanche, "la grande collection de littérature," boasts contributing authors who, since its establishment in 1911, have received the Prix Goncourt, Prix Fémina, and Grands Prix du Roman de l'Académie française, among other literary prizes. Even this exclusive collection's cream-colored cover with familiar red and black type connotes prestige, and Gallimard's website calls its logo "le plus prestigieux générique de la littérature française du vingtième siècle."[13] Bourdieu highlights the value of the Gallimard brand citing "l'effet de label exercé par les couvertures."[14] Yet in the current marketplace the financial needs of this institution, coupled with its prestigious tradition, can at times force to the surface questions of value and taste.

Take, for example, three of Gallimard's highest selling novels from the years 2006 and 2007: *Harry Potter et les reliques de la mort* by J. K. Rowling, *Les Bienveillantes* by the Franco-American writer Jonathan Littell, and *L'Élégance du hérisson* by Muriel Barbery. It should come as no surprise that sales of the French translation of the final installment of the *Harry Potter* series, with an initial print run of 2.3 million copies and published in the series Gallimard Jeunesse, led Antoine Gallimard to comment that for his company 2007 had been an "année exceptionnelle."[15] Littell's work, a novel told from the perspective of an SS officer, had been the Collection Blanche's frontrunner for the 2006 *rentrée scolaire*, the season in book sales when many new books are released, largely to generate "une couverture médiatique" and just in time for the awarding of literary prizes.[16] In fact it went on to sell over 600,000 copies and win the Prix Goncourt. While *Harry Potter* and *Les Bienveillantes* fall easily into neat Bourdieusian cultural categories, (unrestricted and restricted, respectively, or "low" and "high"), the novel by Barbery, a professor of philosophy in her mid-thirties who had already published the moderately successful *La Gourmandise* with Gallimard in 2000, is harder to situate. It was published, like Littell's novel, in the Collection Blanche; like Rowling's best seller, it is in part a coming-of-age novel or even young adult fiction, and it ultimately sold 1.3 million copies in France alone. A popular author with credentials as a *philosophe agrégée*, Barbery is, however, decidedly not ranked by scholars and critics alongside France's elite contemporary authors.[17] Rather she is a liminal cultural figure, and her surprise success with *L'Élégance* challenges fixed categories in the contemporary literary field. Barbery also stages this ambiguous status throughout the novel itself; in this sense, the text evinces—in its plot and literary devices—the same tensions present in the works of some of the nineteenth-century authors examined in this book.

L'Élégance du hérisson was released in late August 2006, but critics cite the simultaneous release of Littell's novel as a factor in forestalling initial sales of Barbery's work: "Surtout, elle a longtemps été masquée par l'effet bulldozer des *Bienveillantes*, dont les 900 pages ont littéralement écrasé les autres livres en compétition l'an dernier."[18] It did not take long, however, for the "phénomène Muriel Barbery," as one reviewer in *L'Express* dubbed it, to take off.[19] Conventional wisdom has it that the novel's sales picked up steam due to word-of-mouth publicity. "En ce moment, tout le monde vous parle d'elle," wrote Alexandre Filon, a 2007 reviewer in *Madame Le Figaro*. "Votre belle-sœur, vos voisins, vos amis. Vous aussi, vous avez sans doute d'ailleurs déjà succombé au charme de Muriel Barbery."[20] A more recent reviewer in *Le Monde* wrote that due to this "bouche-à oreille progressif, une vague de fond irrésistible va très vite déférer sur les points de vente, au mépris de tous les prognostics."[21] The critics' responses show a justifiably clear sense of surprise: not only did the novel begin to sell out its initially low print runs, but sales figures reached the 600,000 mark by late 2007. A novel meant to be sold on a relatively short print run, *L'Élégance du hérisson* remained on best-seller lists for months. Against all odds it had transformed from a best seller into a "succès durable" or, as Gallimard's director of sales, Philippe le Tendre, put it, into a "long-seller: un livre qui, à la différence classique du best-seller, démarre lentement mais dure très longtemps."[22] A long-seller indeed: in 2016 Gallimard continued to list *L'Élégance du hérisson* as the Collection Blanche's number-one best seller. Barbery's novel was later translated by Europa Editions and sold more than 300,000 copies by 2009 and 900,000 copies by 2013 in the United States alone.[23] In this surprise hit—made popular not from conventional marketing tactics but by word-of-mouth promotion—Barbery exposes the variable nature of even our modern marketplace for literary culture.

The novel itself sheds light on its complicated position. The unanticipated best seller is narrated by two female protagonists: Mme Renée Michel, the concierge in a luxurious building on the Rue de Grenelle in Paris's seventh arrondissement, and Paloma Josse, a preadolescent girl living in one of these apartments. Renée is an autodidact whose interests range from Russian novelists and Flemish art to *The Hunt for Red October* (she tries, but fails, to enjoy phenomenology). Paloma is an "enfant surdouée" uninterested in turning out like the members of her family: her father is a "parlementaire socialiste"; her mother has a doctorate in literature but spends her days tending to plants; her sister, a self-important *normalienne*.[24] Paloma plans to commit suicide and burn down the building on her thirteenth birthday. Both protagonists hide their vibrant and intellectual inner lives in order to avoid arousing the suspicions of others. With Renée as narrator, we read accounts of her interactions in the building, her furtive attempts to dissimulate her intellect from her employers, and passages in which she theorizes about art, philosophy, film, and culture. With Paloma, we learn snippets about her daily life through entries in her "journal du movement dans le monde" and her "pensées profondes," in which she observes her surroundings, trying to make sense of whether or not she should enact her plan.[25] The two do not interact for over three-quarters of the novel, yet a sort of virtual kinship forms between them in the eyes of the reader through their many shared interests and ways of negotiating life at 7 Rue de Grenelle. When a new tenant, Kakuro Ozu, moves in, both protagonists begin to let down their guard: Renée enjoys meaningful discussions with him; Paloma meets an adult who engages sincerely with her and does not make her fear growing older. Paloma and Renée discover too that they are "âmes soeurs."[26] Both protagonists begin to envision a fulfilling future, and when Renée dies in an accident with a laundry truck, Paloma vows not to kill herself but rather, inspired by Renée, to continue her search for "la beauté dans ce monde."[27] As this summary makes clear, an antagonism between the categories of value that Bourdieu juxtaposes lies at the very heart of the plot of this novel.

The book's curious title comes from Paloma, who characterizes Renée in the following way: "Mme Michelle, elle a l'élégance du hérisson: à l'extérieur, elle est bardée de piquants, une vraie forteresse, mais j'ai l'intuition qu'à l'intérieur, elle est aussi simplement raffinée que les hérissons, qui sont des petites bêtes faussement indolentes, farouchement solitaires et terriblement élégantes."[28] Paloma herself is also like a hedgehog: brooding on the outside, full of grace on the inside. Part of the book's appeal, in fact, is the eventual peeling off of the characters' rough layers to expose the "elegance" that their reader has come to appreciate. Its appeal also lies in its (arguably clichéd) tropes: two outsiders finding friendship in one another; the arrival of a third party to disrupt the existing order. Barbery's use of an apartment-house plot in *L'Élégance du hérisson* is also familiar, especially to readers of nineteenth-century literature.[29] With some nuances, *L'Élégance*'s apartment story conforms to the genre as laid out by Sharon Marcus: "The apartment-house plot . . . combines the salon novel's emphasis on domestic interiors and microscopic social networks (think *Le Père Goriot*) with the urban novel's emphasis on chance encounters, the interplay between isolation and community, and the sudden transformation of strangers into kin."[30] Barbery's use of this recognizable organizing principle makes visible traces of Balzac and even de Kock in this interior, modern urban novel.

Barbery's style is also, like the hedgehog, "simplement raffinée."[31] Though it contains digressive passages on Husserl and Tolstoy, these more metaphysical parts, themselves written in an accessible manner, are mixed with less cerebral ones. There are comedic scenes (Renée is confounded by Kakuro's Japanese-style toilet) and romantic ones (Renée's practical but tender relationship with her late husband; an evening out with Kakuro). Both narrators delve into the quotidian details of their lives (the food they eat, the habits of their cats); at times these details are pregnant with meaning. Barbery's novel is thus a fine-tuned blend of "high" and "low" culture, and in fact the two narrators address this bathos in their own lives: Mme Michel expounds at length upon her particular blend of tastes, a "mélange brutal entre des oeuvres respectables et d'autres qui l'étaient beaucoup moins," and puts these tastes on display as she freely quotes, for example, *Anna Karenina* and rap songs by Eminem.[32] Paloma balances drinking her mother's *thé au jasmine* (jasmine tea) as she reads her mangas: she calls this "l'élégance et l'enchantement."[33] Barbery consciously stages the dynamics of value in the novel's content and form, in addition to, of course, the questions of class that underpin its plot. This balancing act between elite and popular culture that Barbery exposes throughout the novel can also be said to reflect the position of this novel itself within the contemporary literary market: it is endowed with prestige by virtue of its publication in Gallimard's Collection Blanche and was awarded the Prix des Librairies, the Prix des Bibliothèques pour tous, the Prix Georges Brassens, and the Prix Rotary International, yet unlike Littell's best seller of the same year, which it outsold by almost double, *L'Élégance* did not receive distinction from France's most elite prize-awarding institutions. Barbery's novel, in other words, strikes a balance between the "commercial" and the "aesthetic" both in the form and content of the novel itself and in the conditions of its publication.

It is not always possible to predict what will make a book a best seller, yet critics and readers have pointed to and ruled out promotional and formal factors that may have helped Barbery reach and appeal to such wide audiences. For example, though contemporary French mainstream media provides many forums for authors to discuss and publicize their work, Barbery—unlike Littell—did few media appearances to promote her novel, thus gaining the reputation of a shy, reclusive figure, much like her protagonists.[34] One wonders if this lack of public appearances generated intrigue about the author that translated into sales. Barbery's husband, Stéphane, speculated that the secret of the novel's commercial success was that it was "un livre que les gens offrent comme cadeau à leurs amis," prompting one reviewer in *L'Express* to create the term "gift-seller" in describing the novel.[35] It was, in this sense, a commodity with almost universal appeal.

In terms of the novel's content, reviewers linked the popularity of *L'Élégance du hérisson* to a number of factors, one of which was its uplifting qualities. The novel was unique in that it was touching and inspirational but not sappy. Catherine Simon of *Le Monde* appreciated this balance, writing, "Des livres qui ont de l'émotion, sans être mièvres ni nombrilistes, il n'y en a pas tant que ça."[36] Other reviewers appreciated its keen but not overly scathing satire, a trait the FNAC's website describes as "satire sociale à l'humour tendre."[37] The novel's straightforward class politics also appealed to audiences. In what was actually a condemnation of the novel, a review in the left-leaning *Libération* explained its popularity by asking rhetorically, "Comment ne pas aimer un livre avec lequel il est impossible de n'être pas d'accord et où il est difficile de ne pas s'attendrir sur le miroir qu'ils vous tend."[38] As with the popular *physiologies* whose caricatures were realistic but exaggerated enough so that no one recognized himself or herself in them, this critic suggests "aucun riche ne se sentira menacé par les caricatures qui en sont faites."[39] Through these somewhat stereotyped characters, then, the author of *L'Élégance* is relying on a literary strategy perfected during the advent of commercial literature to reach a wide audience. The novel is perfectly pitched, we might conclude, to be moving, humorous, and critical, but just enough to still be enticing to everyone.

In addition to commenting on its formal qualities, reviewers almost universally called attention to the popularity of the novel and Barbery's newfound status as a popular writer; this consciousness about the novel's success itself may have generated more sales. Reviewers noted that *L'Élégance* had propelled her "parmi les meilleurs auteurs populaires" and described its unexpected sales as a "phénomène d'édition."[40] The enthusiasm of Barbery's fans was played up in reviews: descriptions of copies flying off the shelf "à 4,000 exemplaires par semaine" and a book signing during which "le stand Gallimard a été pris d'assaut" no doubt animated more readers to participate in the phenomenon.[41] Recalling the nineteenth-century critics who evoked the near universal consumption of Sue's *Mathilde* and *Les Mystères*, one of Barbery's reviewers in *Madame Le Figaro* joked that only those who "auraient vécu à l'étranger ou sous terre ces derniers mois" would need to avail themselves of his plot summary.[42] The commercial success of the novel—its impressive sales and the duration of its popularity—led one critic to claim that "le 'Hérisson' représente le rêve de tout éditeur."[43] If editors of the Collection Blanche had not initially banked on such a huge hit, especially during the same *rentrée* as *Les Bienveillantes*, the commercial triumphs of *L'Élégance* only redounded to their credit while also exposing the changing and fluid nature of taste.

Barbery is certainly not the only example of a surprise best seller in today's marketplace for literature, but her novel stages particularly clearly the still-shifting categories of value in the literary field. It was released the same year and in the same prestigious collection as *Les Bienveillantes*, the eventual Goncourt winner, and despite containing lengthy passages on philosophy and engaging openly with questions of aesthetics and culture (thereby connoting a more overtly intellectual status), its subsequent sales dwarfed Littell's, while not quite reaching the same level as Rowling's. By maintaining an equilibrium between the high (aesthetic, metaphysical) and the low (popular culture, commercial), Barbery is not a twenty-first-century corollary to authors like de Kock or Sue, who, if in different ways, almost exclusively produced plot-driven narratives, at times repurposing these plots and characters across different media. Those authors, as well as many of the contributors to the panoramic literary works, might be more akin to contemporary writers working in and repurposing text across different media platforms: think of a blogger turning her work into a novel or podcast or film, or vice versa.[44] Yet like her nineteenth-century predecessor Balzac, whose works testified on the level of form to the difficulty of balancing between commercial and elite impulses, "high" and "low" ambitions, Barbery makes manifest her book's ambiguous status in the literary field. As the marketplace for fiction has developed from the period of the late Restoration and the July Monarchy to the present moment, authors have responded to changing commercial demands using calculated professional strategies—but also formal ones. These formal tactics vary from author to author and have an unpredictable degree of success, as the career of Eugène Sue exemplifies. *Mastering the Marketplace* emerges from the conviction that tracking developments in taste requires not just histories of reading and studies of the material developments of the marketplace but also close analysis of the literature being sold. As debates over online book sales and media conglomerates persist, and as the forms and formats in which books themselves are consumed evolve, authors will continue to test new formal strategies, aesthetic efforts to adapt to the marketplace of culture, and attempt to distinguish themselves within it.

Source Acknowledgments

Portions of chapter 1 were previously published as "*La Grande Ville*: Parisian Observations in the Urban Guides and Novels of Paul de Kock" in *Dix-Neuf* 13 (October 2009): 22–35 and can be found at Taylor and Francis online: http://www.tandfonline.com/doi/10.1179/147873109791499100.

Portions of chapter 2 were previously published as "Paul de Kock and the Marketplace of Culture" in *French Forum* 39, nos. 2–3 (2014): 97–112.

Portions of chapter 4 were previously published as "'[Le] Besoin de définir' and 'le danger de s'embrouiller': Balzac's *Les Employés* and the *physiologies*" in *Dix-Neuf* 20, no. 2 (2016): 162–75 and can be found at Taylor and Francis online: http://www.tandfonline.com/doi/10.1080/14787318.2016.1184849.

Notes

INTRODUCTION

1. Denis, "Paul de Kock," 45. "Become like Paul de Kock." Unless otherwise documented, all translations are mine.
2. Fougère, "Paul de Kock face à la postérité," 9. "What I am writing at present risks becoming like Paul de Kock if I don't give it a profoundly literary shape."
3. Guise, "Balzac et le roman-feuilleton," 322. "Paul de Kock in satin and sequins."
4. Guise, "Balzac et le roman-feuilleton," 312. "I'm doing purely Sue-like work."
5. According to Allen, "the book trade moved from a traditional artisanal craft to a more modern industry in consumer goods by the middle of the nineteenth century. . . . Printers adopted stereotyped plates and mechanical presses that permitted the mass production of classical and popular titles well before 1850." Among other technological developments, Allen counts late eighteenth-century inking techniques, stating that "although eighteenth-century modifications to the hand press made traditional printing more efficient, they did not affect production as radically as the mechanical press built first by William Nicolson, the inventor of the rubber ink roller in 1790" (*Popular French Romanticism*, 103, 112). See also Barbier, "L'industrialisation des techniques."
6. Critics studying the later part of the century, like Lyons and Allen, also credit Jules Ferry's legislation in the 1880s with contributing to mass readership at the end of the century; Mollier acknowledges this importance too but views these reforms as part of a continuum rather than an abrupt change. See Mollier, "Les Lois scolaires de Jules Ferry au miroir de l'histoire."
7. Lyons, "New Readers in the Nineteenth Century," 316. By 1848, Allen reports, "the Paris Chamber of Commerce study stated that 87 percent of the *ouvriers* and 79 percent of the *ouvrières* were completely literate"; he concludes that "the simple ability to read in early nineteenth-century Paris must have been a widespread one, even if the ability to write was not" (*Popular French Romanticism*, 155, 158). See also Lyons, *Readers and Society in Nineteenth-Century France*.

8. Writers, Allen explains, took advantage of this market for financial gain: "Authors born at the turn of the century learned to profit in the literary marketplace" (*Popular French Romanticism*, 7).

9. Barbier, "L'industrialisation des techniques," 229; Barbaret, "Linking Producers to Consumers," 190.

10. As Anne-Marie Thiesse puts it, "L'abonnement collectif, la consultation payante (pour une somme très modique) dans les cabinets de lecture permettent toutefois aux journaux d'atteindre un public plus large que celui de leurs seuls acheteurs" ("Collective subscriptions, paid consultation (for a very modest sum) in the *cabinets de lecture* allowed newspapers to achieve a larger public than that of those who purchased it"). Describing the frequenting of lending libraries by the working class, Allen writes that "lending libraries constituted . . . the public's most accessible source of books [renting books] by the month, by the year, by the sitting, by the volume, or by the day for nominal fees, often as little as 10 centimes per title. This made access to books during the Restoration cheaper than a kilo loaf of bread, well within the means of the Parisian day-laborer who normally earned more than two francs a day." See Thiesse, "Le roman populaire," 457; Allen, *Popular French Romanticism*, 139.

11. Later in the century Louis Hachette, inspired by the British example, would create the *Bibliothèque des chemins de fer* series. Capitalizing on the developments in modern transportation, Hachette had kiosks installed in railway stations that sold works with different colored covers for ease of recognition for travelers who wanted to read on the train. See Martin and Martin, "Le mode des éditeurs."

12. Though this study focuses principally on the political *quotidiens* of the early to mid-nineteenth century, this same period also saw the proliferation of other types of periodicals, for example fashion magazines. In her article "Fashion Discourses in Fashion Magazines and Madame de Girardin's *Lettres parisiennes* in July-Monarchy France (1830–1848)," Hazel Hahn revisits the major fashion magazines of this period and studies them along with the role of advertising.

13. Martin, "La Publicité," 1042. "Entrance of advertising in the press"; "the market for advertisements came together." In 1845 Charles Duveyrier would establish the Société générale des annonces, which standardized the formats and prices of advertisements.

14. De la Motte and Przyblyski, introduction, 2. See also Thérenty and Vaillant's *1836, L'An I de l'ère médiatique*.

15. De la Motte and Przyblyski, introduction, 2. See also Feyel, "Presse et publicité en France."

16. Thérenty, "The Fooliton," 36.
17. Queffélec, *Le Roman-feuilleton français au XIXe siècle*, 9. "A novel published in parts in the 'feuilleton' of the daily papers."
18. Prendergast, *For the People*, 1. According to Maria Adamowicz-Hariasz, "the success of *Les Mystères de Paris* not only made Sue a dominant figure in the literary market (1842), but also created a roman-feuilleton frenzy, as other newspapers and authors tried to profit from his success. . . . In the years 1842–47 the very existence of many papers depended on the success of the serial novels they published, as readers no longer based their decision to subscribe on papers' political affiliations, but on the kind of fictional works offered" ("From Opinion to Information," 164).
19. See Thiesse, *Le roman au quotidien*.
20. Thérenty describes this overlapping in the following way: "Le journal renvoie constamment à la littérature qui se situe dans un étrange rapport d'intériorité/extériorité par rapport à la presse" (The newspaper constantly refers to literature that has a strange relationship of interiority/exteriority with the press). Many authors, including Théophile Gautier and Jules Janin, straddled the line between journalist and writer (poet, novelist, etc.) as they published in and edited journals prolifically in addition to their other literary work; Patrick Berthier characterizes Gautier, for example, as an "écrivain journaliste" (writer-journalist). See Thérenty and Vaillant, *La Presse au XIXe siècle*, 369; Berthier, "Théophile Gautier journaliste," 443.
21. Haynes, *Lost Illusions*, 2, 9.
22. Haynes, *Lost Illusions*, 8.
23. Haynes, "The Politics of Authorship," 102.
24. Mollier, *L'Argent et les lettres*, 12. "Little by little these best-seller factories became businesses, managed intelligently or neglected depending on each case . . . cottage industries and amateurism often gave way to the attentive and astute management of big business."
25. Crubellier, "L'élargissement du public," 39. "The daily salary of a good worker." A new edition of Balzac's *Physiologie du mariage* was one of the first books sold in this format.
26. Martin and Martin, "Le mode des éditeurs," 181.
27. On the phenomenon of the collection, see Isabelle Olivero, *L'invention de la collection*.
28. "All That Is Associated with the Interests of Printing, Bookselling, Type Foundry, Paper Shops, Engraving, Music, Etc."
29. Jacqueline Melet-Sanson and Daniel Renoult explain, "Le décret napoléonien

du 14 octobre 1811 créant 'un journal d'annonces de toutes les éditions d'ouvrages imprimés ou gravés' est considéré comme fondateur de la bibliographie nationale courante officielle" (The Napoleonic decree of October 14, 1811, creating a 'publication announcing all the editions of printed or engraved works,' is considered as the foundation of the current official national bibliography), after the library's "dépôt légal" was suspended during the years following the Revolution of 1789. According to Mollier, the *Feuilleton* stemmed from "un besoin d'information et de communication croissante dans la société" (an increasing need for information and communication in society). See Melet-Sanson and Renoult, *La Bibliothèque nationale de France*, 111; Mollier, *L'Argent et les lettres*, 57.

30. According to Haynes, the *Feuilleton* "functioned as a bulletin board for the book trade" and enabled publishers to "undertake a number of collective activities" (*Lost Illusions*, 98).

31. *Feuilleton*, March 21, 1835. "Such a minimal portion."

32. See Chabrier, "De la chronique au feuilleton judiciaire."

33. *Feuilleton*, December 21, 1833, 3–4. "Can a bookseller publish articles already published in a periodical in another collection?"; "We will report on the decision that is made."

34. *Feuilleton*, March 8, 1834, 4. "Do the submissions required by the printer or the publisher by the decree of February 5, 1810, suffice for conserving the author's property rights? (Yes)."

35. *Feuilleton*, March 20, 1841, 7; *Feuilleton*, May 6, 1837, 7. "It is prohibited for a stenographer to publish a professor's lesson plans; such an act is legally considered counterfeiting"; "Any author who has entered into agreement with a bookseller over the composition of a work is obliged to deliver a readable copy and to correct the proofs himself, under penalty of the termination of agreement."

36. Lyon-Caen, *La lecture et la vie*, 23.

37. Cohen, *The Sentimental Education of the Novel*, 28.

38. See Terni, "A Genre for Early Mass Culture," 222.

39. Lyon-Caen, *La lecture et la vie*, 46. "The denigration of the modern novel and the return to history . . . as one of the most efficient ways to disqualify the novel."

40. As Allen notes, "Balzac, Dumas *fils*, Sand, Hugo and Zola, among others, are known to have prepared review copies of works by close personal friends" (*Public French Romanticism*, 13).

41. Glinoer, "Critique donné(e), critique prostitué(e) au XIXe siècle," 30. "A

professional man of letters who, to survive, had to sell the product of his work to the publishers and newspapers."

42. Lyon-Caen, *La lecture et la vie*, 60–1. "Literary grandeur"; "the most conservative aesthetic and moral positions."

43. Sainte-Beuve recognized that writing has been a profession since the advent of printing, so this concept of "littérature industrielle" is not necessarily a new one. Yet for him it has reached a fever pitch: "La littérature purement industrielle s'affiche crûment" (Purely industrial literature crudely flaunts itself). Sainte-Beuve's commentary was also not a singular expression of displeasure with the state of contemporary literature but rather the culmination of previous discussions: for Anthony Glinoer, "Sainte-Beuve absorbe et reproduit tout un discours social désormais admis" (Sainte-Beuve absorbs and reproduces an entire already-accepted social discourse). See Sainte-Beuve, "De la littérature industrielle," 677; Glinoer, "Classes de textes et littérature industrielle dans la première moitié du XIXe siècle," 3.

44. Sainte-Beuve, "De la littérature industrielle," 679. "Invaded, exploited, reclaimed as rightful owner by such a numerous, disparate and almost organized gang as we see them today and with this single motto inscribed on the flag: Live as a writer."

45. Sainte-Beuve, "De la littérature industrielle," 681. "Why not me too, everyone asks themselves?"

46. Sainte-Beuve, "De la littérature industrielle," 691. "Let us try to advance and to develop this judgment by extracting the good [literature] and by firmly limiting the other."

47. Glinoer, "Classes," 3. "Another literature, dedicated to rareness, inspiration, hard work and esthetic excellence."

48. Nettement, "Études critiques sur le roman feuilleton," 1. "Literary disorder." He attributes this "disorder" to "la naissance de la presse à 40 francs, à l'existence de laquelle l'existence du feuilleton-roman est intimement liée" (the birth of the 40 franc press, the existence of which is intimately connected to the existence of the serial novel [2]).

49. Nettement, "Études critiques sur le roman feuilleton," 3, 18. "Below the level of civilization"; "inundated by its sewers."

50. Of the *Mystères de Paris*, Nettement wrote, "C'est vous dire que les Mystères de Paris échappent à l'analyse. Analyser en effet c'est extraire d'un livre les idées principales en émondant les détails et en supprimant les épisodes. Or comment supprimer les détails là où il n'y a que des détails. Comment laisser de côté les

épisodes quand tout est épisodique dans un ouvrage" (All this to say that *Les Mystères de Paris* escapes analysis. Analysis is, effectively, extracting from a book the primary ideas while pruning the details and eliminating the episodes. But how does one eliminate the details when all there is are details. How does one put aside the episodes when everything in a work is episodic). About Alexandre Dumas's contemporaneous publication *Le Comte de Monte Cristo*: "Comment l'art trouverait-il sa place dans ce chaos, où tout est faux, arbitraire, en dehors de la nature et de la vérité?" (How will art find its place in this chaos where all is fake, arbitrary, and outside of nature and truth? [*Études Critiques*, 249, 407]).

51. Bourdieu, *The Rules of Art*, 24, 121, 58.

52. In the context of Spanish culture, Stephanie Sieburth has discussed the high/low distinctions still relevant in the contemporary discipline of cultural studies. In *Inventing High and Low* she writes that we have "progressed very far from the nineteenth-century critics who inveighed against mass cultural fictions without reading them or consulting those who did, and we have gotten past the dead end of the apocalyptic criticism of Horkheimer and Adorno, who could similarly be accused of not understanding some of the forms they anathematized in the 1940s. But studies of the relationships among different kinds of cultural production that do not resort to the limiting and falsifying categories of 'high' and 'low' are still in their infancy" (9).

53. Cohen, *The Sentimental Education of the Novel*, 21, 6. An early work outside of French studies, Janice Radway's 1984 *Reading the Romance*, also examines the tastes and reading practices of the consumers of romance novels.

54. See Moretti, *Graphs, Maps, Trees* and *Distant Reading*.

55. Bolter and Grusin, *Remediation*, 55.

56. Garvey, "Scissorizing and Scrapbooks," 224.

57. See Whidden, *Models of Collaboration in Nineteenth-Century Literature*, 6. For a recent, in-depth analysis of the of the work of Alexandre Dumas, his life, and celebrity, see Daniel Desormeaux's *Alexandre Dumas, fabrique d'immortalité*.

58. For recent studies on Delphine de Girardin, see Catherine Nesci's "Feuilletons sans frontieres?" and her *Le flâneur et les flâneuses*.

1. POPULAR PANORAMAS

1. *La Presse*, May 5, 1842, 4. "52 deliveries of 16 pages apiece, 'jésus vélin' paper, embellished with four to six sketches by Andrew, Best and Leloir, and inserted in the text." The term *jésus vélin* refers to a fine paper in a standard French format from this period. I am grateful to Mitch Fraas for his assistance with these terms.

2. *La Presse*, May 5, 1842, 4. "Two beautiful in-8° volumes on 'jésus vélin' paper decorated with a rich cover printed in color and drawn by Victor Adam." A way of indicating how many times the paper on which the text was printed had been folded and thus the size of the book: books in octavo format were of medium size, smaller than books *in-folio* or *in-quarto*, larger than books in-12 or in-16. Gérard Genette explains that "au début du XIXe siècle, où les grands volumes étaient devenus plus rares, la différence de dignité passait entre les in-8 pour la littérature sérieuse et les in-12 et plus petit pour les éditions bon marché réservées à la littérature populaire" (*Seuils*, 23; "at the beginning of the nineteenth century when large volumes were becoming rarer, the difference in prestige ran from the in octavo format for serious literature to books in the in-12 format and smaller for cheap works of popular literature"). The physical size of the text therefore implies seriousness or at least a higher quality in the content of *La Grande Ville*.

3. Benjamin, *Charles Baudelaire*, 18. The painted panorama was a representation generally of a historical scene or a landscape, hung on the walls of a rotunda and illuminated from above. It allowed viewers either a "total immersion in history," as Maurice Samuels has argued, or conveyed "absolute dominance," in the words of Bernard Comment. See Samuels, *The Spectacular Past*, 33; Comment, *The Painted Panorama*, 19.

4. On the question of the "scientific" origins of the *physiologies*, according to Andrée Lhéritier, "Le mot physiologie n'avait plus à ce moment . . . aucune valeur sémantique originelle" (At that point the word "physiology" no longer had any of its original semantic value). Richard Sieburth develops this concept further: "If the very title of the *Physiologie* evokes a tradition of confident scientific materialism . . . the inventors of contemporary social types found in these little books would seem rather to derive from the various *études de moeurs* which were quite popular with the growing reading public of the late eighteenth-century and early nineteenth-century." The authors of the *physiologies*, in other words, were by no means engaged in what they deemed to be true physiological studies of society. See Lhéritier, "Les Physiologies," 2; Sieburth, "Same Difference," 164.

5. For Lhéritier, the *physiologie*'s "ton humoristique, plaisant, parfois satirique, convient à ces textes légers qui traitent la plupart du temps des travers et ridicules de certains types sociaux ou des mœurs et coutumes de l'époque" ("Les Physiologies," 9; the *physiologie*'s humorous, amusing, and at times satirical tone works for these light reads that mostly address the quirks and absurdities of certain social types or of the morals and customs of the time). Announcements of the

publications in the *Le Charivari* tended to underscore their comic nature. An article in the February 4, 1842, issue, for example, disclosed the publication of *La Physiologie du viveur*, explaining, "Ce petit manuel de l'art de bien vivre est plein de joyeux préceptes, de piquants aphorismes, de spirituelles saillies et d'ébouriffantes anecdotes. Le rire est chose si bonne et si douce, que plus de 3,000 exemplaires ont été vendus hier" (This little manual on the art of good living is full of merry guidelines, juicy aphorisms, amusing witticisms and astounding anecdotes. Laughter is such a good and pleasant thing that more than 3,000 copies were sold yesterday).

6. According to Richard Sieburth, Philipon's journals "regularly featured satirical physiological vignettes, the most celebrated being Philipon's *Portrait-charge* of Louis-Philippe in the shape of a pear, which in turn inspired Peytel's *Physiologie de la poire* (1832), often cited as the first example of the genre that was to become so successful a decade later" ("Same Difference, 165).

7. See Sandy Petrey's *In the Court of the Pear King*.

8. See Terni, "A Genre for Early Mass Culture," 222.

9. Ferguson, *Paris as Revolution*, 55.

10. See Le Men, "La 'littérature panoramique' dans la genèse de *La Comédie humaine*. Between 1781 and 1788 Mercier, a prolific playwright, essayist, and poet, wrote *Le Tableau de Paris*, a text comprising multiple short scenes of Parisian life, ranging in subject from "Latrines" to "Noblesse," from "Très haut et très puissant seigneur" to "Filles publiques." A revolutionary representation of Paris, as Jeffrey Kaplow has put it, attempted to "tout voir, tout décrire, faire de tout la matière de la littérature" (introduction to *Le Tableau de Paris* 10; "see everything, describe everything, and to make literature from all this material"). Priscilla Ferguson calls his work in *Le Tableau de Paris* a "proclamation that points ahead to the journalistic principles and the realist practice of the next century," and Anthony Vidler has read *Le Tableau* as "a model for poetic flâneurs" and a dramatic restaging of the experience of the citizen in the city. Mercier's work set the scene not only for some of the major literary movements of the nineteenth century but for the massive body of work that attempted to capture the rapidly changing city and its inhabitants produced throughout the nineteenth century as well. See Ferguson, *Paris as Revolution*, 52; Vidler, "Reading the City," 273.

11. Victoria Thompson underscores the class difference between those who purchased the *physiologies* and those who purchased their larger counterparts, stating that the *physiologies*, "written primarily by middle-class authors, were designed for a middle-class audience. While those in its upper ranks bought the lavishly bound

multi-authored *tableaux*, the inexpensive *physiologies* had a broader middle-class audience" ("Telling 'Spatial Stories,'" 524).

12. Cohen, "Panoramic Literature," 233.

13. See Judith Lyon-Caen, Richard Terdiman, Richard Sieburth, Nathalie Preiss, and Priscilla Ferguson. More recently Aimée Boutin has written, "By pinning identities down, and connecting social class with fixed, visible signs such as clothing or accessories, these 'physiologies' and similar visual/verbal texts promised a logical, 'natural' taxonomy through which to understand urban spaces and social groups in the face of a rapidly changing, unsettling, multifaceted city" ("'The Title of Lawyer Leads Nowhere!,'" 59).

14. For example, Parent-Duchâtelet's *La Prostitution à Paris au XIXe siècle* or Honoré-Antoine Frégier's *Des Classes dangereuses de la population dans les grandes villes et des moyens de les rendre meilleures.*

15. Lyon-Caen, "Saisir," 323. "Panoramic literature, novels, and social investigations from the July Monarchy thereby form a textual proximity that blurs the lines of genre and register."

16. As Karlheinz Stierle has shown convincingly, by using the title *Tableaux Parisiens*, Baudelaire was not only openly citing the literary tradition of the *tableaux de Paris*, but he "could be sure that the contemporary reader of his poetry would be familiar with this background, the intertextual relation, established with the title of 'Tableaux Parisiens.'" In other words, not only did Baudelaire revisit and reimagine themes already present in the various nineteenth-century *tableaux de Paris*, such as that of the *flâneur* and the *passant*, but his theories of modernity explored in the *Fleurs du mal* and, in more detail, in *Le Peintre de la vie moderne* can also be seen as stemming from the tradition of the *tableaux de Paris*. According to Stierle, "Baudelaire's poetry of the city . . . is not a spontaneous and unmediated reflection of his own experience. This experience is mediated by a given literary genre, that of the *tableau de Paris*, and this genre itself is reflected theoretically in the context of a theory of modernity which provides an aesthetic justification for passing from a genre of feuilletonistic subliterature to the level of poetry" ("Baudelaire and the Tradition of the *Tableau de Paris*," 345, 353).

17. Benjamin, *Charles Baudelaire*, 170. This reading is reiterated in Richard Sieburth's seminal article on the *physiologies* in which he deems them to be of a "numbing banality" ("Same Difference," 186). Adherence to Benjamin's reading is likely due, in large part, to the critic's groundbreaking studies on nineteenth-century Paris that significantly impacted works on nineteenth-century culture from a wide range of disciplines. See Harvey, *Paris, Capital of Modernity*; Higonnet,

Paris, Capital of the World; Ferguson, *Paris as Revolution*; Weschler, *A Human Comedy*. All these scholarly works acknowledge their indebtedness to Benjamin's characterization of Paris as the "capital of the nineteenth century."

18. Lauster, *Sketches of the Nineteenth Century*, 3–4.

19. Preiss and Stiénon, "'Croqués par eux-mêmes,'" 10. "Privilege not fragmentary writing but fractioned and detached writing, not the whole."

20. See Valérie Stiénon's "La vie littéraire par le kaléidoscope des Physiologies."

21. For example, for a reading of how the 1842 *Physiologie de l'omnibus* captured the ambiguous social and cultural responses to this modern means of transportation, see Masha Belenky's "From Transit to Transitoire: The Omnibus and Modernity."

22. According to Richard Sieburth, far from hiding their commerciality, these works "often allude to the new marketplace conditions which have transformed the author into producer and the reader into consumer" ("Same Difference," 167).

23. Sieburth, "Same Difference," 167.

24. Benjamin, *Charles Baudelaire*, 36; Sieburth, "Same Difference," 167.

25. See Lhéritier, "Les Physiologies."

26. Lhéritier, *Les Physiologies*, 381. "The constant presence of the same in-32 format with the same number of pages (around a hundred), the same price, 1 franc, a relatively good deal at this time."

27. In his book *The Spectacular Past*, Maurice Samuels examines this notion of mastery, not in the context of classifying social types but in terms of history: "By simulating total historical vision, by making details of the past visible with an unimagined degree of specificity, the new spectacles of history purported to reassure spectators that a difficult past could be known and mastered." For Samuels, then, it is not only the present that early July Monarchy writers strove to comprehend fully, to master, but the recent revolutionary past as well. Samuels makes this link—in reverse—when he mentions the physiologies as one of "numerous representational practices [that] posited the detection of visible signs as the key to knowledge in early nineteenth-century France" (8, 8n23).

28. Huart, *Physiologie du flâneur*, 6. "A two-footed animal, without feathers, wearing a coat, smoking and idling."

29. Huart, *Physiologie du flâneur*, 7. "Waste his time."

30. Saint-Amand and Stiénon, "Lectures littéraires du document physiologique," 161. "The editorial imperatives for collections meant to create a loyal readership and invoke stylistic trends."

31. Richard Sieburth calls this a "more or less parodic spoof of the entire genre" ("Same Difference," 169).

32. "GONE TO PRESS. . . . The abundance of material makes us balk at this ad!"

33. *Physiologie des Physiologie*, 6. "This is a goldmine / One says to oneself / One at a time / Before getting out of here / I'm also going to go churn out / My physiology, Oh ho! My physiology."

34. *Physiologie des Physiologies*, 6–7. "A work that is completed in just a few moments"; "If I had only ink and paper I would bet you / that before tomorrow / I could easily describe the entire human race / in a physiology."

35. Amossy, "Types ou stereotypes?," 118. "The main value of these little books lies in how easily they are sold on the market."

36. *Physiologie des Physiologies*, 7. "Mushrooms after rain"; "Every man wished to have his own physiology."

37. *Physiologie des Physiologies*, 6. "No longer cause excitement"; "The readers have had enough, their luck has run out."

38. *Physiologie des Physiologies*, 8. "On this happy day, long live the physiology."

39. *Physiologie des Physiologies*, 23, 28. "Thanks to these little books, made of wit and science, man will be better classified, divided and subdivided than his brothers the animals"; "Take a pinch of Labruyère—a spoonful of *Les Lettres Persannes*. Add *Les Guêpes*; *Les Papillons noirs*; *Les Lettres Cochinchinoises*; *La Revue Parisienne*; *les Nouvelles à la main*; Toss in the feuilletons of *Le Corsaire* and *Le Charivari* and wrap it all up in the *Français*, as invented by M. Curmer."

40. Stiénon, "La vie littéraire par le kaléidoscope des Physiologies," 5. "Basic ingredients, fairly easy to find"; "Mockery of the uncreated creator"; "Creator-genius."

41. For the connection between the *physiologies* and the contemporary *enquêtes sociales*, see Lyon-Caen, "Saisir, décrire, déchiffrer."

42. *Physiologie des Physiologies*, 55. "Everyone recognizes in them the portrait of his neighbor and laughs at it. If he were to recognize himself, he would call it a scandal. That is why everyone waits so impatiently for his physiology . . . to recognize his neighbor and take pleasure in it, without ever recognizing his own self."

43. *Physiologie des Physiologies*, 43. "The term is composed of two Greek words, and it means the following: published in the in-18 format; composed of 124 pages, and any number of vignettes, of *cul-de-lampes* (tailpieces), of silly mistakes and chitter-chatter both done by people ignorant of their nature."

44. *Physiologie des Physiologies*, 96. "So much delicacy and wit of his time."

45. *Physiologie des Physiologies*, 96. "Done so well at furthering himself from the master."

46. *Physiologie des Physiologies*, 96. "In the one, the most exquisite, charming, delicate, gay wit; in these, the most fastidious, crude, heavy, thick wit."

47. *Physiologie des Physiologies*, 101. "The entire book is on the first page"; "physiologie of the dead man."

48. Stiénon, "Le canon littéraire au crible des physiologies," 133–36. "These monographs define themselves as illegitimate through a writing style that voluntarily shows their status as minor texts, uncomplicated texts, even texts of poor quality."

49. *Physiologie des Physiologies*, 23. "Physiologies—physiologies, and everything is a physiology"; "To call a book serious is meaningless today."

50. *Physiologie des Physiologies*, 30.

> Look here—You go into a bookstore and ask for a good book.
> What does the bookseller do?
> He offers you a *physiologie*.
> You push it away with contempt and you are correct to do so—But look around you.
> Scan the entire bookstore. Where are Molière, Racine, Corneille, Montesquieu, Fénalon, Chateaubriand, Lamartine, Hugo? In the back, in the depths of the shadows. They sleep, awaiting resurrection. But what are all those little books, colored in yellow . . .—blue,—red,—that are scattered pell-mell in the aisles,—that are piled on the tables up to the ceiling, and roll out in long lines—winding and unwinding like enormous serpents with changing scales? *Physiologies, physiologies*—and it is all *physiologies*!

51. *Physiologie des Physiologies*, 129, 126. "You have only sharpened your thirst"; "You would be blessed by cobblers, hat-makers and glove-makers—which is good; and you would be heavily paid for your works—which is better."

52. Saint-Amand and Stiénon, "Lectures littéraires du document physiologique," 75 "Counterprogrammatic"; "Its mediocrity, its facility, its commercial goals." Ruth Amossy too finds the criticism of the genre "acerbic," noting that the "*Physiologie des Physiologies* renchérit sur la dérisoire futilité du genre" ("Types ou stereotypes?," 119; "*Physiologie des Physiologies* has the last laugh about the ridiculous futility of the genre").

53. Saint-Amand and Stiénon, "Parodie de la science et réflexivité," 164.

54. "Physiologie des Physiologies," *La Caricature*, October 11, 1840, 4. "The physiology is the art of speaking and writing incorrectly, in the form of a little green, blue, red, or yellow book that does its best to extort a twenty-sous piece from each passerby and to bore him to his heart's content."

55. "Physiologie des Physiologies," *La Caricature*, October 11, 1840, 4. "You fill it with claptrap, one-liners, nonsense, dirty jokes, tangents, poppycock, frivolities. . . .

You sprinkle everything with solecisms, curses. . . . You copy *Les Guêpes* or *La Revue parisienne* for the cover . . . and you serve it up hot."

56. Cuno, "Charles Philipon, La Maison Aubert, and the Business of Caricature in Paris," 353.

57. Lhéritier, "Les Physiologies," 4. "Aubert, mostly by the quality of his illustrations, established himself as the true publisher of physiologies." Saint-Amand and Stiénon deem the "Physiologies-Aubert" "la plus representative de ces collections ("Parodie de la science et réflexivité," 161; "the most representative of these collections").

58. Cuno, "Charles Philipon, La Maison Aubert, and the Business of Caricature in Paris,"353.

59. Lhéritier, "Les Physiologies," 4. "It certainly seems that physiologies as they are presented to the public, in small format and containing multiple illustrated vignettes, were born from a journalist's idea. The invention can be credited to Philipon . . . and from all the productions of La Maison Aubert."

60. Cuno, "Charles Philipon, La Maison Aubert, and the Business of Caricature in Paris," 347, 348, 349.

61. Cuno notes that "*Le Charivari*, on the other hand, would be printed more freely than *La Caricature*; its prints, therefore, would be of lesser quality, and it would be made available to public establishments and those *amateurs* . . . at a more ordinary subscription price of sixty francs per year for the daily journal" ("Charles Philipon, La Maison Aubert, and the Business of Caricature in Paris," 351).

62. Cuno, "Charles Philipon, La Maison Aubert, and the Business of Caricature in Paris," 350.

63. As Cuno describes him, Philipon had a superior business sense. For example, though involved in and ultimately jailed over the infamous caricature of Louis-Philippe as a pear, he nonetheless scaled back on political critique when it was less appealing to the public: "It is the mark of Philipon's business sense that as soon as he recognized this fact he played down the political content of the prints published in his journals and by La Maison Aubert and emphasized rather their incidental and more commercially viable character" ("Charles Philipon, La Maison Aubert, and the Business of Caricature in Paris," 348).

64. Cuno, "Charles Philipon, La Maison Aubert, and the Business of Caricature in Paris," 347.

65. Lhéritier, "Les Physiologies," 4. "On the last page, one would often encounter advertisements for Aubert's collections and sometimes full-page reproductions of vignettes from the physiologies."

66. It should also be noted that this was not the first time Philipon used one of his publications to advertise another: "With each new issue of La Caricature, new publications of La Maison Aubert appeared and were similarly advertised" (Cuno, "Charles Philipon, La Maison Aubert, and the Business of Caricature in Paris," 352). On the distinction between the French terms *publicité* and *réclame*, see Hahn, *Scenes of Parisian Modernity*: "Advertising was understood by contemporaries not only as overt advertising but also as 'editorial advertising,' articles or illustrations created for the purpose of advertising, or articles that included advertising, and therefore appeared as forms of publicity" (5).

67. A *réclame* at the top of the page under "Librairie, beaux-arts et musique" confirms this. "*La Physiologie de l'étudiant*, qui vient d'être mise en vente par la maison Aubert, est appellée à obtenir un succès plus grand encore que *la Physiologie du Garde national*" (*La Physiologie de l'étudiant*, which has just been released by La Maison Aubert, is expected to be an even bigger success than *La Physiologie du Garde national*). This ad refers to the success of the previous installment in the physiologie series—and uses that success to promote the subsequent volume—but it does not make reference to the current vogue of these texts or to the abundance of works in the series.

68. *La Presse*, May 18, 1841. "The sensational collection of volumes in the in-18 format, created by MM Aubert and Co. who have published *La Physiologie de la lorette* as well as those of the *flâneur*, the *storekeeper*, the *entertainer*, and a large number of other works in the same genre."

69. *La Presse*, August 14, 1841. "It is the most fruitful of our authors, M. H. de Balzac, who has been willing to take on the task of describing the bureaucrat, and no one could have done it better"; "This collection of little *physiologies* is better than all others that are published these days." This particular *réclame* announces, "La spirituelle et amusante collection des petites physiologies publiées par M. Aubert vient de s'enrichir de deux nouveaux petits volumes" (The witty and amusing collection of short *physiologies* published by Mr. Aubert has just expanded to include two new little volumes). The other ads focused on the previous successes and the lively aspects of the *physiologie*; this one highlights its quality. Though the publication of Edouard Ourliac's *Physiologie de l'écolier* is also noted here, the advertisement for both of these physiologies places the name Balzac in large type in the upper left-hand corner, by far the largest word of the ad. In this case, as in the previous *réclame*, Aubert is relying on Balzac's renown to sell the *physiologie*; it is a rare example of the author rather than the title being used to promote the series.

70. *La Presse*, November 24, 1841. "It is essential not to confuse this wonderful publication with the hoard of bad books its success has spawned." This particular ad also features a depiction of Aubert et Compagnie's storefront, with passersby and clients lingering in front of the window to gaze at the prints. Jillian Taylor-Lerner has written about other examples of Aubert's depiction of its clients and storefront in ads in her article "The French Profiled by Themselves." The sketch she studies, a poster for the album *Paris-comique*, "indicates the specific urban and social spaces in which the publisher put his products and ads on view." Taylor-Lerner locates in this image—similar to that in the ad from *La Presse*—a "legible" depiction of the store's "middle-class clientele": "The makeup of Aubert's target public is clear" (17). Here too we see La Maison Aubert's keen understanding of its clientele and of the market for its products more generally. "With the help of his gifted brother-in-law Charles Philipon," Taylor-Lerner writes, "Aubert positioned himself as a pioneer and defender of the modern press, specializing in satirical newspapers, lithographic prints, and albums" (17). In her example, as well as the advertisement in *La Presse* we see evidence of this deliberate self-positioning.

71. *La Presse*, May 28, 1841. "The collection of twenty-five wonderful little volumes that can all be put under the title *Physiologie-Aubert*, so as to distinguish them from that mob of bad books its success has spawned."

72. Taylor-Lerner writes of the modularity of these panoramic forms, "Equally at home in literary anthologies, fashion journals, or caricature albums, they could be lucratively recombined and repackaged to create multiple product derivatives." This same phenomenon could be seen with the repackaging of authors' individual works into their collected works ("The French Profiled by Themselves," 10).

73. Lhéritier reiterates the idea that the familiar names of the contributors would have added to sales: "Toute cette publicité, les noms d'artistes tels que Daumier, Gavarni, bien connus des lecteurs du *Charivari*, ne purent que contribuer à imposer la collection Aubert" (*Les Physiologies*, 281; All this publicity, the names of artists like Daumier, Gavarni, who were familiar to the readers of *Le Charivari*, could do nothing but contribute to the dominance of Aubert's collection).

74. See Martin, "La Publicité."

75. Huart, *Physiologie du flâneur*, 29. "Susse, Martinet and Aubert"; "It is difficult to concentrate on a caricature and one's pocket at the same time." Susse was an art dealership and Martinet a publisher.

76. The text also includes a direct reference to "notre ami Ch. Philipon" and counsels

readers to buy "cinq exemplaires de la Physiologie du flâneur" (Huart, *Physiologie du flâneur*, 120; our friend Ch. Philipon; five copies of the *Physiologie du flâneur*).

77. Saint-Amand and Stiénon, "Parodie de la science et réflexivité," 165. "Encoding their readability according to the modes of consumption for the specific kind of literature, these texts insist on mentions that would serve the reading rooms and boutiques that circulated them."

78. *Paris, ou le livre des cent-et-un* (online).

79. *Paris, ou le livre des cent-et-un* (online). The book's publisher, Ladvocat, does indeed gesture toward a new style of book in the preface, which Cohen quotes in English: "This was 'a new book if ever there was one; new in its content, new in its form, new in its procedure of composition which makes it a kind of encyclopedia of contemporary ideas, the monument of a young and brilliant period'" ("Panoramic Literature and Everyday Genres," 229). Nonetheless Ladvocat cites a contemporary review of *Paris, ou le livre des cent-et-un* that claims one of the main reasons for the publication of this text is that "il faut faire pour le Paris d'aujourd'hui ce que Mercier a fait pour le Paris de son temps" (we must do for today's Paris what Mercier did for Paris in his own time), clearly situating the text in the tradition of Mercier. Additionally, in the preface of this book, entitled "Asmodée," Janin also calls the work "le nouveau Diable boiteux." In fact the work was initially to be entitled *Le Diable boiteux à Paris*. See *Paris, ou le livre des cent-et-un* (Ladvocat), vi, 14.

80. Cohen, "Panoramic Literature," 229.

81. Taylor-Lerner, "The French Profiled by Themselves," 10.

82. Taylor-Lerner, "The French Profiled by Themselves," 10. Taylor-Lerner analyzes the promotional strategies used by Curmer to sell *Les Français* and notes that "the new business model embraced by Curmer and his colleagues was extremely risky: these publishers invested substantial amounts of cash up-front, preparing unprecedented inventories of shelf-ready products for retail, and then scrambled to recuperate their costs as sales trickled in. Hence they needed to devise new forms of publicity and display in order to recommend and parade the inventories they could now so rapidly produce" (9).

83. This second volume contained a motley assortment of descriptions and anecdotes about Paris that blend Mercier's vignettes with the popular *physiologie*-style taxonomies and with realist fiction, including Balzac's long treatise on the press, an excerpt from his *Histoire naturelle du Bimane en société*; and Marc Fournier's and Eugène Briffault's respective short-story-style contributions,

"Les Canotiers de la Seine" and "Une actrice de Société: Chronique de l'Hôtel Castellane."

84. Kock, *La Grande Ville: Nouveau tableau de Paris*, 1–2. "A work of tremendous importance, written by the most popular novelist of our time"; "It is not a novel, but it also does not consist of simple tableaux: it is a huge comedy with one hundred different acts.... It is Paris as it is, as Paul de Kock, the most authentic, merriest, most observant author of our time, saw it."

85. *Le Charivari*, August 30, 1842. "The *Tableau de la grande ville*, whose vignettes are replacing our usual lithograph today, is a funny and faithful panorama of Paris. It speaks at once to our eyes and our minds: to our eyes through the sketches from the pencils of our most witty artists; to our minds through a keen, biting, and lively story, just as we have come to expect from the pen of Mr. Paul de Kock."

86. In light of Terdiman's analysis of each section of the daily paper under the July Monarchy, this favorable mention of de Kock's work could likely fall under "editorial publicity," a recommendation that "completely disguised its status as advertisement." According to Terdiman, editors such as Villemessant of *Le Figaro* were not satisfied with an issue unless "every single line within it had been bought and paid for in some way" (*Discourse/Counter-Discourse*, 124–25).

87. Kock, *La Grande Ville: Nouveau tableau de Paris*, 6. "Let us walk at random."

88. On the topic of Parisian literature, de Kock writes, "On a fait beaucoup d'ouvrages sur Paris; sans doute on en fera beaucoup encore!" (There have been many works on Paris, no doubt there are still more to come!). He goes on to explain, "Sans doute aussi, tout en cherchant à dépeindre la grande ville et ce qu'elle renferme de curieux, d'amusant ou de remarquable, nous oublierons bien encore quelque chose" (Without a doubt as well, in trying to depict the great city and the curious, entertaining or remarkable things within it, we will forget something else). On the concept of realism, he explains, "Nous décrirons ce que nous avons vu, c'est le meilleur moyen d'être vrai" (We will describe what we have seen; that is the best way to be realistic [*La Grande Ville ou Paris il y a vingt-cinq ans*, 1–2].

89. Kock, *La Grande Ville: Nouveau tableau de Paris*, 1. "It is not a novel, but it also does not consist of simple tableaux: it is a huge comedy with 100 varied acts."

90. This blending of styles is, for Cohen, "heterogenericity." She explains that this hybrid form is typical of the overarching genre she terms "panoramic literature": "That these authors write in a variety of genres is also an important characteristic of panoramic texts." She argues that this heterogenericity coincides with these multi-authored texts' "panoptic aims": "The panoramic text uses clearly

differentiated genres to represent differing social species" ("Panoramic Literature and Everyday Genres," 233).

91. Kock, *La Grande Ville: Nouveau tableau de Paris*, 61. "Let us listen rather to this conversation between two lovely ladies."

92. Kock, *La Grande Ville: Nouveau tableau de Paris*, 3. "It is only necessary to relate the facts; most authors have the flaw of always placing themselves between the reader and the subject at hand, as if to tell the reader: 'By the way, don't forget that I was the one who wrote this.'"

93. Kock, *La Grande Ville: Nouveau tableau de Paris*, 4. "What does all this do to the reader, who is hardly bothered to know how you came to write this or that work, but who only wants the work to amuse, instruct, or interest him?"

94. Kock, *La Grande Ville: Nouveau tableau de Paris*, 193. "Parisians are not the only ones to have their daguerreotype taken: foreigners who visit Paris don't want to leave without having tried out this invention."

95. Kock, *La Grande Ville: Nouveau tableau de Paris*, 41, 53. "You who warm your feet pleasantly before a good fire . . . a good bourgeois, a civil servant, a businessman, employed with a private income, all of you who without having a big enough fortune to charge your steward or your servants to handle the details of your house"; "You who, in order to get rich, think it is necessary to risk a lot of money." Here the narrator goes on to explain the advent of the *galette* to the uninformed reader, labeling the reader naive and assuming that it will be the role of the narrator to set him or her straight. The reader is thus cast in the position of the outdated, ignorant of vogues and trends, who will be updated by this modern narrator.

96. Ferguson, *Paris as Revolution*, 53.

97. Between 1848 and 1852, for example, though most of the overarching rubrics that comprised this section of the *Bibliographie* ("Théologie," "Jurisprudence," "Sciences et Arts," "Belles-Lettres," etc.) remained the same in 1848, a number of subcategory names were changed.

98. Occasionally a *physiologie* would be placed under the topic it explored. For example, the 1840 *Physiologie du théâtre* was classified under "Théâtre," while another 1840 publication, *Physiologie du chant*, was categorized as "Beaux Arts."

99. Lyon-Caen, "Saisir, décrire, déchiffrer," 323. "The *Bibliographie de la France . . .* rightfully puts panoramic literature and novels in the 'Belles Lettres' section and the *enquêtes sociales* in the 'Economics and Politics' subcategory of the 'Science and Art' section"; "Blur the borders of genres and registers."

100. Larousse, *Grand Dictionnaire Universel du XIXe Siècle*, 279. "The series of all

sorts of works that look at Paris from different points of view"; "Topographical descriptions, guides, maps, prints."

101. Larousse, *Grand Dictionnaire Universel du XIXe Siècle*, 279. "Where the list of all the works, serious or playful, that relate to the physiognomy of Paris and the physiology of its inhabitants is found."

102. Perhaps due to the fact that this bibliography was situated under the dictionary heading "Paris," only the physiologies with the word "Paris" in their title appear in this list: *Physiologie du provincial à Paris* (1841); *Physiologie du Parisien en Province* (1841); *Physiologie des rues de Paris* (1842).

103. *Paris, ou le livre des cent-et-un* (Ladvocat), v–ix. "This drama with 100 different acts; An encyclopedia of modern thought . . . the album of an ingenious and powerful literature."

104. In discussing the nineteenth century's interest in recording and dissecting society, Naomi Schor has characterized this tendency as the "obsessive desire to expose and inventory the real" ("'Cartes Postales,'" 215).

2. THE DE KOCK PARADOX

1. *Le Charivari*, April 12, 1842. "Praised by doorwomen and loved by *grisettes* / for whom his merry novels have immense appeal / Paul de Kock is also admired by the English / and this is understandable because his complete works / are not by a very good Frenchman."

2. Thérenty, *Mosaïques*, 668. "In an industrial manner: one novel after another, each month, year after year."

3. Fougère, "Paul de Kock face à la postérité," 8. "A particular figure in the literary field, that of the bourgeois writer."

4. As Benoît Denis indicates, the name "acquiert la valeur synonymique de 'mauvais style'" ("Paul de Kock," 45; earned the synonymic value of "bad style").

5. I thank Elizabeth Emery for noting the connection between Paul de Kock in the July Monarchy and Georges Ohnet in the last decades of the nineteenth century.

6. Mirecourt, *Paul de Kock*, 33. "The day that a novel by Paul de Kock went on sale there was a veritable riot in the bookstores."

7. Martin and Martin, "Le mode des éditeurs" 180. Even toward the end of his career, de Kock could be counted on to generate sales. According to his biographer Timothée Trimm, in 1865 "la *Petite Presse* monta de 50,000 par jour avec un roman de Paul de Kock, dont le principal héros était un portier" (*La Vie de Ch. Paul de Kock*, 4; the *Petite Presse*'s [readership] rose to 50,000 per day with a novel by Paul de Kock whose protagonist was a doorman).

8. Lyons, "Les Best-sellers," 392.

9. Allen, *Popular French Romanticism*, 94.

10. Martin and Martin, "Le mode des éditeurs," 152.

11. Stiénon, "Paul de Kock relu par les physiologies," 51. "Initial success at distribution"; "delegitimization of an aesthetic belittled for its simplicity and ribaldry"

12. His prominence as a popular novelist is recalled in Margaret Cohen's *Sentimental Education of the Novel*, in which she cites de Kock as being emblematic of the "roman gai." In *Apartment Stories*, Sharon Marcus devotes attention to his novel *La Demoiselle du cinquième* in her larger study of the apartment-house plot. In his 2001 *Readers and Society in Nineteenth-Century France*, Martyn Lyons refers repeatedly to de Kock's work in the context of literary best sellers with high circulation during the period he studies. Allen focuses on de Kock's writing and self-positioning strategies within the mid-nineteenth-century literary market in *In the Public Eye* and posits the novelist as cognizant of the historical shifts in the status of the author.

13. Lyon-Caen, *La lecture et la vie*, 36. "The description and the deciphering of the mechanisms of contemporary society." One exception is a 2011 volume entitled *Lectures de Paul de Kock*, edited by Florence Fix and Marie-Ange Fougère, composed of a number of French scholars' articles that I cite throughout this chapter.

14. In his own time de Kock was taken to task for his "licentious tableaus," as one 1841 reviewer called them. In the later part of the century critics referred to his "grossness and immorality," and the twentieth-century critic Legrand-Chabrier described his work as "'endiablé, excessif et lassant, pris à doses trop fortes, et tout le long d'une lente combinaison de petits faits vulgaires'" (frenzied, excessive and tiresome taken in overly strong doses, alongside a slow-paced collection of slightly crude occurrences). See Cherbuliez, *Revue Critique des livres nouveaux, publiés pendant l'année*, 1841, 2; Bowan, "Romans de Paul de Kock," 300; Fougère, "Paul de Kock face à la postérité," 15.

15. Cherbuliez, *Revue Critique des livres nouveaux, publiés pendant l'année 1837*, 77. "Within the narrow limits of a scene of 5 or 6 pages, it could have been very amusing, because the author excels at painting the absurdities and the idiosyncrasies of the Parisian bourgeoisie; but spread out over a volume, it loses all its value and is nothing but trivial and without wit."

16. Kock, *Un Homme à marier*, 4. "It was nearly five o'clock when Girardière entered into the restaurant."

17. Kock, *Un Homme à marier*, 90. "Now that you are sufficiently aware of M. Girardière's background, kindly return with him to the restaurant."

18. Kock, *Un Homme à marier*, 108. "And the respectable family . . . leaves after having taken care to carry off all of the toothpicks that had been put on the table."

19. Kock, *Un Homme à marier*, 108. "[Augustine's aunt] and her niece had also finished their dinner; they pay, Girardière does the same, and they all leave the restaurant together."

20. Lyon-Caen, *La lecture et la vie*, 35. "Does not aim for posterity, but rather addresses a readership anchored in the present for whom he composes a fictional guide to contemporary society."

21. According to Lyons ("Les Best-sellers"), Fleury's *Cathéchisme historique* was the most successful best seller between 1831 and 1835, selling 100,000 to 130,000 copies; Saint-Pierre's *Paul et Virginie* sold 21,000 to 26,000; La Fontaine's *Fables* sold 95,000 to 120,000.

22. Kock, *Le Cocu*, 3. "I am standing up at the entrance to the salon where I rarely stand for long."

23. Kock, *Le Cocu*, 6. "I am still holding my newspaper, but I am no longer reading it. I'm entertaining myself by considering all of the faces leaning over their pieces of printed paper. It would be a lovely tableau for a genre painter."

24. Kock, *Le Cocu*, 7. "The lamp must be right in front of him, his feet must have a chair to lean upon, and his snuffbox must be placed right next to his newspaper."

25. "The scarecrow of the reading room."

26. Kock, *Le Cocu*, 27. "Something to put him to sleep right away."

27. Kock, *Le Cocu*, 34. "And taking M. Bélan by the arm, I lead him far away from the reading room."

28. Kock, *Le Cocu*, 14. "Tableaux of manners, contemporary scenes."

29. Kock, *Le Cocu*, 14. "A novel that is over twenty years old . . . can not depict contemporary manners."

30. Lyon-Caen, *La lecture et la vie*, 28. "Inscribe their plots into a contemporary setting." Given this idea that a more than twenty-year-old novel cannot depict current mores, it is unsurprising and fitting that later twentieth-century editions of this novel have whittled the *cabinet de lecture* chapter to nearly one third of its original length. The 1925 edition (published by M.-P. Trémois) for example is substantially shorter than the original. A reading of the two chapters side by side shows obvious omissions in the later edition.

31. Kock, *La Jolie fille du faubourg*, 171. "Alexis parks himself on a chair that is against a bed on the other side of the room. After a moment, the conversation and the songs begin again as before the arrival of these men."

32. Cherbuliez, *Revue Critique des livres nouveaux, publiés pendant l'année 1840*, 107. "The true talent of Mr. Paul de Kock."

33. Kock, *La Jolie fille du faubourg*, 172. "Get-together . . . composed of seven young women including the mistress of the dwelling"; "two made flowers like Miss Julienne, one embroidered, one did tapestry work, another mended a beautiful shawl, and finally the last one held the pattern for the bodice of a dress that she turned over and over on her knees."

34. Kock, *La Jolie fille du faubourg*, 163. "It is precisely because I am reasonable that I like to frequent diverse social classes. Those who only want to see one deprive themselves of many curious and interesting tableaux of manners."

35. "Curious tableaux of manners."

36. Lyon-Caen, "Le romancier, lecteur du social dans la France de la Monarchie de Juillet," 5. "To decipher, to decrypt, to unveil, to represent the social world as a readable text, a visible landscape."

37. The narrator notes, for example, that "dans ce temps-là, Paris était bien différent de ce qu'il est aujourd'hui" (at that time, Paris was very different than it is today) and explains that though he does not purport to provide a full history of Paris, "nous avons pensé qu'il était nécessaire de rappeler au lecteur ce qu'était Paris à l'époque où notre barbier existait" (we thought it necessary to remind the reader what Paris was like at the time when our barber was alive). In typical de Kock fashion, the narrator goes so far as to draw a distinction between sixteenth-century social types and those from his own period: "Maintenant nous avons à Paris des artistes en cheveux, des coiffeurs et des perruquiers, mais nous n'avons plus de barbiers" (Kock, *Le Barbier de Paris*, 2–5; Now in Paris we have hair artists, hair stylists and hairdressers, but we no longer have barbers").

38. The author seems to have been so unable to resist these digressions in his works situated in contemporary Paris that even his *Mémoires de Paul de Kock, écrits par lui-même* contain a similar deviation from the plotline of his own life: a short story about a philanderer who was cheated on by his wife. He does state that this story is one that he modified for a novel, presumably *Le Cocu*, yet this digression is one of the lengthiest tales in his autobiography and is reminiscent of those found in his fictional works.

39. Cherbuliez, *Revue Critique des livres nouveaux, publiés pendant l'année 1837*, 295. "*Moeurs Parisiennes* contains several pieces . . . which seem to me to be what the author does best. That, I believe, is the true nature of his talent, which excels at depicting certain ridiculous scenes from everyday life."

40. As Alex Lascar suggests, "Offrir aux lecteurs une vue du monde comme il est,

où ils se reconnaissent, voilà clairement son but" ("Le Roman selon Paul de Kock," 21; His goal is clearly to offer his readers a vision of the world as it is, in which they recognize themselves).

41. Migozzi, review of *Lectures de Paul de Kock*, 145. "Misunderstandings and surprises with a narrative or playful function, coincidences, mistakes or hoaxes"; "farcical episodes and ribaldry."

42. Migozzi, review of *Lectures de Paul de Kock*, 144.

43. Kock, *Memoirs*, 139. "Typical novel of the genre."

44. See Berkovicius, "Visages du bourgeois dans le roman populaire."

45. Kock, *Mon voisin Raymond*, 17. "You see, reader, I am good some of the time."

46. Kock, *Mon voisin Raymond*, 35. "She asked me for hospitality and I was going to take advantage of that to seduce her! That is very bad."

47. Kock, *Mon voisin Raymond*, 88–89. "The man that you have hurt is not well; . . . the damages you have caused in the garden are considerable."

48. Kock, *Mon voisin Raymond*, 90. "His conduct from the previous evening certainly merited this little act of revenge."

49. Kock, *Mon voisin Raymond*, 213. "With a leg caught in a trap, and sitting on a pile of hams on which he had fallen asleep."

50. Kock, *Mon voisin Raymond*, 213. "A dreadful grimace"; "the portly girl laughed until she cried."

51. Kock, *Mon voisin Raymond*, 214. "I could mock my friend about the misfortune that pursues him, but I am generous so I keep quiet."

52. Kock, *Mon voisin Raymond*, 392. "He insisted that he was more capable than anyone, and that he would eat six hard-boiled eggs before eating his lunch and that he would eat more quickly than everyone else."

53. Kock, *Mon voisin Raymond*, 393. "Had just died from the consequences of his bet."

54. "Little vulgar occurrences."

55. Constans, "'Votre argent m'intéresse,'" 82. "Many of Paul de Kock's novels could have as their subtitle 'the trials and triumphs of virtue.'"

56. "Become like Paul de Kock."

57. Bourdieu, *Les Règles*, 123. "Indigenous taxonomy, born of the struggle of rankings found in the literary field."

58. *La France littéraire* (1836), 207. "Practically Paul de Kock in verse."

59. *La France littéraire* (1837), 235. "Announced at the very best a novel in the style of Paul de Kock."

60. *Journal des débats*, April 4,1835. "I am telling you that the play is by Mis-ter-Paul-de-Kock!"

61. The *Journal des débats* was, according to Thérenty, "l'un . . . des plus importants organes de la presse classique" (*Mosaïques*, 705; one of the most important organs of the classic press).

62. *Journal des débats*, March 27, 1841. "New novel by the English Paul de Kock (Charles Dickens) Oliver Twist."

63. A glowing review in a British journal of de Kock's novel *Un Jeune Homme Charmant* held de Kock in much more favor than Charles Dickens: "Giving full awareness of his great merits to Mr. Dickens, we cannot however admit that he is even to be named in the same breath with Paul de Kock. The French author is a man of education, Dickens does not pretend to possess this advantage." De Kock enjoyed much greater critical success in England than in his native France. See *Monthly Review* (London), 1 (1840): 179.

64. Sainte-Beuve, "De la littérature industrielle," 682. "How can we condemn, qualify as detestable and dire that which is heralded and advertised merely an inch away as the marvel of the century."

65. *Journal des débats*, November 28, 1820. "The goal of this novel is a moral one, but the details are not always discreet enough. . . . Mothers will forbid their daughters to read it, . . . but mothers will treat themselves to a reading, and they will enjoy it."

66. *Journal des débats*, August 18, 1821. "Mr. de Kock's play contains comic situations, with lively action; there is cheerfulness in its style and some happy words that make a series of improbabilities acceptable."

67. According to Terni, during the first half of the nineteenth century, though coauthoring popular theatrical works was common, "joint authorship became synonymous in the public mind with commercial production, literary prostitution, and shoddy fare" ("A Genre for Early Mass Culture," 223).

68. *Journal des débats*, August 10, 1825. "Combined in it his double talent as novelist and playwright."

69. *Journal des débats*, August 10, 1825. "Nothing would be easier than to make a good four-volume novel from this opera."

70. *Journal des débats*, August 10, 1825. A commendable work in many respects."

71. *Journal des débats*, February 14, 1828. "Presented a subject that offers such happy developments through new forms. . . . *Jean* is one of the merriest novels he has composed so far."

72. *Journal des débats*, April 17, 1834. "Mr. Paul de Kock has not gone to great creative lengths to botch this supposed *folie-vaudeville*; he quite simply transcribed a section of his novel."

73. *L'Indépendant*, May 15, 1834. "It is settled that, when Mr. Paul de Kock writes any play, it is always with one of his novels.... This saves Mr. Paul de Kock the trouble of coming up with something, and saves us the trouble of speaking about his plays."

74. *Journal des débats*, July 27, 1840. "He writes, it is true, like a barbarian, he doesn't invent anything, his tales are commonplace, his characters are of a deplorable triviality"; "Like all the other stories by the same author, one of those terrible tales that he improvises with little shamelessness and so much good spirit."

75. *L'Indépendant*, July 7, 1842. "Despite the warmth and the prose of Mr. Paul de Kock, the perilous and really extraordinary practices of the *Marocains* can draw a crowd."

76. *Journal des débats*, September 14, 1846 ; *Journal des débats*, September 27, 1847. "A farce that the Palais-Royal Theater would not have wanted during carnival season."

77. Sainte-Beuve, "De la littérature industrielle," 677, 676. "Almost ten years ago, an abrupt revolution disrupted the series of fast-developing studies and ideas, [and] an initial and lengthy anarchy ensued.... But in literature, as in politics, as the exterior causes of disruption ceased, the interior symptoms and a profound disorganization could be more clearly seen."

78. By underscoring the repeated praise of wit—*esprit* or *gaîté*—in reviews of de Kock, I am not arguing that critics viewed this quality as one that rendered the author's works erudite or made them consider de Kock on the same literary level as authors generally considered intellectual. As Jennifer Tsien notes in her study on eighteenth-century literary taste, *The Bad Taste of Others*, writers—Voltaire among them—have historically pointed to wit (*bel-esprit*) as indicative of a lack of substance or philosophy. This consistent praise of de Kock's wit points nonetheless to an appreciation of his work, despite his style, and contradicts the idea that his oeuvre was simply disregarded by critics.

79. *Le Monde Dramatique* 5 (1837): 191. "Don't go looking for anything extraordinary in *Tourlourou*"; "there is the joyfulness of a cabaret, the great foolishness of the barracks, the wit of lower classes, and all of it uproarious. We therefore laughed a lot without worrying about much else."

80. *Journal des débats*, August 31,1835. "That revolting volume"; "horrible pleasure"; "It is in this type of work, that rejects taste, good sense, style, imagination, everything that makes man reasonable ... that the author unknowingly mixed in something that nothing can replace and that replaces all other things, spirit, genius, invention and style.... Consider what this great strength is—cheerfulness!" Marie-Pierre Rootering reads this review as negative: "[Janin] pointe du doigt la terrible

arme littéraire que constitue le comique pour Paul de Kock" ("La Réception dans la presse des adaptations théâtrales de Paul de Kock," 113; Janin points out the awesome literary weapon that Paul de Kock's comedic style constitutes). While Janin and others are dismissive of the author's style, they nonetheless acknowledge a redemptive sense of wit that enables readers to overlook stylistic flaws.

81. Rootering, "La Réception dans la presse des adaptations théâtrales de Paul de Kock," 113. "A reading of the reception of theatrical adaptations of Paul de Kock's novels show an author fallen victim to his popularity." One September 4, 1842, reviewer of *Les Trois Culottes* deemed the vaudeville's script lacking in originality, yet he recommends that readers consider de Kock's work "au point de vue de l'observation, souvent au point de vue de la morale et de la raison, plus souvent encore à celui de l'esprit, et [ils verront] si une grande partie des œuvres de M. Paul de Kock ne sont pas dignes de leur immense popularité" (from the perspective of observation, often from the perspective of morality and reason, more often still from that of wit, and they will see if a good portion of the works of Mr. Paul de Kock are not worthy of their immense popularity). In part for its keen observations, but above all for its wit, de Kock's popularity is, for this critic, understandable. See *L'Indépendant*, September 4, 1842.

82. *Journal des débats*, June 29, 1833. "Faithfulness of observations in the variety of situations and customs"; "[The authors] Mr. Paul de Kock, like Mr. Charles Nodier, are equally at ease in the domain of imagination and heart, where the art of writing finds no other rules and limits but the need to please or to connect. These gifted writers have imbued their work with such particular genius that their other works taught us to know and to love."

83. *Journal des débats*, August 19 1833. "Absurd, false, tiring, and boring."

84. Martin, "La Publicité," 1042. "Editorial advertisement, disguised as an article." Thérenty, "La réclame de librairie dans le journal quotidien au XIXe siècle," 95. "On the third or fourth page before the ads with which they often functioned in tandem."

85. *Journal des débats*, September 25, 1841. "A text full of wit and observation."

86. *Journal des débats*, February 13, 1842.

87. *Le Charivari*, November 14, 1842. "Spread all the cheerfulness, all the character that have made him the painter of the Parisian bourgeoisie."

88. *Le Charivari*, September 14, 1845. "These little tableaux of manners at which he excels; he included a few too many. . . . The tableau is not new, but it is merry."

89. Cherbuliez, *Revue Critique des livres nouveaux, publiés pendant l'année 1840*, 107.

"There are three or four scenes which are, in a slightly trivial genre no doubt, little masterpieces of truth and observation . . . which deserve to be cited as samples of Mr. Paul de Kock's true talent."

90. Cherbuliez, *Revue Critique des livres nouveaux, publiés pendant l'année 1837*, 295. "Once one has read one novel by Paul de Kock, one can say that one knows, not only all that he has written, but also all that he will write. Never has a novelist's imagination been less fertile than his."

91. Minor, *The Militant Hackwriter*, 18.

92. Prevost, *Dictionnaire de Biographie Française*, 1236. "Paul de Kock has only ever written one novel whose setting and details he has endlessly varied, by shifting around the same features and the same adventures."

93. Rootering, "La Réception dans la presse des adaptations théâtrales de Paul de Kock," 105. "The majority of his dramatic works were derived from his own novels."

94. See Terni, "A Genre for Early Mass Culture," 223.

95. See Rootering, "La Réception dans la presse des adaptations théâtrales de Paul de Kock," 105–6. "The largest audience."

96. See Rootering, "La Réception dans la presse des adaptations théâtrales de Paul de Kock," 105.

97. As we have seen, de Kock's recycling of novels into vaudevilles and vice versa was often referenced in critiques of his work.

98. "The huge comedy with one hundred different acts."

99. Kock, *La Grande Ville ou Paris il y a vingt-cinq ans*, 1. "I published this tableau of sorts in 1842. Today, I am leaving it exactly as I wrote it 25 years ago, and I am making no changes to it; I am persuaded that many readers for whom new, modern representations of Paris are made every minute, will not be displeased to know an older version. Moreover, in terms of the customs, the absurdities, the follies of society, readers will be surprised to see that there has been little change among Parisians."

100. Thérenty, *Mosaïques*, 124. "Change of title which permitted the same collection to be sold twice to the same reader."

101. Haynes, *Lost Illusions*, 37.

102. Mirecourt, *Paul de Kock*, 23. "[Barba] thereby set out to exploit singlehandedly Paul de Kock's talent and not to let others tap into it."

103. Trimm, *La Vie de Ch. Paul de Kock*, 177. "Was not very high. But it was worth more than his first work [which he self-published for free]."

104. Though de Kock did publish novels with other publishing houses after his

contract with Barba came to an end in 1840, he continued working with Barba until the late 1840s.

105. De Kock was by no means the only author or publisher with whom Gustave Barba had legal dealings.

106. Rootering, "La Réception dans la presse des adaptations théâtrales de Paul de Kock," 109. "One either loved him or hated him."

107. Stiénon, "Paul de Kock relu par les physiologies," 52. "Thematisation of the values of the bourgeois urban universe"; "a short-term, practical and amusing reception, even at the risk of making his work a sales order production."

108. Kock, *Mon voisin Raymond*, 11–12. "I always tried to show the consequences of misbehavior, to prove where our passions can take us, to turn vice into ridicule. . . . In the eyes of many, I will always be guilty, but I am counting on the indulgence of the majority of people."

109. Bourdieu, *Les Règles*, 153. "Which flattered the public by showing it its own image in the form of a hero directly transcribed from the daily life of the petite bourgeoisie."

110. Allen, *Popular French Romanticism*, 94.

111. Couleau, "Paul de Kock," 118. "If in reality everyone in high society from Gregory VI to Chateaubriand had read him, it looked bad to call oneself his reader."

112. See Maza, *The Myth of the French Bourgeoisie*.

3. THE ADAPTABLE EUGÈNE SUE

1. *Revue de Paris* 1, no. 1 (1844): 518. "Because the undeniable success of *Les Mystères de Paris* . . . has increased the number of readers of M. Eugène Sue's previous books, many of these books have been reprinted. People will want to reread *Mathilde, Arthur, la Salamandre* and all of the author's books that preceded *Les Mystères de Paris*."

2. With the exception of the six-volume *Mathilde* (his 1840–41 more moderate best seller), all of Sue's other works are composed of less than half the number of volumes of *Les Mystères de Paris*; some are printed in the standard octavo format; others are printed in the in-18 format, a smaller, cheaper formatting option.

3. Brooks, introduction to *The Mysteries of Paris*, xiii.

4. Queffélec, *Le Roman-feuilleton français au XIXe siècle*. "Astonishing success." Cohen's *The Novel and the Sea* is a notable exception; in it, she examines Sue's maritime fiction at length.

5. See Queffélec, *Le Roman-feuilleton français au XIXe siècle*.

6. According to Thiesse, despite *Le Journal des Débat*'s subscription rate of 80

francs, "la publication des *Mystères de Paris* . . . fit augmenter les ventes de plusieurs milliers d'exemplaires" ("Le roman populaire," 457; "the publication of *Les Mystères de Paris* raised sales by multiple thousands of copies"). Theisse also reiterates, importantly, as does Prendergast (*For the People?*), that this rate implies a bourgeois (*petit* and *moyen*) reading public and not a working-class one. René Guise cites this as the moment in which "le roman-feuilleton . . . trouva sa forme la plus achevée" ("Balzac et le roman-feuilleton," 285; "The *roman-feuilleton* . . . found its most complete form").

7. Regarding Pierre Orecchioni's calculations, Thérenty writes, "Il s'agit d'une fourchette large peut-être sous-estimée" ("Présentation"; "It is a large and perhaps underestimated range").

8. In their introduction to *Les Mystères urbains au XIXe siècle* Thérenty and Kalifa calculate that there were at least twenty English translations (ten in England and nine in the United States), twelve Spanish translations, twelve Italian, seven German, six Portuguese, three Catalan, and four Danish. See also Aron, "Les mystères des *Mystères de Bruxelles*"; Powers, "Charles Testut and *Les Mystères de la Nouvelle-orléans.*" These examples come from a multiauthored publication by the *Medias 19* group entitled *Les Mystères urbains au XIXe siècle: Circulations, transferts, appropriations* edited by Thérenty and Kalifa that studies the global phenomenon of the urban mysteries genre. For an in depth examination of the rewritings of Sue's *Mystères* see Wigelsworth, *Rewriting "Les Mystères de Paris."*

9. Queffélec argues that readers were fascinated with and drawn in by "l'exotisme et le pittoresque de cette représentation des 'sauvages' de Paris" (*Le Roman-feuilleton français au XIXe siècle*, 14; "the exoticism and folklore of this representation of Paris's 'savages'").

10. Illustrations would be "un accessoire qui vient poliment offrir à [son] livre une auréole dont il n'a nul besoin" (Burette, introduction to *Les Mystères de Paris*, 284; "an accessory that nicely offers [his] book a halo that it doesn't need").

11. Burette, introduction to *Les Mystères de Paris*, 285. "But trends dictate it." Reissuing works of fiction accompanied by vignettes was a popular and lucrative practice in the 1830s and 1840s. Gustave Barba's series *Romans populaires illustrés* was among the most widely read. On popular illustrated editions, see Ségolène Le Men's "La vignette et la lettre"; on the *Romans populaires illustrés*, see Thiesse's "Imprimés du pauvre, livres de fortune."

12. Burette, introduction to *Les Mystères de Paris*, 284. "Your success troubles you." Burette evokes the readers for whom "le coeur est en émoi depuis l'apparition de

Mathilde" ("whose hearts have been in turmoil since the appearance of *Mathilde*" [285]).

13. Brooks notes, "Sue, before *The Mysteries of Paris*, was the moderately success-ful author of seafaring tales and sentimental fiction." Queffélec comments on Sue's previous successful publications, calling them "très remarqué[es]" ("very noteworthy"), but does not examine them at length. Lyons contends that Sue "discovered the medium of the serialized novel in 1841 . . . first in *Les Mystères de Paris* and then in *Le Juif errant*." Brooks, introduction to *The Mysteries of Paris*, xiv; Queffélec, *Le Roman-feuilleton français au XIXe siècle*, 13; Lyons, *Readers and Society in Nineteenth-Century France*, 31.

14. Sue's biographer Bory repeats this notion of "evolution" in his characterization of Sue's serial novel as the confluence of his ideological leanings from the begin-ning to the end of his career.

15. Cohen, *The Novel and the Sea*, 136.

16. *Constitutionnel*, November 23, 1844. "In 1830, an old artillery comrade said to M. Eugène Sue: 'Cooper's books made the seas fashionable; you should write down your memories of being on the water and create a maritime novel in France.' This idea pleased our author."

17. Sue, *Romans de mort et d'aventures*, 1315. "I thought it better to make my debut modestly as a *genre* painter."

18. Cohen labels this the "internationally resonant and flexible" genre of "sea fic-tion." Lacassin writes that France was "sous le charme d'un genre littéraire alors inédit, le roman maritime" ("under the charm of a literary genre hitherto unseen, the maritime novel"). Cohen, *The Novel and the Sea*, 170; Lacassin, preface to *Romans de mort et d'aventures*, iii.

19. Bory, *Eugène Sue*, 93. "What's Eugène to do? As everyone does: write literature. A bit. Just enough for someone who wants to be a part of high society."

20. Bory observes that Sue's initial literary endeavors "ne signifie[nt] pas que Sue, suivant l'exemple de ses amis, va se consacrer exclusivement à la littérature" (*Eugène Sue*, 94; "do not mean that Sue, following his friends' example, will dedicate himself entirely to literature").

21. Sue was reputed to be "beau, riche, couvert de femmes" (Bory, *Eugène Sue*, 112; "handsome, rich, and draped with women").

22. Lacassin, preface to *Romans de mort et d'aventures*, v. "The sea and the ship just serve as the canvas for a wild drama."

23. Sue, *Romans de mort et d'aventures*, 35. "She could not finish, for a cannonball, whistling in by the stern, shattered her head, cut Carlos in two, and broke the

crates of flowers and the birdcages." Emilie Pézard cites this scene of murder as an example of a contemporary literary trend, what he calls "romantisme frénétique." While there was not necessarily "un corpus auquel serait assignée une étiquette fixe" ("La vogue romantique de l'horreur" 43; "a corpus to which a fixed label could be assigned"), Pezard explains, in the period of the 1820s and 1830s that we associate with romanticism, and perhaps in response to the trauma endured in the Napoleonic wars, literary tastes tended to be morbid: "ce constat est répété depuis des années par la critique comme par les écrivains qui fournissent avec une complaisance plus ou moins cynique son lot d'horreurs au public" ("the trend was for the macabre: this assessment had been repeated for years by critics and by the authors who provided the public with their share of horror with more or less cynical deference" [41]).

24. Bory, *Eugène Sue*, 123. "License to a literary life was thus the author's only ambition."

25. Sue noted elsewhere that he would prefer to slide "inaperçu parmi le monde littéraire" (Bory, *Eugène*, 125; "unnoticed in the literary world").

26. *Revue Encyclopédique* (January–May 1831), 204. "No natural scenes have gone less untapped in France than the adventures of maritime life."

27. *Le Figaro*, January 28, 1831. "Has not yet been explored by our literature"; "the young specialty of the author of *The Pilot* and *The Red Corsaire*."

28. *Journal des débats*, March 13, 1831. "A sailor like Cooper"; "familiarity with the ocean and the sky."

29. Sue was conscious of the conventions of the genre, writing in his preface to *La Salamandre*, "En tâchant d'introduire, le premier, la littérature maritime dans notre langue, j'ai dû toucher à toutes les parties de ce genre. . . . J'ai tenté dans *Kernok* de mettre en relief le pirate, d'en donner le prototype ; dans *El Gitano* de donner le prototype du contrebandier ; dans *Atar-Gull*, du négrier; dans *La Salamandre*, du marin militaire" (Bory, *Eugène Sue*, 161; "In trying to bring maritime literature into our language, I've had to explore all aspects of the genre. . . . In *Kernok* I've tried to give the profile of a pirate, to create the prototype; in *El Gitano* to give the prototype of the smuggler; in *Atar-Gull* the slave trader; in *La Salamandre* the military mariner").

30. *Revue encyclopédique* (January–May 1831), 204. "Supple, clear, picturesque." *Le Figaro*, January 28, 1831. "Lively, vivid, brilliant." *Journal des débats*, March 13, 1831. "Lively, picturesque, passionate . . . in an adventurous and animated style."

31. *La Caricature*, February 5, 1831, 110–11. "To taint the subjects by a critical analysis"; "sketched an admirable portrait of a pirate"; "a few pretty sailor girls,

with charming figures." This review corresponds to the period of time during which Sue and Balzac collaborated, a time marked by "camaraderie . . . peut-être amitié" (Lascar, "Le Roman selon Paul de Kock," 201; "camaraderie . . . maybe friendship"). This friendship ended rather coldly as Sue's success became more evident; he represented for Balzac the "pioupious littéraires" he wished to demolish ("literary babies" [210]).

32. *Le Figaro*, January 18, 1831; *Gazette des Théâtres* February 24, 1831. "All the poetry"; "a book entirely of art and poetry."

33. *Gazette littéraire*, March 10, 1831, 227. "Well-executed"; "His talent has a future."

34. *Le Figaro*, January 18, 1831; *Gazette des Théâtres* February 24, 1831. "The modern school in all its spirit"; "It's Cooper, it's Balzac, what do I know?"

35. *Journal des débats*, March 13, 1831. "Modeled on Lord Byron's sailors much more than on those of Cooper, Kernock is the hero of the genre."

36. There were, to be sure, also negative assessments of *Plik et Plok*. Reviewers took Sue to task for the lack of "signification morale" ("moral significance"). Others claimed that the novel lacked verisimilitude and would benefit from more focus on "la vie réelle et ordinaire des marins" ("the real and ordinary life of sailors"). The first critic offers possible ways for Sue to improve his work instead of dismissing it: "Nous engageons M. Sue à réfléchir là-dessus: ses réflexions décideront de son avenir littéraire" ("We encourage M. Sue to reflect on this: his thoughts will decide his literary future"). See *Revue encyclopédique* (January–May 1831), 205; *Le Figaro*, January 18, 1831.

37. *Gazette littéraire*, March 10, 1831, 227. "The rarer secret, interesting us in this story."

38. *Gazette littéraire*, March 10, 1831, 227. "It is clear that he met his goal, that the book deserves success and the name of author merits his reputation."

39. *Gazette littéraire*, March 10, 1831, 227. "Success in the deeper meaning of the word . . . success of art and of the public"; "he does not strive for them."

40. Sue, *Correspondance générale d'Eugène Sue*, 1: 182. "Sir, I read *Atar Gull* . . . which was a very enjoyable experience. It's possible that the prudes will reproach you, but be assured that everyone will read you."

41. Sue, *Correspondance générale d'Eugène Sue*, 1: 225. "We have reason to be satisfied about what your future holds because wherever we read your name it is preceded or followed by a respectable or benevolent epithet."

42. Bory, *Eugéne Sue*, 125. "M. Eugéne Sue in *La Mode* has given us the delightful seascape of *Kernok* and, later, *le Gitano*, modestly showing a fresh and graceful talent that will grow, for he is young, very young."

43. Lascar, "Balzac et Sue," 204. Sue's early success also coincides with the emergence

of the historical novel in France, a phenomenon that scholars like Claudie Bernard in *Le passé recomposé* have studied in depth.

44. *Le Charivari*, January 7, 1833. "Those notebooks of assorted swatches that tailors always have in their pockets."

45. *Le Charivari*, January 7, 1833. "A little story full of charm and interest"; "a second representative of what is called maritime literature." Auguste Jal, a contemporary of Sue, was an author and historian who served as the official historiographer of the marines and the curator of their official archives.

46. *Le Charivari*, January 7, 1833. "Ingeniously placed and artfully developed contrasts"; "One of the most extraordinary things to come from the pen of M. Sue."

47. *Le Charivari*, January 7, 1833. "An industrial operation."

48. *Le Charivari*, July 20, 1833. "A call to all the literary celebrities who could take part in the success of his operation. MM. Charles Nodier, E. Sue, Jules Janin, A. Jal, Saintines, le comte de Peyronnet, Ancelot, Alexandre Dumas . . . knew to give a variety of works, at once substantial and attractive to this select gathering."

49. Sue, *Correspondance générale d'Eugène Sue*, 1: 294. "A distinguished writer who makes our era proud."

50. See Lyon-Caen, *La lecture et la vie*.

51. *Revue de Paris* 54 (1833): 28. "the leader of the women's section"; "M. Eugène Sue is always on a boat, just as M. de Balzac is always in the bedroom. It's always the same exaggerated love, always the same monotonous passion, always the same ship or the same woman. Zounds! Gadzooks! Captain Sue, unfurl the sails!"

52. Sue, *Correspondance générale d'Eugène Sue*, 1: 316. "Amiable spitefulness"; "the preface of a huge curse of a book, that I (God willing, this will be the last), that I finished about six weeks ago. Four huge volumes in-8°. I wanted, to use a vulgar expression, to empty my sack one last time. And then I'm finished when it comes to novels, oh! How finished! If I have the time to be lazy, I will try to do a few dramas. These are, truthfully, more fun (to do)."

53. *Le Charivari*, April 30, 1840. "In literature, the sea is becoming an unimportant accessory."

54. One 1840 critic even wrote rather caustically that this study "obtint beaucoup de succès dans les ports de mer, près des midshipmen qui ne savaient pas le français, et fut très répandue par de magnifiques prospectus tirés à cent mille exemplaires, mais elle ne se vendit pas du tout" ("achieved much success in the seaports with the midshipmen who do not know French, and was well publicized

through magnificent prospectuses with a print run of one hundred thousand copies, but it sold poorly"). *Le Charivari*, April 30, 1840.

55. *Le Charivari*, April 30, 1840. "Mr. Sue has deigned to make land."

56. Bory writes, "Ce roman, *Le Commandeur de Malte*, qui cherche à unir Scott et Cooper sous la forme du roman maritime et historique comme avait déjà pu le faire *La Vigie de Koat-Ven*.... Hélas ! Kernok a perdu ses griffes, El Gitano son panache extravagant" (*Eugène Sue*, 191; "This novel, *La Commandeur de Malte*, which attempts to unify Scott and Cooper under the form of the maritime and historical novel as *La Vigie de Koat-Ven* had already done.... Alas! Kernok has lost his claws, El Gitano his extravagant spirit").

57. *La Sylphide*, December 6, 1840, 266. "The ephemeral popularity of *Mathilde*"; "one of the most fashionable books right now"; "full of the most lively interest." This critic offers a word of advice to the novelist, counseling him to keep things simple in his subsequent works ("préférer désormais le simple à l'étrange"; "to prefer henceforth the simple to the bizarre"), suggesting that this will be the only way to ensure sustainable ("durable") literary success. If Sue's "exaggerated" account of high-society July Monarchy constituted "l'étrange," *Les Mystères de Paris*'s recourse to "real life" and non-"mondain" Paris suggests that Sue, if indirectly, took this critic's advice to heart (267).

58. *Journal des débats*, April 14, 1841. "That eagerly attracts the attention of a certain milieu"; "will have huge success . . . [and] it will earn this success through its charming style and its dramatic interest."

59. *Revue Pittoresque I* (1843), 90. "Devoured the work in installments in *La Presse*, . . . savored it in long draughts, and, as it were, hour by hour, interest is still growing for this long drama."

60. *Tribune dramatique*, October 2, 1842, 120. "It's the dramatic incarnation of the famous *Mathilde* that moved all the women who read it last year, and provoked so many literary controversies among men who write."

61. *Tribune dramatique*, October 2, 1842, 121. "It is clear that Parisians, who all read the novel *Mathilde*, as well as the country-folk who are beginning to read it, and the foreigners who are translating it, will find themselves for four months at the theater of Porte-Saint-Martin."

62. *Journal des débats*, September 26, 1842. "I saw the entire attentive room enjoying the memory of its past reading. I heard men who said out loud—that's Mlle Ursule!—Women who said, in all seriousness;—that's Monsieur de Rochegune! One might have said it was a piece of history or at least a fairy tale that everyone

was so happy to hear told a second time. Thus the book's success reached its final results!"

63. *Revue des Deux Mondes*, April 28, 1841, 1012, 1004. "The most striking example we could cite in support of what we said against the gloomy mode of publication most of our writers have adopted"; "its psychological pretentions, its interminable dull passages, its somewhat puerile affectations of worldly elegance"; "to a certain point the interest surrounding it."

64. The critic notes that the novel is "médité . . . avec soin par M. Sue," that its descriptions of clothing and drapery "vous fait éprouver un peu de plaisir" and its "splendides décorations servent à un théâtre dont les acteurs sont choisis parmi les plus nobles et les plus brilliants" ("thought over with care by M. Sue"; "makes you feel a bit of pleasure"; "splendid decorations are used at a theater whose actors are chosen from among the noblest and the brightest"). *Revue des Deux Mondes*, April 28, 1841, 1005–6.

65. *Revue des Deux Mondes*, April 28, 1841, 1009. "Quite far from having the style of disdain that most writers seem to affect; on the contrary, he very often tends toward that which demands the most care and delicacy in the art of writing."

66. *Revue des Deux Mondes*, April 28, 1841, 1009–10. "Influence of hasty work that the press imposes"; *Mathilde* has eminent qualities and even, so we maintain, some parts that are entirely praiseworthy."

67. *La Presse*, August 7, 1842. "Excited the greatest interest."

68. Cherbuliez, *Revue Critique des livres nouveaux, publiés pendant l'année 1842*, 289. "It seemed to us that underneath these brilliant exteriors were hidden customs and weaknesses that are no more noble than those of the *tapis-franc*'s patrons."

69. Kirill Tchekalov points out, in a discussion of Iris's suicide, that "il n'y a pas de vrai repentir, à la différence des *Mystères de Paris*" ("La Bohémienne dans *L'Hôtel Lambert* d'Eugène Sue," 220; "there is no real remorse as opposed to *Les Mystères de Paris*").

70. Sue, *Paula Monti*, 172. "We will lead readers to several different theater boxes where they will find many different characters from this story whose general curiosity drew them to this dramatic ceremony."

71. *Journal des débats*, September 7, 1842. "This work is a contemporary *tableau de moeurs* and can be favorably situated next to *Mathilde* and *Thérèse Dunoyer*."

72. Sue, *Romans de mort et d'aventures*, 3. "November night, dark and cold."

73. Sue, *Romans de mort et d'aventures*, 3. "Of wretched appearance"; "horrible and revolting"; "multitude of bones, horse and dog cadavers, bloody skins, and other debris."

74. Sue, *Romans de mort et d'aventures*, 3. "Yellow, wrinkled face."

75. Sue, *Romans de mort et d'aventures*, 4. "In bursts, a stupid and convulsive laugh, wipes his injury with his long black hair, and huddles under the mantle of a huge chimney."

76. Sue, *Romans de mort et d'aventures*, 5. "Luckily, someone knocks on the door of the shack."

77. Sue, *Les Mystères de Paris* (1989), 32. "December 13, 1838, on a rainy and cold night."

78. Sue, *Les Mystères de Paris* (1989), 33. "Having a few rare windows with frames, worm-eaten and almost without window panes"; "black, revolting alleys [that] lead to stairways that were even blacker and yet more revolting."

79. Sue, *Les Mystères de Paris* (1989), 39. "Physiognomies were ferocious or brutish"; "rude or licentious cheer."

80. Sue, *Les Mystères de Paris* (1989), 31. "Hideous, frightening characters [who] swarm in these impure cesspools like reptiles in a swamp."

81. Sue, *Romans de mort et d'aventures*, 8–9. "Large square build that indicated athletic vigor . . . swarthy features . . . large sideburns [that] gave him a hardened, savage air"; "pretty enough, if not for the extraordinary mobility of his thick eyebrows." Lascar views Kernok as having influenced some of Sue's more devious characters, Jacques Ferrand and the Maître d'école; however, these hints at Kernok's subtle beauty alongside his athletic build point toward an obvious connection with Rodolphe. See Lascar, "Balzac et Sue," 206.

82. Sue, *Les Mystères de Paris* (1989), 41. "Medium size, slender, perfectly proportioned"; "perhaps too beautiful for a man"; "the hardness of the lines of his mouth, his sometimes imperious and brazen way of holding his head, which indicated him to be a man of action whose physical force and daring would always give him the upper hand over the masses." Lascar notes another repetition within Sue's oeuvre: "Les premiers héros de Sue, dont maints criminels, ont d'abord plutôt des yeux sombres. Mais ceux d'Arthur de Cerval, un être pacifique, sont . . . d'un 'brun de velours, à l'iris orangé.' Rodolphe a comme Arthur de 'grands yeux d'un brun orangé'" ("Balzac et Sue," 206; "Sue's first heroes, many of whom are criminals, have dark eyes. But those of Arthur de Cerval, a peaceful person, are . . . velvety brown with an orangey iris. Rodolphe, like Arthur, has big, orangey-brown eyes"). Though both Arthur and Rodolphe differ in eye color from the pirates of Sue's earlier works, the author is nonetheless reworking the tactic of conveying moral distinction through the physical traits of his characters, here specifically through their eyes.

83. Sue, *Les Mystères de Paris* (1989), 35. "My goose is cooked." For a study of footnotes, both slang and plot related, see Wigelsworth, "Au Seuil des bas-fonds."

84. Sue, *Romans de mort et d'aventures*, 14. "Egad! Zounds! Gadzooks! What an intrepid brig *L'Épervier* is!"

85. Pezard, "La vogue romantique de l'horreur," 41. "The representation of horrible subjects"; "The trend was for the macabre." On the "littérature terrifiante" or "frénétique" so popular under the Restoration, see Glinoer, "Du monstre au surhomme."

86. "The king of the popular novel." *Eugène Sue: Le roi du roman populaire* is the title of Bory's biography.

87. Sue, like Balzac, appropriates the conventions of the panoramic literary texts. Elizabeth Erbeznik argues, for example, that "*Les Mystères de Paris* begins like a *physiologie*, a text describing and often caricaturizing popular urban figures of the July Monarchy such as the *flâneur* or *portière*" that he borrows from "the familiar characterizations propagated by popular panoramic literature[.] Sue's novel contains a vast assortment of recognizable types—including, of course, the *grisette*" ("Workers and Wives as Legible Types in Eugène Sue's *Les Mystères de Paris*," 68). According to Lascar, Sue and Balzac engaged in mutual borrowing despite their ultimate professional rivalry. Lascar notes, among other examples, Sue's reworking of the parable of the Mandarin in *Arthur* (1837), which was also famously cited in Balzac's *Le Père Goriot*. It is worth mentioning that Lascar shows Balzac borrowing from Sue as well. To give one example, he writes, "Dans les années 1830–1832, Balzac avait emprunté à Sue pour de petits tableaux maritimes" ("Balzac et Sue," 212; "Between 1830 and 1832, Balzac had borrowed little maritime *tableaux* from Sue").

88. Killen, *Le Roman "térrifiant" ou roman "noir" de Walpole à Anne Radcliffe*, 204. "The whole apparatus that had made the popular novel lucrative since its origins: undergrounds, muffled voices, mysteries and recognitions, the persecution of innocent victim, ghosts (at least in the imagination of the actors), flashes of lightning and bolts of thunder."

89. Adamowicz-Hariasz writes, "A successful *roman-feuilleton* made frequent use of clichés, it privileged dialogue over description, and it delighted readers through swift action and rapidly and unexpectedly changing events.... The fragmentary style of the *roman-feuilleton* reflected the novelty-oriented content and the look of the new press and further strengthened their symbiotic connection" ("From Opinion to Information," 165).

90. Sue, *Les Mystères de Paris* (1989), 111. "Sire, sire, remember January 13th!"

91. Sue, *Paula Monti*, 41. "There is no one in the world except Osorio and M. de Brévannes who could have told you what happened in Venice, three years ago, on the night of April 13th!"

92. The strategy of the mysterious date in *Les Mystères* and *Paula Monti* is perhaps facilitated by these novels' omniscient narrators, unlike the first-person narrator present for the majority of *Mathilde*.

93. Sue, *Mathilde*, 1:199. "Oh, February 15th; I remember that day, that date, those circumstances as if it all happened yesterday."

94. Sue, *Romans de mort et d'aventures*, 10. "Yellowed, wrinkled face"; "a hideous smile."

95. Sue, *Romans de mort et d'aventures*, 10. "Old hag"; "talons"; "hide."

96. Sue, *Mathilde*, 1: 118. "It would be hard to imagine a more interesting face, a sweeter or more friendly smile."

97. Sue, *Mathilde*, 1:133. "The cunning, the skill of my cousin frightened me."

98. Sue, *Mathilde*, 4:41. "Beautiful . . . oh, definitely beautiful . . . with that sensual beauty that has, as they say, so much power over men."

99. Sue, *Mathilde*, 4:56, 186, 67, 76. "Ferocious vulture," "panther," "that diabolical woman," "that devilish Ursule."

100. Sue, *Paula Monti*, 113. "Bohemian or Moor."

101. Sue, *Paula Monti*, 112. "Somewhat regular features"; "something virile"; "This girl had been able to pass for a man."

102. Sue, *Paula Monti*, 114. "That young girl"; "abandoned child"; "Iris was just coming out of childhood."

103. Sue, *Paula Monti*, 112. "It was a blind, savage fondness that one would have almost called heartless, so exclusive was it."

104. Sue, *Paula Monti*, 115. "Specific to the canine race"; "gloomy exaggeration of her attachment."

105. Sue, *Paula Monti*, 114. "Amorality expressed through ferocious jealousy."

106. Sue, *Paula Monti*, 114. "She surrounded herself with an impenetrable façade"; "that savage elation"; "ferocious jealousy."

107. Sue, *Paula Monti*, 236. For Tchekalov, Sue also creates "une certaine ambiguïté du personnage" by blurring the lines between traditional tropes of the "femme fatale ou criminelle" ("La Bohémienne dans *L'Hôtel Lambert* d'Eugène Sue," 218; "a certain ambiguity of character").

108. Sue, *Les Mystères de Paris* (1989), 198. "Audacious mestizo." Ferrand is not only responsible for selling Fleur-de-Marie to the Chouette and passing her off as

dead, framing Mme Georges's and the Maître d'école's son Germain and for a
number of murders, but also for sexually assaulting and impregnating Louise
Morel, daughter of the impoverished gem cutter Morel.

109. Sue, *Les Mystères de Paris* (1989), 892. "As beautiful as she was perverted, as
much an enchantress as she was dangerous."

110. Sue, *Les Mystères* (1989), 932–33. "A tall, slim figure"; "an elegant plump neck";
"black hair"; "eyelids fringing with long lashes, the bluish transparency of the
eye itself"; "mouth, loving and insolent . . . a lively purple"; "Let us say that
this tall Creole, at once slender and fleshy, vigorous and supple like a panther,
was the incarnation of the brutal sensuality that only burns in the fires of the
tropics. Everyone had heard of these colored girls fatal to Europeans, of these
vampire enchantresses who, intoxicating their victim with terrible seductions,
suck from them every drop of gold and blood. . . . Such was Cecily." Carolyn
Vellenga Berman thinks the familiarity Sue assumes his reader will have with
this Creole type is striking: "While exotic local knowledge might be required
to identify a Creole woman of color, the (French) community addressed by Sue
already knows—or is presumed to know—what to make of this information,
since 'everybody has heard' of 'those bewitching vampires,' nineteenth-century
femmes fatales who 'suck' a European victim dry" (*Creole Crossings*, 30).

111. Sue, *Les Mystères* (1989), 935. "First instinct"; "sudden action."

112. Sue, *Les Mystères* (1989), 949. "Agile like a panther."

113. Lyon-Caen and Vaillant, "La Face obscene du romantisme," 55. "An overwhelming
spectacle of delight, then flees without letting herself be touched."

114. "Perverted enough."

115. Prendergast, *For the People*, 1.

116. Martin, "La Publicité," 1042; Feyel, "Presse et publicité en France," 858. Feyel
describes this format as one that "ne présente aucun effet typographique, les
lignes en sont plus courtes et imprimées en plus petits caractères" ("does not
present any typographical effects, the lines are shorter and printed in smaller
font" [33]).

117. For Thérenty these ads showcased "autant la fonction éditoriale que la respons-
abilité auctoriale" ("La réclame de librairie dans le journal quotidien au XIXe
siècle," 92; "the editorial function as much as the authorial responsibility").

118. This header was not exclusive to ads of *Les Mystères de Paris* or to ads of Sue's
work more generally.

119. Sue was also grouped with Gosselin's other authors in excerpts from the catalogue of the Comptoir Central de la Librairie, a corporation "intended to

serve as a clearinghouse between the publishers of Paris and the booksellers of the provinces," according to Haynes (*Lost Illusions*, 107). In the case of this daily catalogue, Sue seems meant not to stand out but simply to add to an impressive roster.

120. *Journal des débats*, September 7, 1842. "The book's success was massive."

121. *Journal des débats*, December 7, 1842. "The success of this work is such that the editions published up until now were quickly sold, despite a large print run." These ads "disguised" as articles were found, according to Thérenty, "à la page 3 ou 4 juste avant les announces avec qui elle fonctionne souvent en binôme" ("on the third or fourth page right before the advertisements with with they often worked in tandem"). The elaborate homages to the novel's success and quality are in keeping with Thérenty's observations about the genre of the "réclames," which "vit sous le régime de l'hyperbole et se caractérise par une gradation de superlatifs et d'adjectifs emphatiques frôlant parfois l'adynaton" ("in which hyperbole reigns supreme and which are characterized by a steady increase of superlatives and emphatic adjectives that verge on the ridiculous"). See Thérenty, "La réclame de librairie dans le journal quotidien au XIXe siècle," 95, 92.

122. *Le Constitutionnel*, October 31, 1843. "On sale at all bookstores, *Les Mystères du Grand Monde*. Mr. Eugène Sue depicted the vices of the People. We are going to reveal High Society's crimes."

123. Bettina Lerner writes about other promotional materials for the *Almanach des Mystères de Paris* that could have been "very easily . . . mistaken" for the *Mystères de Paris*, noting in particular that the similarity of its title and cover were "hardly accidental." See Lerner, "Seriality and Modernity," 133.

124. Thérenty writes of the *réclame* that it "ne s'insère pas dans une rubrique spécifique et titrée qui permettrait de l'identifier" ("La réclame de librairie dans le journal quotidien au XIXe siècle," 95; "was not inserted into a specific rubric or titled in a way that it could be identified"). Feyel points out that "la publicité a acquis une fort mauvaise réputation" ("Presse et publicité en France," 33; "advertising acquired a very bad reputation").

125. Charle, "Le champ de la production littéraire," 152.

126. Charle, "Le champ de la production littéraire," 152.

127. Lyons, "Les Best-sellers."

128. Lyon-Caen credits Sue with having invented "une manière très personnelle d'être le représentant du peuple dans le monde de l'écrit" ("Un magistère social," 20; "a very personal way of being the representative of the people in the world of writing").

129. Lyons, "Les Best-sellers," 382.

130. Bory, *Eugène Sue*, 249. "*Les Mystères de Paris* created its author. Or rather the success of *Les Mystères de Paris*—but all of that is inseparable."

4. BALZAC, HIGH AND LOW

1. Chollet and Vachon, *A l'écoute du jeune Balzac*, 575. "Paul de Kock in satin and sequins"; "Paul de Kock does not make Victor Hugo jealous."

2. Chollet and Vachon write that in "*Un grand homme de province à Paris*, Balzac— par la bouche de Lousteau—appelait Paul de Kock 'un commerçant'–ce mot ayant été substitué au 'commençant' du manuscrit. Cette variante, qu'elle qu'en soit l'origine, ou cette bévue du typographe avalisée par l'auteur, semble refléter la médiocre estime de Balzac, en 1839, pour son concurrent 'populaire,' dont le nom n'apparaît d'ailleurs jamais dans la *Correspondance* générale" (*A l'écoute du jeune Balzac*, 575; "Balzac—by way of Lousteau—calls Paul de Kock 'a shopkeeper'— this word having been substituted for 'beginner'—in the manuscript. This variation, whatever its origin, or this typo supported by the author seems to reflect the low regard Balzac held in 1839 for his 'popular' competitor, whose name would never appear in the *Correspondance*").

3. Lascar, "Balzac et Sue," 207. "Balzac would never stop fighting him, convinced that he was being persecuted, driven by the impression of an immense injustice, both material (he was obsessed by Sue's stupendous profits) and above all liter- ary, which he countered with all his might." As Lascar shows in his thorough examination of Balzac's rivalry with Sue, the author frequently insulted Sue and his talent, claiming that "Sue n'a jamais été autre chose qu'un débutant, qu'il n'a fait aucun progrès" ("Sue was never anything but a beginner, and he has made no progress" [219]). Yet the two often borrowed freely from each other's works.

4. Rouvillois notes, "Tout au sommet, les écrivains à la mode, comme Victor Hugo et Paul de Kock, sont tirés à 2,500 exemplaires (soit environ 20% des ventes totales de leurs derniers chefs-d'oeuvre respectifs, *Notre-Dame de Paris* et *Le Cocu*). En dessous, des auteurs plus confidentiels, comme Balzac, tirés à 1500 exemplaires" ("At their peak, the popular writers like Victor Hugo and Paul de Kock were printing 2,500 copies (about 20% of the total sales of their latest masterpieces, *Notre-Dame de Paris* and *Le Cocu*, respectively"). Authors with a more limited distribution, like Balzac, had 1,500 copies printed). Rouvillois, *Une histoire des best-sellers*, 34.

5. As Chollet and Vachon show in their engagement with Balzac's early works throughout the 1820s, "si l'activité du jeune Balzac est profondément liée aux pratiques d'écriture et d'édition de la Restauration, elle suit aussi, cela va sans

dire, un parcours personnel, concret et, risquons le mot, pécuniaire" (*A l'écoute du jeune Balzac*, 17; "if the young Balzac's activity was strongly connected to writing and publishing during the Restoration, it goes without saying that it was also personal, concrete, and, dare we say it, pecuniary").

6. Balzac's biographers and critics give a mixed picture of his willingness to follow the contemporary trend started by Scott. For Gerson, Balzac calculated that he could make his mark with the historical novel, and Chollet and Vachon note that in the lead-up to the publication of *Les Chouans*, the author "s'est secrètement interrogé plusieurs années durant la plume à la main sur l'art et la technique de Walter Scott" ("secretly wondered for years on end with pen in hand about the art and technique of Walter Scott"). Maurois claims, however, that Balzac "was not content to be merely an imitator of Scott. He expressed his view of the matter some years later in the words of Daniel d'Arthez, talking to Lucien de Rubempré in *Illusions perdues*: 'If you don't want to be Walter Scott's shadow you must find other methods, instead of simply imitating him.'" See Gerson, *The Prodigal Genius*, 87; Chollet and Vachon, *A l'écoute du jeune Balzac*, 21; Maurois, *Prometheus*, 132. Claudie Bernard also remarks on Balzac's comprehension of the once popular, now waning trend of the historical novel: "L'usure du genre fut bientôt à la mesure de son immense succès. Les créateurs entretiennent une attitude mêlée d'admiration et de lassitude, d'émulation et de dédain vis-à-vis de ce que Balzac appelle, dès la préface de *La Peau de chagrin* (1831), le récit "walterscotté" (52, "The weakening of the genre was soon commensurate with its great success. The creators kept up an attitude of mixed admiration and weariness, emulation and disdain toward what Balzac called, in the preface of *La Peau de chagrin* [1831], the 'Walter Scottified' story").

7. Maurois writes, "At the end of eight months, Urbain Canel had sold only 450 copies, [and] when Latouche drew up his balance sheet, he had not even got his money back" (*Prometheus*, 141).

8. As we have seen, Brillat-Savarin published his *Physiologie du goût* in 1826. Balzac claimed, however, after the *physiologie* series grew in popularity, that his own *Physiologie* dated back to 1820 and that he was therefore the instigator of the genre. "Grâce à la date de 1820, Balzac fait remonter le projet analytique en deça de ses oeuvres de jeunesse, comme si la connaissance positive, méthodique et exhaustive du fait social que constitue le mariage avait donné naissance au reste de la production Romanesque signée de son nom" (Nesci, *La Femme mode d'emploi*, 42; "Thanks to the date of 1820, Balzac moves back this analytic project to well before his early works, as though the positive, systematic, and

exhaustive knowledge of the social fact that is marriage had given birth to the rest of the fictional production with his name on it").

9. Gerson, *Prodigal Genius*, 92.

10. Marcus quotes Nesci's important observation that "Balzac also affiliated his text with medical physiology by publishing his book in the octavo format used for serious scientific works, rather than in the smaller formats used for novels and the satiric *Codes*." In *À l'écoute du jeune Balzac*, Chollet and Vachon signal a material difference between *Les Chouans* and *La Physiologie du mariage*, notably that the latter was published in the less expensive in-12 format while the former was published in the in-8° format, indicating market value. See Marcus, introduction to *The Physiology of Marriage*, xii.

11. Nesci, *La Femme mode d'emploi*, 13. "The young writer into a stylish author, the idol of women and of the editors of journals."

12. Marcus, introduction to *The Physiology of Marriage*, xix; Gerson, *Prodigal Genius*, 93. Robb writes, "Letters from Balzac's admirers—too numerous for them all to be included in his published correspondence and, by one account, totaling more than 10,000—began to arrive at the Rue Cassini in 1831" (*Balzac*, 167). For an in-depth analysis of letters from Balzac's readers, see Lyon-Caen's *La lecture et la vie*.

13. Lyons, "Les Best-sellers," 394.

14. Gerson, *Prodigal Genius*, 92; Robb, *Balzac*, 171.

15. Chollet and Vachon, *À l'écoute du jeune Balzac*, 194n3. "Big hit in the bookstores." The publication of *La Physiologie du mariage* solidified Balzac's popularity, and over the course of the next year he would produce many pieces of commercial writing, notably articles for *La Silhouette*, *Le Voleur*, and *La Mode*. His 1831 *La Peau de Chagrin* was both a commercial and a critical success even if Gosselin overstated original sales figures to sell more copies. Lyons estimates that, by 1850, with eight editions in France, it had sold approximately 20,000 copies. When it went on sale in August 1831, after a publicity campaign and positive reviews (likely written by Balzac himself), "it sold out before it reached the bookshops," and a second edition was "rushed out in September with twelve other tales." See Rouvillois, *Une histoire des best-sellers*, 18; Lyons, "Les Best-sellers," 394; Robb, *Balzac*, 180–81.

16. Marcel Reboussin recalls, for example, the "colère" and "sauvagerie" with which Balzac represents the press of the Restauration: "Selon lui, ce sont tous des médiocres et des coquins" ("Balzac et la presse dans les 'Illusions perdues,'" 130; "Anger," "savagery"; "According to him, everyone was a mediocre scoundrel").

17. Chollet and Vachon, *A l'écoute du jeune Balzac*, 36. "Thousands of wretched reading rooms that are killing our literature."

18. Rouvillois, *Une histoire des best-sellers*, 102. "There is something in me (I don't know what) that stops me from conscientiously doing poorly. It's a matter giving a future to a book, to make it either toilet paper or a work worthy of a library."

19. Chollet, *Balzac Journaliste*, 135. "The system of publishing in journals gave Balzac a literary and commercial solution to the problems of everyday crises and impending economic disaster he faced after the publication of the *Physiologie du marriage*: how to survive without ending his career as a novelist?"

20. Chollet, *Balzac Journaliste*, 135. "Within the scope of *La Comédie humaine*, important works that appeared in *La Mode, La Revue de Paris, La Revue des Deux Mondes* keep the stigma of their journalistic origins. Additionally, Balzac the journalist exercised a considerable influence as early as 1830 on the development of the literary press in the 19th century."

21. Chollet and Vachon, *A l'écoute du jeune Balzac*, 577, 21. "Paul de Kock belongs to another world, a world Balzac declined"; "the ideological and commercial constraints of his time . . . he managed to surpass them."

22. The larger project of his *Comédie humaine* has been viewed too as participating in this genre. Lyon-Caen argues that "l'essor du projet balzacien . . . ne peut se comprendre hors de cette explosion de 'littérature panoramique'" ("Une Histoire de l'imaginaire social par le livre en France au premier XIXe siècle," 169; "the rise of the Balzacian project . . . cannot be understood outside this explosion of 'panoramic literature'"). Marcus too finds a link between Balzac's 1829 work and his larger project: "The *Physiology* [*du mariage*]'s deployment of representative individuals divided into multiple subcategories prefigures *The Human Comedy*'s desire to classify contemporary social types and exhaustively account for all their possible plots. It also signals the influence of natural science, one of the many discourses that shaped the *Physiology*" (introduction to *The Physiology of Marriage*, x).

23. Lhéritier, "Les Physiologies," 4; Weschler, *A Human Comedy*, 32. Andrée Lhéritier writes that with "codes, les arts de . . . et les physiologies qu[e Balzac] écrivit entre 1824 et 1842, on n'est point étonné qu'il ait revendiqué la paternité de la littérature physiogique" ("Les Physiologies," 5; "codes, arts of . . . and the physiologies that Balzac wrote between 1824 and 1842, one cannot be surprised that he claimed to be the father of physiological literature").

24. Balzac, "Monographie de la presse parisienne," 190. "If he is not counted among the participants of whichever undertaking, he attacks it."

25. Stiénon, "La consécration à l'envers," n72; Balzac, "Monographie de la presse parisienne," 190. "Mocking shortcut"; "Today, the physiology is the art of speaking and writing incorrectly about anything, in the form of a small blue or yellow book that extorts twenty sous from each passerby, under the pretext of making them laugh, and that makes them crack up."

26. Balzac, "Monographie de la presse parisienne," 191. "Physiologies are like Panurge's sheep; they all run after each other."

27. Balzac, "Monographie de la presse parisienne," 191. "These little books are written by the wittiest people of our age."

28. Lhéritier, "Les Physiologies," 4. "Who, under the title of *'physiologies,'* produced serious studies, treated with a tone that tried to be light-hearted, picturesque and pleasant."

29. Lyon-Caen, "Saisir, décrire, déchiffrer," 320, 320n62. "One can read *La Comédie humaine* as a huge gallery of types anchored in recent history"; "the relationships between types and characters in Balzac are nevertheless more complex, each character tending to incarnate, create, and surpass their types at the same time."

30. Lyon-Caen, "Saisir, décrire, déchiffrer," 320. "Typologizing disposition."

31. Sieburth, "Same Difference," 171.

32. Weiner, "Gender-rising the Revolution," 111. According to Carl Weiner, Balzac's "bitterness at the unsatisfactory outcome of his love affair with the Marquise de Castries, an aristocratic *grande dame* of the bluest blood, is commonly held to have inspired him to write it."

33. Balzac, *La Comédie humaine*, 5:923–24. "What in France goes by the name of the Faubourg Saint-Germain is neither a quarter of Paris, nor an institution, nor anything clearly definable. The Place Royale, the Faubourg Saint-Honoré and the Chaussée-d'Antin also possess mansions in which the atmosphere of the Faubourg Saint-Germain prevails. Thus the Faubourg is not strictly confined to its own territory. . . . The manners, speech, in a word the Faubourg Saint-Germain tradition, has been in Paris, during the last forty years, what the Court formerly had been, what the Hôtel Saint-Paul had been in the fourteenth century. . . . This separatism with its periodic variations offers ample material for reflection to those desirous of studying or depicting the different social zones." Unless otherwise noted, all translations of *La Duchesse de Langeais, La Fille aux yeax d'or*, and *Ferragus* come from Hurbert J. Hunt's *History of the Thirteen*.

34. Critics of *La Duchesse de Langeais* have traditionally focused on this section as an explicit political introduction to the ensuing novelistic treatment of the *faubourg*, a treatise in accord with Balzac's own opinion of the Restoration.

Weiner, for example, ties this section to Balzac's budding friendship with the Duc de Fitz-James, "a legitimist politician who clearly saw the futility of the aristocratic disdain for politics that Balzac had forcefully criticized in his political essays and would again dissect mercilessly in the first pages of the second chapter of *Langeais*" ("Gender-rising the Revolution," 112). David Bell too has highlighted this political criticism as it functions to delay the main action of the narrative: "After a mysteriously unexplained preliminary incident, *La Duchesse de Langeais* lingers for a while on a discussion of the weaknesses in the position of the French aristocracy within Restoration society and politics before getting onto the narration meant to explain that incident" (*Circumstances*, 118).

35. Balzac, *La Comédie humaine*, 5:932, 924. "Semi-political glimpse"; "those desirous of studying or depicting the different social zones."

36. Balzac, *La Comédie humaine*, 5:926. "As its foremost characteristic feature, the Faubourg Saint-Germain possesses the splendour of its mansions, its great gardens and their silence, formerly in harmony with the magnificence of its territorial fortunes."

37. Balzac, *La Comédie humaine*, 5:927. "Aristocratic châteaux and palaces, the luxury of their details, the unvarying sumptuousness of their furnishings, the *orbit* in which, unconfined and unencumbered, the fortunate landowner moves, born as he is with a silver spoon in his mouth."

38. Though she refers to this passage as "une brillante et solide étude sur le faubourg Saint-Germain" (*Balzac*, 42; "a brilliant and solid study of the *faubourg Saint-Germain*"), Jeannine Guichardet contends that this section, a "copieuse 'digression historique,'" mixes "le vrai, le faux et d'approximatives vérités pour expliquer le peuplement du noble faubourg" ("wordy historical digression"; "truth, falsehood, and approximate truths to explain the people of the aristocratic *faubourg*" [135]).

39. Balzac, *La Comédie humaine*, 5:927. "Here and there, in the Faubourg Saint-Germain, fine characters are met with, exceptions which prove the rule notwithstanding the general egoism which has caused the downfall of this segregated society."

40. Balzac, *La Comédie humaine*, 5:793. "In Paris there are certain streets which are in as much disrepute as any man branded with infamy can be. There are also noble streets; then there are streets which are just simply decent." In her article "La mélancolie de *Ferragus*," Paule Petitier remarks, "Une typologie des rues de la capitale introduit l'idée d'une diversité presqu'infinie, fixée cependant dans un cadre spatial" ("A typology of the capital's streets introduces the idea of an

almost infinite diversity, nevertheless fixed in a spatial context" [45]). Bell asserts that the narrator of *Ferragus* "begins his story with a series of remarks in which he attempts to create a typology of Parisian streets. . . . The typology of streets constructed by the narrator as *Ferragus* opens is directed toward a specific type of reader" (*Circumstances*, 118).

41. Balzac, *La Comédie humaine*, 5:796. "A person of impeccable and delightful character with whom he was secretly and passionately in love." Bell has linked the narrator of *Ferragus* to the figure of the *flâneur*, both occupied with leisurely strolling the Parisian streets, and has focused on the *flâneur* as a locus of chance: "The *flâneur*, that category of idle observer invented by Balzac, Baudelaire, and their contemporaries, is not only a Parisian, he is the very embodiment of the potential for chance encounters" (*Circumstances*, 118).

42. Balzac, *La Comédie humaine*, 5:793. "Human qualities and such a physiognomy as leaves us with impressions against which we can put up no resistance."

43. Balzac, *La Comédie humaine*, 5:793. "Some of them, like the Rue Montmartre, are like mermaids—lovely heads, but fish-tails at the other extremity. . . . Stock Exchange Square is all rattle, bustle and harlotry. It is beautiful only in the moonlight, at two in the morning."

44. Balzac, *La Comédie humaine*, 5:794. "Narrow streets facing north"; "justice today fights shy of them."

45. Balzac, *La Comédie humaine*, 5:794. "Outside Paris would have no application."

46. Balzac, *La Comédie humaine*, 5:794. "Most delightful of monsters"; "its head is in the garrets, inhabited by men of science and genius; the first floors house the well-filled stomachs; on the ground floor are the shops, the legs and feet."

47. Balzac, *La Comédie humaine*, 5:794. "Invisibly operated by thirty thousand men or women, every one of whom occupies a space of six square feet per person"; "Then it roars and stirs its thousand legs."

48. Balzac, *La Comédie humaine*, 5:795. "Every individual, every bit of a house is a lobe in the cellular tissue of that great harlot whose head, heart and unpredictable behavior are perfectly familiar to them . . . this restless queen of cities."

49. Balzac, *La Comédie humaine*, 5:795. "Here it is: there are streets."

50. Lichtlé, introduction to *Ferragus*, 17.

51. Bell, *Circumstances*, 118.

52. Balzac, *La Comédie humaine*, 5:1039. "The general aspect of the Parisian population."

53. Jean Larose, in his article on melancholy, refers to the "tableau de Paris qui ouvre *la Fille aux yeux d'or*" ("Travail et mélancolie," 18; "the *tableau de Paris* that opens *La Fille aux yeux d'or*"). Lucette Czyba evokes the "'tableau' qui sert

d'ouverture à la *Fille aux yeux d'or*" ("Misogynie et gynophobie dans *La Fille aux yeux d'or*," 167; "'tableau' that functions as an introduction to *La Fille aux yeux d'or*"). Judith Weschler too places the passage not only in the tradition of the *tableau de moeurs* but in that of early nineteenth-century scientific writing as well: "This portrait of the *moeurs* of the petit bourgeois derives its form both from Buffon's descriptions of animal species and the characterizations of La Bruyère. It is a report on the physiology, habits and inclinations of the genus" (*A Human Comedy*, 29). In *Balzac et la provinciale à Paris*, Aurée d'Esneval notes that the author "ne fait que suivre une tradition vivante depuis le *Tableau de Paris* de L. S. Mercier" ("is simply following a tradition that has been alive and well since L. S. Mercier's *Tableau de Paris*" [25]). Petitier also evokes the tradition of Mercier in *Ferragus*, stating that "son ouverture en 'tableau de Paris' . . . dresse une image mythique de la capital" ("La mélancholie de *Ferragus*," 45; "his opening of a portrait of Paris sets up a mythical image of the capital").

54. Prendergast has underscored the importance of the first words of this novella— "un des spectacles" (one of the sights)—linking them to "the positioning of the observing subject at a point sufficiently distant from its object for it to be taken in as a whole, at a 'single view'" (*Paris and the Nineteenth Century*, 53). The narrator implies a totalizing view of the urban scene and therefore a mastery of this landscape.

55. Balzac, *La Comédie humaine*, 5:1039. "A few reflections on Paris as a moral entity may help to explain the reasons for its cadaverous physiognomy."

56. Prendergast, *Paris and the Nineteenth Century*, 53.

57. Balzac, *La Comédie humaine*, 5:1044, 1040. "Spheres of Paris"; "Gold or pleasure." He writes, for example, "Cette ambition introduit la pensée dans la seconde des sphères parisiennes. Montez donc un étage et allez à l'entresol; ou descendez du grenier et restez au quatrième" ("That kind of ambition brings our attention to the second of the spheres of Paris. So let us mount one storey to the *entresol*, or descend from the garret and linger on the fourth floor" [5:1040]).

58. Harvey, *Paris, Capital of Modernity*, 36.

59. Once again this points to Prendergast's argument about Balzac's desire to achieve a totalizing view of the city. He evokes the "famous quasi-demiurgic Balzacian gaze, looking out, over and down—the universe seen from the point of view of the universe" (*Paris and the Nineteenth Century*, 53).

60. Balzac, *La Comédie humaine*, 5:1039–40. "It is not only in jest that Paris has been called an inferno"; "that huge stucco cage, that human beehive with black runnels marking its sections."

61. One passes from "Paris as field, then as theater (the motif of the mask), then as workshop, then as hell, then as volcano." See Prendergast, *Paris and the Nineteenth Century*, 58.

62. Prendergast, *Paris and the Nineteenth Century*, 58.

63. Balzac, *La Comédie humaine*, 5:1039–40. "There all is smoke, fire, glare, ebullience; everything flares up, falters, dies down, burns up again, sparkles, crackles and is consumed."

64. Another sentence whose enumeration serves to underscore its literary qualities rather than to describe an actual Parisian type is the following: "Le fabricant, le je ne sais quel fil secondaire dont le branle agite ce peuple qui, de ses mains sales, tourne et dore les porcelaines, coud les habits et les robes, amincit le fer, amenuise le bois, tisse l'acier, solidifie le chancre et le fil, satine les bronzes, festonne le cristal, imite les fleurs, brode la laine, dresse les chevaux, tresse les harnais et les galons, découpe le cuivre, peint les voitures, arrondit les vieux ormeaux, vaporise le coton, souffle les tulles, corrode le diamant, polit les métaux, transforme en feuilles le marbre, lèche les cailloux, toilette la pensée, colore, blanchit et noircit tout; et bien, ce sous-chef est venu promettre à ce monde de sueur et de volonté, d'étude et de patience, un salaire excessif, soit au nom des caprices de la ville, soit à la voix du monstre nommé Spéculation" (Balzac, *La Comédie humaine*, 5:1041; "The intermediary string pulling and moving these puppets who with grimy hands model and gild the potter's clay, stitch coats and dresses, beat out iron, shave and plane wood, temper steel, spin and weave hemp and flax, burnish bronzes, festoon crystal with floral decorations, embroider woollens, train horses, plait and braid harness, cut out copper, paint carriages, pollard aged elms, steam-dye cotton, dry out tulle, polish diamonds and metals, foliate marble, round off precious stones, give thought a graceful form in print, deck it out in colour or plain black and white—the aforesaid middleman has approached that sweating, willing, patient, industrious populace and promised it a lavish wage, either in order to cater for a city's whims or on behalf of the monster we call Speculation"). The narrator, in one large breath, describes all the labors of this world of "sweat and will," and despite the number of actions mentioned in this one sentence, the piles upon piles of professions encompassed in this sentence underscore its nontypological nature. Readers are given a lengthy list of what all members of an entire class do, rather than a lengthy description of one of these individuals.

65. Balzac, *La Comédie humaine*, 5:1051. "Such a picture of Paris from the moral point of view proves that, physically speaking, Paris could not be other than it is."

66. Despite my contention that this passage represents a more "novelistic" treatment of Paris, as opposed to the fragmentary tableaux, I take seriously Andrea Goulet's argument about the inconsistency of Balzac's vision of Paris in this section: "Grammatically, there is no clear movement between specific and general, example and group. The working class appears variably as a singular type ... as a plural subject ... and as a collective ... each granted its own long list of active verbs, while descriptions of the other classes just as inconsistently jumble grammatical plurals and singulars into a thematic hodgepodge of collectives and individuals. Why is this notable? Because it problematizes, within the scope of narrative description, the methodological tension underlying Balzac's proposed 'constructional unity.' If, indeed, the world is composed of a hidden unified structure and a manifest plurality of forms, how does one go about knowing—and describing—it? Does one observe, inductively, its multiple parts and add them up to form a sense of the whole, or does one deduce the individual forms from a preexisting theory of the whole?" (*Optiques*, 63).

67. This passage from *La Fille aux yeux d'or* can be found in the 1834 Béchet edition of Balzac's *Études de moeurs au XIXe siècle* that also includes the second section of *La Duchesse de Langeais*, then entitled *Ne touchez pas la hache*. According to Maurice Bardèche, the multivolume *Études*, for which Balzac earned the hefty sum of 27,000 francs, included "la réimpression de toutes ses oeuvres à l'exclusion des *Romans et Contes Philosophiques* et des romans historiques" (*Balzac, romancier*, 457; "the reprinting of all his works with the exception of *Romans et Contes Philosophiques* and historical novels"). Despite minor word and punctuation changes, there are no major differences between the "physionomie parisienne" passage published in the *Études de moeurs* and the one that would eventually be incorporated into the completed edition of *La Fille aux yeux d'or*. The reprinting of this text in different publications, while not exemplary of Balzac's recycling across genres, underscores nonetheless the tactically commercial nature of Balzac's oeuvre.

68. Schor, "'Cartes postales,'" 215.

69. Schor, "'Cartes Postales,'" 215.

70. In her study of *Ferragus* Petitier notes that there is nearly constant interruption of the "le fil narratif par des tableaux, des typologies, des portraits de types," and that these textual digressions become "un récit ambulatoire, dont la marche mime celle du flâneur parisien" ("La mélancholie de *Ferragus*," 47; "the narrative thread by tableaux, typologies, and character sketches"; "an ambulatory narrative whose pace mimics that of the Parisian *flâneur*").

71. Balzac, *La Comédie humaine*, 5:814–15. "When this happens a pedestrian in Paris has to stop short, take refuge in a shop or a café—if he has enough money to pay for the hospitality he is obliged to seek— or, if urgency demands, under a *porte-cochère*, where poor or shabbily dressed people take shelter. Why is it that none of our painters has yet tried to make a lifelike sketch of a swarm of Parisians grouped, during a downpour, under the dripping porch of some mansion or other? Where else could so rich a picture be found? . . . Every member of this chance assembly, conforming to his own particular bent, scans the heavens, hops this way and that, either in order to avoid the mud, or because he is in a hurry, or because he sees other citizens rushing along helter-skelter, or because the courtyard behind the *porte-cochère* is sodden and terribly likely to give him a mortal cold if he ventures into it, so that he feels it would be like stepping from the frying-pan into the fire. There is only one other kind of pedestrian—the prudent one who, before he steps out again, looks for breaks in the clouds, and patches of blue sky."

72. Balzac, *La Comédie humaine*, 5:814. "The lead-grey atmosphere"; "the wayward spewings from the bubbling, frothing spouts."

73. Balzac, *La Comédie humaine*, 5:814. "The voluble pedestrian who complains and converses with the portress as she stands poised on her broomstick like a grenadier on his rifle"; "the business pedestrian armed with a satchel or carrying a parcel, computing the gains or losses the downpour will cause"; "the genuine bourgeois of Paris, the man with the umbrella."

74. Balzac, *La Comédie humaine*, 5:850–51. "This *demoiselle* was a type of woman one only meets with in Paris"; "a *grisette* in all her glory." The *grisette*, a young working-class woman, is a type found throughout the literature of the mid-nineteenth century. Hugo's Fantine from *Les Misérables* is perhaps the most well-known example.

75. Balzac, *La Comédie humaine*, 5:851. "She has many times been hit off by the draughtsman's crayon, the caricaturist's brush, the black-and-white artist's graphite, but she eludes all analysis because she is as uncapturable in all her moods as is Nature herself, as mercurial as Paris itself is."

76. Petitier argues that these typologies, coupled with the movement of the city and what she sees as the blurring of character, actually serve to undermine the project of classification so pervasive in the mid-nineteenth century. In particular, she argues, the typologies give way to the subsequent descriptions of the poor that defy the very categories of classification: "L'accentuation du mouvement entraîne l'impossibilité de la taxinomie, la disparition des repères" ("La mélancholie de

Ferragus," 47; "The accentuation of the movement leads to the impossibility of taxonomy, the disappearance of points of reference"). The city's dual nature, on the one hand fixed and decoded, and on the other left to chance, comes to bear on the actual form of the narrative, which in turn is made up of these (stable) typologies and these (unstable) meanderings.

77. Balzac, *La Comédie humaine*, 5:1059. "In fact, the young men of Paris are unlike the young men of any other city. They are divided into two categories: the young man who has possessions and the young man who has none; alternatively the young man who perpends and the young man who spends."

78. Balzac, "Les Jeunes gens," 326. "At first glance then it is natural to believe that the two types of young men who cultivate an elegant lifestyle are very distinct from one another."

79. Balzac, *La Comédie humaine*, 5:1059. "An amiable corporation to which Henri de Marsay belonged."

80. Balzac, "Les Jeunes gens," 333. "One fine day, if you were to ask so-and-so if he knows Paul de Manerville, landed heir, so-and-so would respond thusly: 'You're asking me what Paul is? Paul. . . . Why he's Paul de Manerville.'"

81. Balzac, "Les Jeunes gens," 333. "The negationist is one who, knowing nothing, denies everything so as to put an end to every type of thing"; "The cultists are a cult formed to oppose the negationists."

82. Preiss and Stiénon helpfully conceive of the "type" as "ce personnage surdé-terminé qui réunit en lui toutes les caractéristiques d'un genre, d'un groupe . . . comme individualité, figure saillante, qui peut même signifier 'caricature' dans le vocabulaire de l'illustration du temps" ("'Croqués par eux-mêmes,'" 9; "a prede-termined character who contains all the characteristics of a genre or a group . . . as an individual, a prominent figure, which can even connote caricature in the vocabulary of the time").

83. Scott, "Variations between the First and the Final Edition of Balzac's *Les Employés*," 315. "I have a preface to stitch, like a ruff, to *La Femme supérieure*, and a fourth part with a twist in it, since the seventy-five columns of *La Presse* have furnished but a small volume."

84. Critics have noted the "indebtedness of Balzac's *Employés* to Henri Monnier['s]" 1835 *Scènes de la vie bureaucratique*, which provides "much of the ground-work for Balzac's novel," as the inspiration for certain characters, plotlines, and dia-logue. Six scenes in the novel are structured in a "manière dramatique" much like Monnier's *Scènes* ("dramatic manner"). See Fess, "Les Employés et Scènes de la vie bureaucratique," 236, 241; Schuerewegen, *Balzac contre Balzac*, 56.

85. Balzac, *La Femme supérieure*, xii. "That no longer expresses the subject of this study in which the heroine, if she is indeed superior, is nothing but an extra face instead of the main character."

86. Balzac, *La Femme supérieure*, li. "If you find here many bureaucrats and not many superior women, this fault can be explained by the following reasons: the bureaucrats were ready, accommodated, finished, and the superior women were yet to be painted."

87. In his preface to *Les Employés*, Raymond Chollet argues that the novel is best read in tandem with Balzac's unfinished *Les Petits Bourgeois*, as it offers the "complément anecdotique et le prolongement esthétique" of *Les Employés* ("anecdotal complement and the aesthetic lengthening"). For Chollet, "l'action traditionnelle, dans *Les Employés*, passait au second plan, au profit de l'étude du milieu" ("traditional action in *Les Employés* is secondary to the study of the environment"). But read in conjunction with *Les Petits bourgeois*, the characters become less caricatured or *croquis*-like. The risk that "aucune passion ne les inscrit dans notre mémoire avec le tracé lumineux des grandes destinées de *La Comédie humaine*" is blunted ("no passion will inscribe them in our memory with the luminous trace of the grand destinies in *La Comédie humaine*" [15, 23]).

88. Stierle, "Baudelaire and the Tradition of the *Tableau de Paris*," 361.

89. Many passages describing the bureaucrats and their customs undergo a tense change between editions: "In discussing some institution or custom there is a noticeably frequent shift from the past tense in the Werdet [1838] to the present tense in the two later editions." This grammatical shift plays into the notion that the author is solidifying the relevance and importance of the subject matter. See Scott, "Variations between the First and the Final Edition of Balzac's *Les Employés*," 326.

90. In both his ambition and his professional failure, Xavier Rabourdin is reminiscent of another of Balzac's characters, the eponymous protagonist of *Z. Marcas*, a novella narrated by Charles Rabourdin, Xavier's son.

91. Balzac, *La Comédie humaine*, 7:898. "In Paris, where men of thought and study bear a certain likeness to one another, living as they do in a common center, you must have met some like Monsieur Rabourdin" (Balzac, *The Bureaucrats*, 5).

92. Balzac, *La Comédie humaine*, 7:898. "Many similar figures."

93. Balzac, *La Comédie humaine*, 7:919. "One of those men whom the tide of political events brings to the surface for a few years" (Balzac, *The Bureaucrats*, 29).

94. Balzac, *La Comédie humaine*, 7:1042. "Des Lupeaulx was one of those men

who, to satisfy a passion, are quite able to store away revenge in some remote corner of their hearts" (Balzac, *The Bureaucrats*, 165).

95. Balzac, *La Comédie humaine*, 7:933. "One of those persons who escape portraiture through their utter repulsiveness, yet who ought nevertheless to be sketched because they are specimens of that Parisian petite bourgeoisie, situated above the wealthy artisans and below the upper classes" (Balzac, *The Bureaucrats*, 47).

96. Bordas, "Un stylème," 43, 34. "The French style from about 1830 to 1890"; "ideal passage from the specific to the general."

97. Balzac, *La Comédie humaine*, 7:954. "In Paris, nearly all [offices] resemble each other."

98. Balzac, *La Comédie humaine*, 7:954. "In whatever ministry you go to, to ask some slight favor or to obtain redress for a trifling wrong, you will find dark corridors, poorly lighted stairways, doors with oval panes of glass like eyes, just like at the theater" (Balzac, *The Bureaucrats*, 73).

99. Balzac, *La Comédie humaine*, 7:957. "Perhaps it would do to portray the division of Monsieur de La Billardière in order to give foreigners and those who live in the country a clear idea of the inner workings of the offices, for their principal characteristics are surely the same in any of the European administrations" (Balzac, *The Bureaucrats*, 76).

100. Scott, "Variations between the First and the Final Edition of Balzac's *Les Employés*," 321–22.

101. Pierrot, introduction to *Physiologie de l'employé*, ii. "Significant to this descriptive method of different 'social types.'"

102. Meininger, introduction to *Les Employés*, 9. "He places so much significance on the bureaucrats that they take over the main role in *La Femme supérieure*."

103. Balzac, *La Femme supérieure*, 82. "There are only two kinds of supernumeraries: rich and poor."

104. Balzac, *La Femme supérieure*, 82. "The young man with whom Rabourdin was speaking was a poor supernumerary named Sébastien de La Roche."

105. Balzac, *Physiologie de l'employé*, 68. "The poor supernumerary is thus the real and only supernumerary."

106. Balzac, *Physiologie de l'employé*, 68–69. "Almost always lodged in a neighborhood where the rent is not expensive"; "So he can . . . wait out the nine hours that separate his lunch from his dinner."

107. Bijaoui-Baron, "L'ironie de Balzac dans la *Physiologie de l'employé*," 70. "Implicit

code of the *physiologie* that requires sticking only to the surface of things";
"banter without consequences."

108. Balzac, *La Comédie humaine*, 7:946. "At this point we might explain, as much
for foreigners as for our own grandchildren, what a supernumerary in Paris is
(Balzac, *The Bureaucrats*, 61)."

109. Balzac, *La Comédie humaine*, 7:949. "The young man with whom Rabourdin
was speaking was a poor supernumerary named Sébastien de La Roche" (Balzac, *The Bureaucrats*, 64). Scott notes that though several typologies from the
Physiologie are omitted from the novel, many characters still bear a striking
resemblance to people described in the *physiologies*: "There are in the *Physiologie
de l'employé* a number of passages besides the parallel ones listed that suggest
in varying degrees parts of *Les Employés*. The *cumulard* [*Physiologie*, 349], for
instance, has several traits in common with Colleville as pictured in the Furne
and Conard editions" ("Variations between the First and the Final Edition of
Balzac's *Les Employés*," 325).

110. Scott notes in her comparison between the *Physiologie* and *Les Employés*, "Balzac
used 641 lines and discarded 101" ("Variations between the First and the Final
Edition of Balzac's *Les Employés*," 323).

111. Balzac, *La Comédie humaine*, 7:968. "Make sure you distinguish between [a
bureaucrat] in Paris and [a bureaucrat] in the country. In the country, the [bureau-
crat] is happy: he is spaciously housed . . . he drinks good wine at a good price,
doesn't end up eating horse meat. . . . Finally, the [bureaucrat] in the country
is *something*, while the [bureaucrat] in Paris is hardly even *someone*" (Balzac,
The Bureaucrats, 88–89). Foulkes occasionally uses the terms "state employee"
and "employee" interchangeably with "bureaucrat," the title of his translation
and also the term I have chosen to use. I have standardized the translation of
"employé" as "bureaucrat" to avoid confusion.

112. Balzac, *La Comédie humaine*, 7:967. "Now before diving into this drama, we must
sketch the main characters in La Billardière's division" (Balzac, *The Bureaucrats*, 88).

113. Balzac, *La Comédie humaine*, 7:968. "Once again the title of this essentially
Parisian study."

114. Balzac, *Physiologie de l'employé*, 31. "We distinguish the Parisian bureaucrat
from the country bureaucrat. This Physiology completely ignores the country
bureaucrat."

115. Balzac, *Physiologie de l'employé*, 34. "The bureaucrat of this *Physiologie* is thus
exclusively the Parisian bureaucrat"; "The country bureaucrat is *someone*, while
the Parisian bureaucrat is *something*."

116. Balzac, *La Comédie humaine*, 7:967. "The oldest man in the ministry" (Balzac, *The Bureaucrats*, 88).

117. Balzac, *La Comédie humaine*, 7:967. "Uncle Antoine . . . since you're so talkative this morning, just what do you think a bureaucrat is?" (Balzac, *The Bureaucrats*, 88).

118. Balzac, *La Comédie humaine*, 7:967. "A man who writes sitting in an office. And just what do I mean by that? Without the [bureaucrat], what would we be? . . . Go along and look after your stoves, and the rest of you, mind you never speak ill of the [bureaucrat]!" (Balzac, *The Bureaucrats*, 88).

119. Balzac, *La Comédie humaine*, 7:957. "A clear idea of the inner workings of the offices" (Balzac, *The Bureaucrats*, 76).

120. Balzac, *La Comédie humaine*, 7:967. "Antoine positioned himself on the landing, a vantage point from which he could see all the [bureaucrats] from under the porte-cochere; he knew everyone in the ministry and observed their manner, noting the differences in their dress" (Balzac, *The Bureaucrats*, 88).

121. Balzac, *La Comédie humaine*, 7:1106–9. "B: Before you leave here, perhaps you would care to know what you are . . . to be able to define, explain, fathom, and analyze precisely what a bureaucrat is. Do you know what he is? P: . . . It's someone paid by the government to do a job. B: Well then, a soldier is a bureaucrat. P: . . . Why, no. B: But he is paid by the state to do work, to go on guard and pass in review. . . . P: . . . Well then, Monsieur, a bureaucrat is, logically speaking, a man who needs his salary to live, is not free to quit his post, and cannot do anything except push papers. B: Ah! Now we're getting at a solution. . . . So the bureau is the [bureaucrat's] shell. No [bureaucrat] without a bureau, no bureau without a [bureaucrat]. But what, then, of a customs officer. . . . Where does the [bureaucrat] end up? That's a serious question. Is a prefect a [bureaucrat]? P: . . . He's a functionary. B: Ah! You are implying the contradiction that a functionary is not a [bureaucrat]! . . . I wanted to prove to you, monsieur, that nothing is simple. . . . I wish to point out that, 'Right alongside the need to define lies the danger of getting stuck.'" (Balzac, *The Bureaucrats*, 238–40).

122. Balzac, *La Femme supérieure*, 187. "Pack of good-for-nothings"; "Go along and look after your stoves." See Balzac, *The Bureaucrats*, 87.

123. Balzac, *Physiologie de l'employé*, 5–7. "What is a bureaucrat?"; "The best definition of a bureaucrat is this one: A man who needs his salary to live and who is not free to leave his station, not knowing how to do anything but paperwork!"

124. Balzac, *Physiologie de l'employé*, 7–9. "Obviously, the French king cannot be a bureaucrat. . . . Even more evidently a soldier is not a bureaucrat; he wishes too

much to leave his station. . . . According to this gloss, a state employee must be a man who writes seated in a bureau. No bureaucrat without a bureau, no bureau without a bureaucrat. . . . Where does the bureaucrat end up? That's a serious question. Is a prefect a bureaucrat? This Physiology does not think so."

125. Balzac, *Physiologie de l'employé*, 9. "First Axiom: where the bureaucrat ends the statesman begins"; "Second Axiom: there are no bureaucrats with a salary over twenty thousand francs."

126. Balzac, *Physiologie de l'employé*, 11. "Right alongside the need to define lies the danger of getting stuck"; "Let us stop defining!"

127. Balzac, *Physiologie de l'employé*, 11. "To parody Louis XVIII's famous statement, let us pose this axiom."

128. Balzac, *La Comédie humaine*, 7:1109. "To borrow an expression from Louis XVIII." In both cases the author refers not to Louis XVIII but to "un de ses ministres, Molé" who supposedly said, "A côté de l'avantage d'innover, il y a le danger de détruire" ("Next to the advantages of innovation lies the danger of destruction"). See Meininger, introduction to *Les Employés*, 335n206.

129. Balzac, *Physiologie de l'employé*, 12. "The subject thus worn out, dissected, divided"; "What is the purpose of a bureaucrat?"

130. Bijaoui-Baron, "L'ironie de Balzac dans la *Physiologie de l'employé*," 69. "The physiologies present themselves as studies of customs, to which a scientific framework gives the appearance of a serious work; but their real goal is to amuse the public by the casualness of their definitions." Bijaoui-Baron sees a distinction between Balzac's *Physiologie de l'employé* and others, when she argues, "Derrière la raillerie, la *Physiologie de l'employé* est le plus féroce réquisitoire contre la bureaucratie"("Behind the ridicule, *La Physiologie de l'employé* is the fiercest indictment against bureaucracy" [70]).

131. Schuerewegen, *Balzac contre Balzac*, 68. "Sort of a miniature *La Comédie humaine*."

132. Schuerewegen, *Balzac contre Balzac*, 68. "A 'declassification' . . . 'a new nomenclature,' that is to say . . . a kind of taxonomy."

133. Rouvillois, *Une histoire des best-sellers*, 34.

CONCLUSION

1. See Mollier, *L'Argent et les lettres*.

2. Dorel and Evain, *L'Industrie du livre en France et au Canada*, 19; Vigne, *Le Livre et l'éditeur*, 22. "A major crisis"; "the global upheaval of reading in France."

3. For a complete history of the company, see Hachette Livre, "Les dates clés," http://www.hachette.com/fr/presentation/dates-cles.

4. Dorel and Evain, *L'Industrie du livre en France et au Canada*, 23 See, for example, Editis's website: http://www.editis.com/content.php?lg=en&id=9.

5. Dorel and Evain, *L'Industrie du livre en France et au Canada*, 23. "The rapid concentration of editorial structures and commercialization tools, as well as methods of management brought up to the standards of global markets, has produced many upheavals, in particular the new emergence of huge editorial marketing."

6. Dorel and Evain insist, "Le livre n'est pas un produit commercial comme les autres" (*L'Industrie du livre en France et au Canada*, 58; "The book is not a commercial product like any other").

7. The law in its entirety can be found at the following website: https://www.legifrance.gouv.fr/affichTexte.do?cidTexte=LEGITEXT000006068716&dateTexte=20090602.

8. Haynes notes that the Lang Law is "an embodiment of the idea, common even among liberal publishers in France, that the book is a unique commodity" (*Lost Illusions*, 243).

9. Enguérand Renault, "Comment Amazon a contourné la loi anti-Amazon," *Le Figaro*, November 7, 2014, accessed May 23, 2016, http://www.lefigaro.fr/secteur /high-tech/2014/07/11/32001-20140711ARTFIG00035-comment-amazon-a -contourne-la-loi-anti-amazon.php. "Never mind."

10. Hannah Ellis-Peterson, "Amazon and Publisher Hachette End Dispute over Online Book Sales," *Guardian*, November 13, 2014, accessed May 23, 2016, https://www.theguardian.com/books/2014/nov/13/amazon-hachette-end -dispute-ebooks.

11. Bourdieu, "Une Révolution conservatrice dans l'édition," 14. "The older big companies that accumulate all forms of capital: economic, commercial and symbolic."

12. Dorel and Evain, *L'Industrie du livre en France et au Canada*, 111. "The phenomenon of best sellers."

13. "The big collection of literature"; "the most prestigious logo of twentieth-century French literature." See Gallimard's website: http://www.gallimard.fr/Catalogue /gallimard/Blanche.

14. Bourdieu, "Une Révolution conservatrice dans l'édition," 4. "The label effect given off by its covers."

15. "An exceptional year." Mazel, "Le Marketing du livre," 14.

16. Dorel and Evain, *L'Industrie du livre en France et au Canada*, 99. "Media coverage."

17. For example, in his assessment of Blankeman and Havercroft's *Narrations d'un nouveau siècle*, a collection based on a colloquium at the elite Cerisy, Simon Kemp writes that the volume "is also deliberately high-culture in its remit, with no room for Muriel Barbery, Nicolas Fargues, or David Foenkinos, let alone Fred Vargas, Marc Levy or Guillaume Musso," authors of "novels actually being read" (139).

18. Alain Beuve-Méry, "Livres: Anatomie d'un succès durable," *Le Monde*, October 1, 2007, accessed May 23, 2016, http://www.lemonde.fr/livres/article/2007/10 /01/livres-anatomie-d-un-succes-durable_961580_3260.html. "Above all, she was hidden for a long time by the bulldozer effect of *Les Bienveillantes* whose 900 pages literally crushed the other books competing the previous year."

19. Jérôme Depuis, "Le petit hérisson qui monte, qui monte," *L'Express*, April 5, 2007, accessed May 23, 2016, http://www.lexpress.fr/culture/livre/le-petit-herisson -qui-monte-qui-monte_822064.html.

20. Alexandre Fillon, "Muriel Barbery, la surprise de l'année," *Madame Le Figaro*, June 20, 2007, accessed May 23, 2016, http://madame.lefigaro.fr/art-de-vivre /muriel-barbery-surprise-de-lannee-200607-24053. "Right now, everyone is talking about her. Your sister-in-law, your neighbors, your friends. You too have no doubt already succumbed to the charms of Muriel Barbery."

21. Frédéric Potet, "Muriel Barbery, après le 'Hérisson,'" *Le Monde*, March 11, 2015, accessed May 23, 2016, http://www.lemonde.fr/livres/article/2015/03/11/muriel -barbery-apres-le-herisson_4591558_3260.html. "Progressive word-of-mouth, an irresistible groundswell will quickly impose itself on points of sale irrespective of all predictions."

22. Beuve-Méry, "Livres." "Lasting success"; "a long-seller: a book that, as opposed to the best-seller, begins slowly but lasts a long time."

23. See "Facts and Figures 2009 Revised"; Marie, "Why Do French Books Sell Abroad?"

24. Barbery, *L'Élégance du hérisson*, 252. "An overly gifted child"; "a socialist parliamentarian"; "student of the École Normale Supérieure."

25. Barbery, *L'Élégance du hérisson*, 34, 19. "Journal of movement in the world"; "deep thoughts."

26. "Soul mates."

27. Barbery, *L'Élégance du hérisson*, 356. "Beauty in this world."

28. Barbery, *L'Élégance du hérisson*, 153. "Mme Michelle has the elegance of the hedgehog: on the outside, she is covered in spikes, a true fortress, but I have

the sense that on the inside, she is as simply refined as hedgehogs, which are deceptively lazy, fiercely solitary, and terribly elegant."

29. We might also think of Georges Perec's 1978 *La Vie mode d'emploi* as a novel with an "apartment-house plot."

30. Marcus, *Apartment Stories*, 11.

31. Barbery, *L'Élégance du hérisson*, 153. "Simply refined."

32. Barbery, *L'Élégance du hérisson*, 71. "A brutal mix of respectable works and much less respectable ones."

33. Barbery, *L'Élégance du hérisson*, 98. "Elegance and charm."

34. For a recent study of mainstream media promotion of literature—in this case literature by North African immigrants—see Kleppinger's *Branding the Beur Author*.

35. Depuis, "Le petit hérisson qui monte, qui monte." "A book that people offer as a gift to their friends."

36. Catherine Simon, "Dans la peau d'un livre," *Le Monde*, August 18, 2011, accessed May 23, 2016, http://www.lemonde.fr/livres/article/2011/08/18/dans-la-peau -d-un-livre_1560763_3260.html. "Books that have emotion without being mushy and navel-gazing are few and far between." *Le Monde*'s Frédéric Potet calls Barbery's novel an example of "cette littérature antidéprime" ("Muriel Barbery, après le 'Hérisson'"). An article in *L'Express* characterized it as "tendre, humor- istique et teinté de philosophie" ("antidepressive literature"; "tender, humorous and tinted with philosophy"). Jérome Depuis, "Le petit hérisson qui monte, qui monte . . . ," *L'Express*, April 5, 2007, accessed May 23, 2016, http://www.lexpress .fr/culture/livre/le-petit-herisson-qui-monte-qui-monte_822064.html.

37. "Social satire with tender humor." Another critic characterized Paloma's contri- butions as a "journal savoureux d'une préadolescente, au regard lucide et acéré" (Beuve-Méry, "Livres"; "The charming diary of a preteen with a lucid and keen gaze"). FNAC's web page on Barbery is http://www4.fnac.com/Muriel-Barbery /ia383653.

38. Philippe Lançon, "Faut-il écraser le Hérisson?," *Libération*, July 5, 2007, accessed May 23, 2016, http://next.liberation.fr/livres/2007/07/05/faut-il-ecraser-le -herisson_97601. "How can one not like a book with which it is impossible not to be in agreement and in which it is difficult not to be moved by the mirror it offers you."

39. Lançon, "Faut-il écraser le Hérisson?" "No rich person will be threatened by the caricatures that are made of them."

40. "Muriel Barbery," *Elle*, accessed May 23, 2016, http://www.elle.fr/Personnalites /Muriel-Barbery. "Among the best popular authors"; Jérome Depuis, "Le petit

hérisson qui monte, qui monte . . . ," *L'Express*, April 5, 2007, accessed May 23, 2016, http://www.lexpress.fr/culture/livre/le-petit-herisson-qui-monte-qui -monte_822064.html. "Publishing phenomenon." A biography in *Le Figaro* describes Barbery as "un écrivain majeur de la littérature populaire" ("a major writer of popular literature"). "Muriel Barbery: Ecrivain française," *Le Figaro*, August 4, 2011, accessed May 23, 2016, http://evene.lefigaro.fr/celebre/biographie /muriel-barbery-22943.php.

41. Depuis, "Le petit hérisson qui monte, qui monte." "At a rate of 4,000 copies a week"; "the Gallimard booth was taken by storm."

42. Fillon, "Muriel Barbery, la surprise de l'année." "Might have lived abroad or underground for the past few months."

43. Beuve-Méry, "Livres." "*Hérisson* represents the dream of all publishers."

44. I thank Elizabeth Emery for her observation that the American blogger Julie Powell is a modern-day example of working across commercial outlets. Powell's initial blog on cooking Julia Child's recipes was repurposed into a novel, *Julie and Julia: 365 Days, 524 Recipes, 1 Tiny Apartment Kitchen* (2005), and later adapted into the film *Julie and Julia* (2009). For another contemporary corollary, the website and Facebook platform *Humans of New York* has been offering photographic and written profiles of individual New Yorkers since 2010; a selection of pieces was published in 2015 and became a *New York Times* best-selling book. It resembles panoramic literature in its predictable structure, focus on urban types, and appearance in different formats.

Bibliography

Adamowicz-Hariasz, Maria. "From Opinion to Information: The *Roman Feuilleton* and the Transformation of the Nineteenth-Century French Press." In *Making the News: Modernity and the Mass Press in Nineteenth-Century France*, edited by Dean de la Motte and Jeannene M. Przyblyski, 160–84. Amherst: University of Massachusetts Press, 1999.

Allen, James Smith. *In the Public Eye: A History of Reading in Modern France, 1800–1940*. Princeton NJ: Princeton University Press, 1991.

——. *Popular French Romanticism: Authors, Readers and Books in the 19th Century*. Syracuse NY: Syracuse University Press, 1981.

Amossy, Ruth. "Types ou stéréotypes? Les 'Physiologies' et la littérature industrielle." *Romantisme* 19, no. 64 (1989): 113–23.

Aron, Paul. "Les mystères des *Mystères de Bruxelles*." In *Les Mystères urbains au XIXe siècle: Circulations, transferts, appropriations*, edited by Dominique Kalifa and Marie-Ève Thérenty. *Médias 19*. http://www.medias19.org/index.php ?id=17039.

Balzac, Honoré de. *The Bureaucrats*. Translated by Charles Foulkes. Evanston IL: Northwestern University Press, 1993.

——. *History of the Thirteen*. Translated by Hurbert J. Hunt. London: Penguin Classics, 1975.

——. *La Comédie humaine*. Vol 1. Paris: Éditions Gallimard, 1976.

——. *La Comédie humaine*. Vol 5. Paris: Editions Gallimard, 1977.

——. *La Comédie humaine*. Vol 7. Paris: Éditions Gallimard, 1977.

——. *La Femme supérieure*. Brussels: Meline, Cans et Cie, 1837.

——. "Les Jeunes gens." In *Nouveaux Tableaux de Paris*, 4: 325–34. Paris: Librairie de Charles Béchet, 1834.

——. "Monographie de la presse parisienne." In *La Grande ville: Nouveau tableau de Paris*, 2: 129–208. Paris: Bureau Central des Publications Nouvelles, 1842.

———. *Physiologie de l'employé*. Paris: Honoré Champion, 1979.

Barbaret, John R. "Linking Producers to Consumers: Balzac's 'Grande Affaire' and the Dynamics of Literary Diffusion." In *Making the News: Modernity and the Mass Press in Nineteenth-Century France*, edited by Dean de la Motte and Jeannene M. Przyblyski, 185–204. Amherst: University of Massachusetts Press, 1999.

Barbery, Muriel. *L'Élégance du hérisson*. Paris: Editions Gallimard, 2006.

Barbier, Frédéric. "L'industrialisation des techniques." In *Histoire de l'édition française*, vol. 3, edited by Roger Chartier and Henri-Jean Martin, 57–67. Paris: Promodis, 1985.

Bardèche, Maurice. *Balzac, romancier: La formation de l'art du roman chez Balzac jusqu'à la publication du "Père Goriot" (1820–1835)*. Geneva: Slatkine Reprints, 1967.

Belenky, Masha. "From Transit to Transitoire: The Omnibus and Modernity." *Nineteenth-Century French Studies* 35, no. 2 (2007): 408–21.

Bell, David. *Circumstances*. Lincoln: University of Nebraska Press, 1993.

Benjamin, Walter. *Charles Baudelaire, a Lyric Poet in the Era of High Capitalism*. London: Verso, 1983.

Berkovicius, André. "Visages du bourgeois dans le roman populaire (1800–1830)." *Romantisme* 17–18 (1977): 139–55.

Berman, Carolyn Vellenga. *Creole Crossings: Domestic Fiction and the Reform of Colonial Slavery*. Ithaca NY: Cornell University Press, 2006.

Bernard, Claudie. *Le Passé recomposé, le roman historique français au dix-neuvième siècle*. Paris: Hachette, 1996.

Berthier, Patrick. "Théophile Gautier journaliste: De quelques pratiques d'écriture." In *Presse et plumes: Journalisme et littérature au XIXe siècle*, edited by Marie-Ève Thérenty, 443–55. Paris: Nouveau Monde Éditions, 2004.

Bijaoui-Baron, Anne-Marie. "L'ironie de Balzac dans la *Physiologie de l'employé*." *L'Année balzacienne* 1 (1980): 69–74.

Blankeman, Bruno, and Barbara Havercroft, eds. *Narrations d'un nouveau siècle: Romans et récits français (2001–2010)*. Paris: Presses Sorbonne nouvelle, 2013.

Bolter, Jay, and Richard Grusin. *Remediation: Understanding New Media*. Cambridge MA: MIT Press, 1998.

Bordas, Éric. "Un Stylème dix-neuviémiste: Le déterminant discontinu un de ces … qui. …" *L'Information Grammaticale* 90 (2001): 32–43.

Bory, Jean-Louis. *Eugène Sue: Le roi du roman populaire*. Paris: Hachette, 1962.

Bourdieu, Pierre. *Les règles de l'art: Genèse et structure du champ littéraire*. Paris: Editions du Seuil, 1998.

————. *The Rules of Art*. Stanford: Stanford University Press, 1996.

————. "Une Révolution conservatrice dans l'édition." *Actes de la recherche en sciences sociales* 126–27 (March 1999): 3–28.

Boutin, Aimée. "'The Title of Lawyer Leads Nowhere!' The 'Physiology' of the Law Student in Paul Gavarni, Emile de la Bedollierre and George Sand." *Nineteenth-Century French Studies* 40, no.1 (2011): 57–80.

Bowan, Francis. "Romans de Paul de Kock." *North American Review* 56, no. 119 (1843): 271–300.

Brooks, Peter. Introduction to *The Mysteries of Paris*. Translated by Carolyn Betensky and Jonathan Loesberg, xiii–xv. New York: Penguin Books, 2015.

Burette, Jean-Baptiste Théodore. Introduction to *Les Mystères de Paris*. Paris: Éditions Charles Gosselin, 1843.

Chabrier, Amélie. "De la chronique au feuilleton judiciaire: Itinéraires des 'causes célèbres.'" *CONTEXTES* 11 (2012). Accessed March 10, 2017. http://contextes.revues.org/5312.

Charle, Christophe. "Le champ de la production littéraire." In *Histoire de l'édition française*, vol. 3, edited by Roger Chartier and Henri-Jean Martin, 126–57. Paris: Promodis, 1985.

Cherbuliez, Joël, ed. *Revue Critique des livres nouveaux, publiés pendant l'année 1837*. Paris: Librairie Cherbuliez, 1837.

————. *Revue Critique des livres nouveaux, publiés pendant l'année 1840*. Paris: Librairie Cherbuliez, 1840.

————. *Revue Critique des livres nouveaux, publiés pendant l'année 1841*. Paris: Librairie Cherbuliez, 1841.

————. *Revue Critique des livres nouveaux, publiés pendant l'année 1842*. Paris: Librairie Cherbuliez, 1842.

Chollet, Roland. *Balzac Journaliste: Le tournant de 1830*. Paris: Klincksieck, 1983.

————. Preface to *Les Employés* by Honoré de Balzac. Geneva: Edito-Sérvice, 1981.

Chollet, Roland, and Stéphane Vachon. *À l'écoute du jeune Balzac: L'écho des premières oeuvres publiées (1822–1829)*. Saint-Denis, France: Presses Universitaires de Vincennes, 2012.

Cohen, Margaret. *The Novel and the Sea*. Princeton NJ: Princeton University Press, 2012.

————. "Panoramic Literature and Everyday Genres." In *Cinema and the Invention of Modern Life*, edited by Leo Charney and Vanessa Schwartz, 227–52. Berkeley: University of California Press, 1995.

————. *The Sentimental Education of the Novel*. Princeton NJ: Princeton University Press, 1999.

Comment, Bernard. *The Painted Panorama*. New York: Henry N. Abrams, 1999.

Constans, Ellen. "'Votre argent m'intéresse': L'argent dans les romans de Paul de Kock." *Romantisme* 53 (1986): 71–82.

Couleau, Christine. "Paul de Kock: Le choix du lisible." In *Lectures de Paul de Kock*, edited by Florence Fix and Marie-Ange Fougère, 117–32. Dijon: Editions Université de Dijon, 2011.

Cuno, James. "Charles Philipon, La Maison Aubert, and the Business of Caricature in Paris, 1829–1841. " *Art Journal* 43, no. 4 (1983): 347–54.

Crubellier, Maurice. "L'élargissement du public." In *Histoire de l'édition française*, vol. 3, edited by Roger Chartier and Henri-Jean Martin, 25–45. Paris: Promodis, 1985.

Czyba, Lucette. "Misogynie et gynophobie dans *La Fille aux yeux d'or*." In *La Femme au XIXe siècle: Littérature et idéologie*, edited by Jean-Françoios Tetu et al., 144–55. Lyon: Presses Universitaires de Lyon, 1978.

de la Motte, Dean, and Jeannene M. Przyblyski. Introduction to *Making the News: Modernity and the Mass Press in Nineteenth-Century France*, edited by Dean de la Motte and Jeannene M. Przyblyski, 1–14. Amherst: University of Massachusetts Press, 1999.

Denis, Benoît. "Paul de Kock: Un orgue de Barbarie littéraire." In *Lectures de Paul de Kock*, edited by Florence Fix and Marie-Ange Fougère, 35–49. Dijon: Editions Université de Dijon, 2011.

D'Esneval, Aurée. *Balzac et la provinciale à Paris*. Paris: Nouvelles Éditions Latines, 1976.

Desormeaux, Daniel. *Alexandre Dumas, fabrique d'immortalité*. Paris: Classiques Garnier, 2014.

Dorel, Frédéric, and Christine Evain. *L'Industrie du livre en France et au Canada: Perspectives*. Paris: L'Harmattan, 2008.

Echo de la littérature française et des beaux-arts en France et à l'étranger. Paris: Bureau Rue Saint-Hyacinthe, 1846.

Erbeznik, Elizabeth. "Workers and Wives as Legible Types in Eugène Sue's *Les Mystères de Paris*." *Nineteenth-Century French Studies* 41, nos. 1–2 (2012–13): 66–79.

"Facts and Figures 2009 Revised." *Publishers Weekly*, April 5, 2010. Accessed May 23, 2016. http://www.publishersweekly.com/pw/by-topic/industry-news/financial-reporting/article/42695-facts-figures-2009-revised.html.

Ferguson, Priscilla. *Literary France: The Making of Culture*. Berkeley: University of California Press, 1987.

———. *Paris as Revolution: Writing the Nineteenth-Century City*. Berkeley: University of California Press, 1994.

Fess, G. M. "*Les Employés* and *Scènes de la vie bureaucratique.*" *Modern Language Notes* 43, no. 4 (1928): 236–42.

Feyel, Gilles. "Presse et publicité en France (XVIIIe et XIXe siècles)." *Revue Historique* 628, no. 4 (2003) 837–68.

La France littéraire. Vol. 2. Paris: Bureau de la France Littéraire, 1832.

———. Vol. 5.24. Paris: Bureau de la France Littéraire, 1836.

———. Vol. 2.3. Paris: Bureau de la France Littéraire, 1837.

Fougère, Marie-Ange. "Paul de Kock face à la postérité." In *Lectures de Paul de Kock,* edited by Florence Fix and Marie-Ange Fougère, 7–19. Dijon: Editions Université de Dijon: 2011.

Garvey, Ellen Gruber. "Scissorizing and Scrapbooks: Nineteenth-Century Reading, Remaking, and Recirculating." In *New Media 1740–1915,* edited by Lisa Gitelman and Geoffrey B. Pingree, 207–28. Cambridge MA: MIT Press, 2004.

Genette, Gérard. *Seuils.* Paris: Éditions du Seuil, 1987.

Gerson, Noel. *The Prodigal Genius: The Life and Times of Honoré de Balzac.* New York: Doubleday, 1972.

Glinoer, Anthony. "Classes de textes et littérature industrielle dans la première moitié du XIXe siècle." *CONTEXTES,* May 26 2009. Accessed June 3, 2016. https://contextes.revues.org/4325?lang=en.

———. "Critique donné(e), critique prostitué(e) au XIXe siècle." *Études littéraires* 40, no. 3 (2009): 29–41.

———. "Du monstre au surhomme: Le Roman frénétique de la Restauration." *Nineteenth-Century French Studies* 34, no. 3 (2006): 223–34.

Goulet, Andrea. *Optiques: The Science of the Eye and the Birth of Modern French Fiction.* Philadelphia: University of Pennsylvania Press, 2006.

Guichardet, Jeannine. *Balzac: "Archéologue" de Paris.* Paris: Sedes, 1986.

Guise, René. "Balzac et le roman-feuilleton." *Année Balzacienne* (1964): 283–338.

Hahn, Hazel. "Fashion Discourses in Fashion Magazines and Madame de Girardin's *Lettres parisiennes* in July-Monarchy France (1830–1848)." *Fashion Theory* 9, no. 2 (2005): 205–27.

———. *Scenes of Parisian Modernity: Culture and Consumption in Nineteenth-Century Paris.* New York: Palgrave Macmillan, 2009.

Harvey, David. *Paris, Capital of Modernity.* New York: Routledge, 2006.

Haynes, Christine. *Lost Illusions.* Cambridge MA: Harvard University Press, 2010.

———. "The Politics of Authorship: The Effects of Literary Property Law on Author-Publisher Relations." *Nineteenth-Century French Studies* 39, nos. 1–2 (2010–11): 99–118.

Higonnet, Patrice. *Paris, Capital of the World.* Translated by Arthur Goldhammer. Cambridge, Harvard University Press, 2005.

Huart, Louis. *Physiologie du flâneur.* Paris: Aubert, 1841.

Kaplow, Jeffrey. Introduction to *Le Tableau de Paris*, by Louis-Sébastien Mercier, 1–13. Paris: La Découverte, 1998.

Kemp, Simon. Review of *Narrations d'un nouveau siècle: Romans et récits français (2001–2010)*, edited by Bruno Blankman and Barbara Havercroft. *French Studies: A Quarterly Review* 68, no. 1 (2014) : 139–40.

Killen, Alice. *Le Roman "térrifiant" ou roman "noir" de Walpole à Anne Radcliffe et son influence sur la littérature française jusqu'en 1840.* Paris: Honoré Champion, 1967.

Kleppinger, Kathryn. *Branding the Beur Author: Minority Writing and the Media in France, 1983–2013.* Liverpool: Liverpool University Press, 2016.

Kock, Paul de. *La Grande Ville: Nouveau tableau de Paris, comique, critique et philosophique.* Paris: Bureau Central des Publications Nouvelles, 1842.

———. *La Grande Ville ou Paris il y a vingt-cinq ans.* Paris: Ferdinand Sartorius, 1867.

———. *La Jolie fille du faubourg.* Paris: H. Delloye, 1840.

———. *Le Barbier de Paris.* Paris: Ambroise Dupont, 1827.

———. *Le Cocu.* Paris: G. Barba, 1831.

———. *Memoirs of Paul de Kock, Written by Himself.* London: Leonard Smithers, 1899.

———. *Moeurs parisiennes, novelles.* Paris: Gustave Barba, 1837.

———. *Mon voisin Raymond.* Paris: Gustave Barba, 1842.

———. *Paris au kaléidoscope.* Paris: Dolin, 1845.

———. *Un Homme à marier.* Paris: L.-E. Herran, 1837.

———. *Un Mari dont on se moque.* Paris: Ferdinand Sartorius, 1869.

Lacassin, Francis. Preface to *Romans de mort et d'aventures*, by Eugène Sue, i–xiv. Paris: Éditions Robert Laffont, 1993.

Lanoux, Armand. Introduction to *Les Mystères de Paris*, by Eugène Sue, 1–18. Paris: Éditions Robert Laffont, 1989.

Larose, Jean. "Travail et mélancolie." *Études françaises* 27, no. 3 (1991): 9–26.

Larousse, Pierre. *Grand Dictionnaire Universel du XIXe Siècle: Français, Historique, Géographique, Mythologique, Bibliographique, Littéraire, Artistique, Scientifique, etc.* Vol. 9, part 2, I–K. Geneva: Slatkine, 1982.

Lascar, Alex. "Balzac et Sue: Échanges à feuilletons mouchetés." *L'Année balzacienne* 1, no. 11 (2010): 201–21.

———. "Le Roman selon Paul de Kock: Esquisses et propositions." In *Lectures de Paul de Kock*, edited by Florence Fix and Marie-Ange Fougère, 22–34. Dijon: Éditions Université de Dijon, 2011.

Lauster, Martina. *Sketches of the Nineteenth Century: European Journalism and Its Physiologies, 1830–50*. New York: Palgrave Macmillan, 2007.

Le Men, Ségolène. "La 'littérature panoramique' dans la genèse de *La Comédie humaine*: Balzac et *Les Français peints par eux-mêmes*." *L'Année balzacienne* 1, no. 3 (2002): 73–100.

———. "La vignette et la lettre." In *Histoire de l'édition française*, vol. 3, edited by Roger Chartier and Henri-Jean Martin, 312–27. Paris: Promodis, 1985.

Lerner, Bettina. "Seriality and Modernity: *L'almanach des Mystères de Paris*." *L'Esprit Créateur* 55, no. 3 (2015): 127–39.

Lhéritier, Andrée. "Les Physiologies." *Études de Presse* 9, no. 17, 4th trimester (1957): 1–38.

———. *Les Physiologies: 1840–1845*. Paris: Service International de Microfilms, 1966.

Lichtlé, Michel. Introduction to *Ferragus: La Fille aux yeux d'or*, by Honoré de Balzac, 9–62. Paris: Flammarion, 1988.

Lyon-Caen, Judith. *La lecture et la vie: Les usages du roman au temps de Balzac*. Paris: Editions Tallandier, 2006.

———. "Le romancier, lecteur du social dans la France de la Monarchie de Juillet." *Revue d'histoire du XIXe siècle* 24 (2002): 15–32.

———. "Saisir, décrire, déchiffrer: Les mises en texte du social sous la Monarchie de Juillet." *Revue Historique* 630 (2004): 303–31.

———. "Une Histoire de l'imaginaire social par le livre en France au premier XIXe siècle." *Revue de synthèse* 6, nos. 1–2 (2007): 165–80.

———. "Un magistère social: Eugène Sue et le pouvoir de représenter." *Le Mouvement social* 3, no. 224 (2008): 75–88.

Lyon-Caen, Judith, and Alain Vaillant. "La Face obscene du romantisme." *Romantisme* 167 (2015): 41–59.

Lyons, Martyn. "Les Best-sellers." In *Histoire de l'édition française*, vol. 3, edited by Roger Chartier and Henri-Jean Martin, 369–97. Paris: Promodis, 1985.

———. "New Readers in the Nineteenth Century: Women, Children, Workers." In *A History of Reading in the West*, edited by Guglielmo Cavallo and Roger Chartier, 313–44. Amherst: University of Massachusetts Press, 1999.

———. *Readers and Society in Nineteenth-Century France: Workers, Women, Peasants*. Houndmills, UK: Palgrave, 2001.

Marcus, Sharon. *Apartment Stories: City and Home in Nineteenth-Century Paris and London*. Berkeley: University of California Press, 1999.

———. Introduction to *The Physiology of Marriage*, by Honoré de Balzac, vii–xxi. Baltimore: Johns Hopkins University Press, 1997.

Marie, Laurence. "Why Do French Books Sell Abroad?" French Embassy in the United States, December 17, 2013. Accessed May 23, 2016. http://frenchculture .org/books/news/why-do-french-books-sell-abroad.

Martin, Henri-Jean, and Odile Martin. "Le mode des éditeurs." In *Histoire de l'édition française*, vol. 3, edited by Roger Chartier and Henri-Jean Martin, 159–215. Paris: Promodis, 1985.

Martin, Marc. "La Publicité." In *La Civilisation du journal: Histoire culturelle et littéraire de la presse française au XIXe siècle*, edited by Dominique Kalifa, Philippe Régnier, Marie-Ève Thérenty, and Alain Vaillant, 1041–47. Paris: Nouveau Monde editions, 2011.

Maurois, André. *Prometheus: The Life of Balzac*. New York: Harper and Row, 1965.

Maza, Sarah C. *The Myth of the French Bourgeoisie: An Essay on the Social Imaginary, 1750–1850*. Cambridge MA: Harvard University Press, 2009.

Mazel, Christophe. "Le Marketing du livre. Quand le nom de l'auteur devient une marque: Le cas de la littérature." MA Thesis, Université Robert Schuman, Institut d'Études Politiques de Strasbourg, 2008.

Meininger, Anne-Marie. Introduction to *Les Employés*, by Honoré de Balzac, 7–28. Paris: Gallimard, 1985.

Melet-Sanson, Jacqueline, and Daniel Renoult. *La Bibliothèque nationale de France: Collections, services, publics*. Paris: Éditions du Cercle de la Librairie, 2001.

Minor, Lucien. *The Militant Hackwriter: French Popular Literature 1800–1848. Its Influence, Artistic and Political*. Bowling Green OH: Bowling Green University Popular Press, 1975.

Mirecourt, Eugène de. *Paul de Kock*. Paris: Gustave Havard, 1856.

Migozzi, Jacques. Review of *Lectures de Paul de Kock*, edited by Florence Fix and Marie-Ange Fougère. *Romantisme* 157 (2012): 143–45.

Mollier, Jean-Yvez. *L'Argent et les lettres: Histoire du capitalisme d'édition 1880–1920*. Paris: Fayard, 1988.

———. "Les Lois scolaires de Jules Ferry au miroir de l'histoire." In *L'école, un enjeu républicain*, edited by Armelle Le Bras-Chopard, 49–62. Paris: Éditions Créaphis, 1995.

Moretti, Franco. *Distant Reading*. London: Verso: 2013

———. *Graphs, Maps, Trees: Abstract Models for Literary History*. London: Verso, 2007.

Nesci, Catherine. "Feuilletons sans frontières? Le 'Monde' selon Delphine de Girardin." *Études littéraires* 40, no. 3 (2009): 61–72.

———. *La Femme mode d'emploi: Balzac, de la Physiologie du mariage à La Comédie humaine*. Lexington KY: French Forum, 1992.

———. *Le flâneur et les flâneuses. Les femmes et la ville à l'époque romantique.* Grenoble: Ellug, 2007.

Nettement, Alfred. *Études critiques sur le roman-feuilleton.* Paris: Lagny Frères, 1847.

Olivero, Isabelle. *L'invention de la collection: De la diffusion de la littérature et des savoirs à la formation du citoyen au XIXe siècle.* Collection "In Octavo." Paris: Editions de la Maison des Sciences de l'Homme, 1999.

Paris, ou le livre des cent-et-un. Paris: Ladvocat, 1831.

Paris, ou le livre des cent-et-un. 1831–34. Editionsprojekt Karl Gutzkow, University of Exeter. http://projects.exeter.ac.uk/gutzkow/Gutzneu/gesamtausgabe/GuLex/livreeng.htm.

Petitier, Paule. "La mélancolie de *Ferragus.*" *Romantisme* 32, no. 117 (2002–3): 45–58.

Petrey, Sandy. *In the Court of the Pear King: French Culture and the Rise of Realism.* Ithaca NY: Cornell University Press, 2005.

Pézard, Emilie. "La vogue romantique de l'horreur: Roman noir et genre frénétique." *Romantisme* 160 (2013): 41–51.

Physiologie des physiologies. Paris: Desloges, 1841.

Pierrot, Roger. Introduction to *Physiologie de l'employé,* by Honoré de Balzac, i–ii. Paris: Honoré Champion, 1997.

Powers, Rebecca. "Charles Testut and *Les Mystères de la Nouvelle-orléans*: Journalism in Exile." In *Les Mystères urbains au XIXe siècle: Circulations, transferts, appropriations,* edited by Dominique Kalifa and Marie-Ève Thérenty. *Médias 19.* Accessed February 24, 2015. http://www.medias19.org/index.php?id=21315.

Preiss, Nathalie, and Valérie Stiénon. "'Croqués par eux-mêmes': Le panorama à l'épreuve du panoramique." *Interférences littéraires/Literaire interferenties* 8 (2012): 7–14.

Prendergast, Christopher. *For the People by the People? Eugène Sue's "Les Mystères de Paris": A Hypothesis in the Sociology of Literature.* Oxford: Legenda, 2003.

———. *Paris and the Nineteenth Century.* Oxford: Blackwell, 1992.

Prevost, M., et al. *Dictionnaire de Biographie Française.* Vol. 18: *Humann–Lacombe.* Paris: Librairie Letouzey et ainé, 1994.

Queffélec, Lise, ed. *La Querelle du roman-feuilleton: Littérature, presse et politique, un débat précurseur 1836–1848.* Grenoble: Université Stendhal, 1999.

———. *Le Roman-feuilleton français au XIXe siècle.* Paris: Presses Universitaires de France, 1989.

Radway, Janice. *Reading the Romance: Women, Patriarchy and Popular Literature.* Chapel Hill: University of North Carolina Press, 1984.

Reboussin, Marcel. "Balzac et la presse dans les 'Illusions perdues.'" *French Review* 32, no. 2 (1958): 130–37.

Robb, Graham. *Balzac: A Bibliography*. New York: Norton, 1994.

Rootering, Marie-Pierre. "La Réception dans la presse des adaptations théâtrales de Paul de Kock." In *Lectures de Paul de Kock*, edited by Florence Fix and Marie-Ange Fougère, 105–15. Dijon: Editions Université de Dijon, 2011.

Rouvillois, Frédéric. *Une histoire des best-sellers*. Paris: Flammarion, 2011.

Saint-Amand, Denis, and Valérie Stiénon. "Lectures littéraires du document physiologique: Méthodes et perspectives." *MethIS* 2 (2009): 71–85.

Saint-Amand, Denis, and Valérie Stiénon. "Parodie de la science et réflexivité." *MethIS* 3 (2010): 159–83.

Sainte-Beuve, Charles-Augustin. "De la littérature industrielle." *Revue des Deux Mondes* 4, no. 19 (1839): 675–91.

Samuels, Maurice. *The Spectacular Past: Popular History and the Novel in Nineteenth-Century France*. Ithaca NY: Cornell University Press, 2004.

Schor, Naomi. "'Cartes Postales': Representing Paris 1900." *Critical Inquiry* 18, no. 2 (1992): 188–244.

Schuerewegen, Franc. *Balzac contre Balzac: Les cartes du lecteur*. Toronto: Les Éditions Paratexte, 1990.

Scott, Mary. "Variations between the First and the Final Edition of Balzac's *Les Employés*." *Modern Philology* 23, no. 3 (1926): 315–36.

Sieburth, Richard. "Same Difference: The French *Physiologies*, 1840–1842." In *Notebooks in Cultural Analysis: An Annual Review*, edited by Norman F. Cantor, 163–99. Durham NC: Duke University Press, 1984.

Sieburth, Stephanie. *Inventing High and Low: Literature, Mass Culture, and Uneven Modernity in Spain*. Durham NC: Duke University Press, 1994.

Stiénon, Valérie. "La consécration à l'envers: Quelques scénarios physiologiques (1840–1842)." *CONTEXTES* 2010. Accessed August 21, 2012. https://contextes.revues.org/4654.

———. "La vie littéraire par le kaléidoscope des Physiologies." *La vie littéraire et artistique au XIXe siècle*. 2011. http://etudes-romantiques.ish-lyon.cnrs.fr/vielitteraire.html.

———. "Le canon littéraire au crible des physiologies." *Revue d'Histoire Littéraire de la France* 114, no. 1 (2014): 131–41.

———. "Paul de Kock relu par les physiologies." In *Lectures de Paul de Kock*, edited by Florence Fix and Marie-Ange Fougère, 51–60. Dijon: Editions Université de Dijon, 2011.

Stierle, Karlheinz. "Baudelaire and the Tradition of the *Tableau de Paris.*" *New Literary History* 11, no. 2 (1980): 345–61.

Sue, Eugène. *Arthur.* Paris: Renée Desforges, 1977.

———. *Correspondance générale d'Eugène Sue.* Vol. 1: *1826–1840.* Edited by Jean-Pierre Galvan. Paris: Honoré Champion, 2010.

———. *Correspondance générale d'Eugène Sue.* Vol. 2: *1841–1845.* Edited by Jean-Pierre Galvan. Paris: Honoré Champion, 2013.

———. *Les Mystères de Paris.* Paris: Éditions Charles Gosselin, 1843.

———. *Les Mystères de Paris.* Paris: Editions Robert Laffont, 1989.

———. *Mathilde: Mémoires d'une jeune fille.* 6 vols. Paris: Paulin, 1845.

———. *Paula Monti.* Paris: Paulin, 1845.

———. *Romans de mort et d'aventures.* Paris: Éditions Robert Laffont, 1993.

Taylor-Lerner, Jillian. "The French Profiled by Themselves: Social Typologies, Advertising Posters, and the Illustration of Consumer Lifestyles." *Grey Room* 27 (Spring 2007): 6–35.

Tchekalov, Kirill. "La Bohémienne dans *L'Hôtel Lambert* d'Eugène Sue." In *La bohémienne, figure poétique de l'errance aux 18e et 19e siècles,* edited by Pascale Auraix-Jonchière and Gérard Loubinoux, 215–22. Clermont-Ferrand: Presses Universitaires Blaise Pascal, 2005.

Terdiman, Richard. *Discourse/Counter-Discourse: The Theory and Practice of Symbolic Resistance in Nineteenth-Century France.* Ithaca NY: Cornell University Press, 1985.

Terni, Jennifer. "A Genre for Early Mass Culture: French Vaudeville and the City, 1830–1848." *Theatre Journal* 52, no. 8 (2006): 221–48.

Thérenty, Marie-Eve. "The Fooliton: A French Media Invention." *Victorian Review* 38, no. 2 (2012): 35–38.

———. "La réclame de librairie dans le journal quotidien au XIXe siècle: Autopsie d'un objet textuel non identifié." *Romantisme* 155, no. 1 (2012): 91–103.

———. *Mosaïques: Être écrivain entre presse et roman (1829–1836).* Paris: Éditions Honoré Champion, 2003.

———. "Présentation: Les mystères urbains au prisme de l'identité nationale." In *Les Mystères urbains au XIXe siècle: Circulations, transferts, appropriations,* edited by Dominique Kalifa and Marie-Ève Thérenty. *Médias 19.* Accessed February 15, 2014. http://www.medias19.org/index.php?id=15580.

Thérenty, Marie-Eve, and Dominique Kalifa. Introduction to *Les Mystères urbains au XIXe siècle: Circulations, transferts, appropriations,* edited by Dominique Kalifa and Marie-Ève Thérenty. *Médias 19.* Accessed January 20, 2016. http://www.medias19.org/index.php?id=17039.

Thérenty, Marie-Eve, and Alain Vaillant, eds. *La Presse au XIXe siècle: Les modes de diffusion d'une industrie culturelle*. Paris: Nouveau Monde, 2004.

Thérenty, Marie-Eve, and Alain Vaillant. *1836: L'An I de l'ère médiatique. Étude littéraire et historique du journal "La Presse" d'Emile de Girardin*. Paris: Nouveau Monde Editions, 2002.

Thiesse, Anne-Marie. "Imprimés du pauvre, livres de fortune." *Romantisme* 14, no. 43 (1984): 91–109.

———. *Le roman du quotidien: Lecteurs et lectures populaires à la Belle Époque*. Paris: Le Chemin vert, 1984.

———. "Le roman populaire." In *Histoire de l'édition française*, vol. 3, edited by Roger Chartier and Henri-Jean Martin, 455–69. Paris: Promodis, 1985.

Thompson, Victoria E. "Telling 'Spatial Stories': Urban Space and Bourgeois Identity in Early Nineteenth-Century Paris." *Journal of Modern History* 75 (September 2003): 523–56.

Trimm, Timothée. *La vie de Ch. Paul de Kock*. Paris: Éditions Gustave Barba, 1873.

Tsien, Jennifer. *The Bad Taste of Others: Judging Literary Value in Eighteenth-Century France*. Philadelphia: University of Pennsylvania Press, 2011.

Vidler, Anthony. "Reading the City: The Urban Book from Mercier to Mitterand." *PMLA* 122, no. 1 (2007): 235–51.

Vigne, Eric. *Le Livre et l'éditeur*. Paris: Klincksieck, 2008.

Weiner, Carl D. "Gender-rising the Revolution: *La Duchesse de Langeais*." In *The French Revolution in Culture and Society*, edited by David G. Troyansky et al., 111–20. New York: Greenwood Press, 1991.

Weschler, Judith. *A Human Comedy: Physiognomy and Caricature in 19th Century Paris*. Chicago: University of Chicago Press, 1982.

Whidden, Seth, ed. *Models of Collaboration in Nineteenth-Century Literature*. New York: Routledge, 2016.

Wigelsworth, Amy. "Au Seuil des bas-fonds: Footnotes in the mystères urbains." *Dix-Neuf* 16, no. 3 (2012): 243–59.

———. *Rewriting "Les Mystères de Paris": The "Mystères Urbains" and the Palimpsest*. Cambridge, UK: Legenda, 2016.

Index

Page numbers in italic indicate illustrations.

9 781496 201980